Sarah C. Michalak
Editor

Portals and Libraries

Portals and Libraries has been co-published simultaneously as *Journal of Library Administration*, Volume 43, Numbers 1/2 2005.

Pre-publication
REVIEWS,
COMMENTARIES,
EVALUATIONS . . .

The Haworth Information Press®
An Imprint of The Haworth Press, Inc.

Portals and Libraries

Portals and Libraries has been co-published simultaneously as *Journal of Library Administration*, Volume 43, Numbers 1/2 2005.

Portals and Libraries, edited by Sarah C. Michalak, MLS (Vol. 43, No. 1/2, 2005). *An examination of the organization of Web-based and other electronic information resources with a review of different types of portals, attached services, and how to make the best use of them.*

Licensing in Libraries: Practical and Ethical Aspects, edited by Karen Rupp-Serrano, MLS, MPA (Vol. 42, No. 3/4, 2005). *Presents state-of-the-art information on licensing issues, including contract management, end-user education, copyright, e-books, consortial licensing software, legalities, and much more.*

Collection Management and Strategic Access to Digital Resources: The New Challenges for Research Libraries, edited by Sul H. Lee (Vol. 42, No. 2, 2005). *Examines how libraries can make the best use of digital materials, maintain a balance between print and electronic resources, and respond to electronic information.*

The Eleventh Off-Campus Library Services Conference, edited by Patrick B. Mahoney, MBA, MLS (Vol. 41, No. 1/2/3/4, 2004). *Examines–and offers solutions to–the problems faced by librarians servicing faculty and students who do not have access to a traditional library.*

Libraries Act on Their LibQUAL+™ Findings: From Data to Action, edited by Fred M. Heath, EdD, Martha Kyrillidou, MEd, MLS, and Consuella A. Askew, MLS (Vol. 40, No. 3/4, 2004). *Focuses on the value of LibQUAL+™ data to help librarians provide better services for users.*

The Changing Landscape for Electronic Resources: Content, Access, Delivery, and Legal Issues, edited by Yem S. Fong, MLS, and Suzanne M. Ward, MA (Vol. 40, No. 1/2, 2004). *Focuses on various aspects of electronic resources for libraries, including statewide resource-sharing initiatives, licensing issues, open source software, standards, and scholarly publishing.*

Improved Access to Information: Portals, Content Selection, and Digital Information, edited by Sul H. Lee (Vol. 39, No. 4, 2003). *Examines how improved electronic resources can allow libraries to provide an increasing amount of digital information to an ever-expanding patron base.*

Digital Images and Art Libraries in the Twenty-First Century, edited by Susan Wyngaard, MLS (Vol. 39, No. 2/3, 2003). *Provides an in-depth look at the technology that art librarians must understand in order to work effectively in today's digital environment.*

The Twenty-First Century Art Librarian, edited by Terrie L. Wilson, MLS (Vol. 39, No. 1, 2003). *"A MUST-READ addition to every art, architecture, museum, and visual resources library bookshelf." (Betty Jo Irvine, PhD, Fine Arts Librarian, Indiana University)*

The Strategic Stewardship of Cultural Resources: To Preserve and Protect, edited by Andrea T. Merrill, BA (Vol. 38, No. 1/2/3/4, 2003). *Leading library, museum, and archival professionals share their expertise on a wide variety of preservation and security issues.*

Distance Learning Library Services: The Tenth Off-Campus Library Services Conference, edited by Patrick B. Mahoney (Vol. 37, No. 1/2/3/4, 2002). *Explores the pitfalls of providing information services to distance students and suggests ways to avoid them.*

Electronic Resources and Collection Development, edited by Sul H. Lee (Vol. 36, No. 3, 2002). *Shows how electronic resources have impacted traditional collection development policies and practices.*

Information Literacy Programs: Successes and Challenges, edited by Patricia Durisin, MLIS (Vol. 36, No. 1/2, 2002). *Examines Web-based collaboration, teamwork with academic and administrative colleagues, evidence-based librarianship, and active learning strategies in library instruction programs.*

Evaluating the Twenty-First Century Library: The Association of Research Libraries New Measures Initiative, 1997-2001, edited by Donald L. DeWitt, PhD (Vol. 35, No. 4, 2001). *This collection of articles (thirteen of which previously appeared in ARL's bimonthly newsletter/ report on research issues and actions) examines the Association of Research Libraries' "new measures" initiative.*

Impact of Digital Technology on Library Collections and Resource Sharing, edited by Sul H. Lee (Vol. 35, No. 3, 2001). *Shows how digital resources have changed the traditional academic library.*

Libraries and Electronic Resources: New Partnerships, New Practices, New Perspectives, edited by Pamela L. Higgins (Vol. 35, No. 1/2, 2001). *An essential guide to the Internet's impact on electronic resources management past, present, and future.*

Diversity Now: People, Collections, and Services in Academic Libraries, edited by Teresa Y. Neely, PhD, and Kuang-Hwei (Janet) Lee-Smeltzer, MS, MSLIS (Vol. 33, No. 1/2/3/4, 2001). *Examines multicultural trends in academic libraries' staff and users, types of collections, and services offered.*

Leadership in the Library and Information Science Professions: Theory and Practice, edited by Mark D. Winston, MLS, PhD (Vol. 32, No. 3/4, 2001). *Offers fresh ideas for developing and using leadership skills, including recruiting potential leaders, staff training and development, issues of gender and ethnic diversity, and budget strategies for success.*

Off-Campus Library Services, edited by Ann Marie Casey (Vol. 31, No. 3/4, 2001 and Vol. 32, No. 1/2, 2001). *This informative volume examines various aspects of off-campus, or distance learning. It explores training issues for library staff, Web site development, changing roles for librarians, the uses of conferencing software, library support for Web-based courses, library agreements and how to successfully negotiate them, and much more!*

Research Collections and Digital Information, edited by Sul H. Lee (Vol. 31, No. 2, 2000). *Offers new strategies for collecting, organizing, and accessing library materials in the digital age.*

Academic Research on the Internet: Options for Scholars & Libraries, edited by Helen Laurence, MLS, EdD, and William Miller, MLS, PhD (Vol. 30, No. 1/2/3/4, 2000). *"Emphasizes quality over quantity. . . . Presents the reader with the best research-oriented Web sites in the field. A state-of-the-art review of academic use of the Internet as well as a guide to the best Internet sites and services. . . . A useful addition for any academic library." (David A. Tyckoson, MLS, Head of Reference, California State University, Fresno)*

Management for Research Libraries Cooperation, edited by Sul H. Lee (Vol. 29. No. 3/4, 2000). *Delivers sound advice, models, and strategies for increasing sharing between institutions to maximize the amount of printed and electronic research material you can make available in your library while keeping costs under control.*

Integration in the Library Organization, edited by Christine E. Thompson, PhD (Vol. 29, No. 2, 1999). *Provides librarians with the necessary tools to help libraries balance and integrate public and technical services and to improve the capability of libraries to offer patrons quality services and large amounts of information.*

Library Training for Staff and Customers, edited by Sara Ramser Beck, MLS, MBA (Vol. 29, No. 1, 1999). *This comprehensive book is designed to assist library professionals involved in presenting or planning training for library staff members and customers. You will explore ideas for effective general reference training, training on automated systems, training in specialized subjects such as African American history and biography, and training for areas such as patents and trademarks, and business subjects.* Library Training for Staff and Customers *answers numerous training questions and is an excellent guide for planning staff development.*

Collection Development in the Electronic Environment: Shifting Priorities, edited by Sul H. Lee (Vol. 28, No. 4, 1999). *Through case studies and firsthand experiences, this volume discusses meeting the needs of scholars at universities, budgeting issues, user education, staffing in the electronic age, collaborating libraries and resources, and how vendors meet the needs of different customers.*

The Age Demographics of Academic Librarians: A Profession Apart, by Stanley J. Wilder (Vol. 28, No. 3, 1999). *The average age of librarians has been increasing dramatically since 1990. This unique book will provide insights on how this demographic issue can impact a library and what can be done to make the effects positive.*

Portals and Libraries

Sarah C. Michalak
Editor

Portals and Libraries has been co-published simultaneously as *Journal of Library Administration*, Volume 43, Numbers 1/2 2005.

The Haworth Information Press®
An Imprint of The Haworth Press, Inc.

New York • London • Victoria (AU)
www.HaworthPress.com

Published by

The Haworth Information Press®, 10 Alice Street, Binghamton, NY 13904-1580 USA

The Haworth Information Press® is an imprint of The Haworth Press, Inc., 10 Alice Street, Binghamton, NY 13904-1580 USA.

Portals and Libraries has been co-published simultaneously as *Journal of Library Administration*™, Volume 43, Numbers 1/2 2005.

The development, preparation, and publication of this work has been undertaken with great care. However, the publisher, employees, editors, and agents of The Haworth Press and all imprints of The Haworth Press, Inc., including The Haworth Medical Press® and Pharmaceutical Products Press®, are not responsible for any errors contained herein or for consequences that may ensue from use of materials or information contained in this work. Opinions expressed by the author(s) are not necessarily those of The Haworth Press, Inc. With regard to case studies, identities and circumstances of individuals discussed herein have been changed to protect confidentiality. Any resemblance to actual persons, living or dead, is entirely coincidental.

Cover design by Lora Wiggins.

Library of Congress Cataloging-in-Publication Data

Portals and libraries / Sarah C. Michalak, editor.
     p. cm.
     "Portals and Libraries has been co-published simultaneously as Journal of Library Administration, Volume 43, Numbers 1/2."
     Includes bibliographical references and index.
     ISBN-13: 978-0-7890-2931-7 (hc. : alk. paper)
     ISBN-10: 0-7890-2931-6 (hc. : alk. paper)
     ISBN-13: 978-0-7890-2932-4 (pbk. : alk. paper)
     ISBN-10: 0-7890-2932-4 (pbk. : alk. paper)
     1. Libraries and the Internet. 2. Web portals. I. Michalak, Sarah. II. Journal of library administration.
tration.

Z674.75.I58 P67 2005
020'.285'4678–dc22

2005002821

Indexing, Abstracting & Website/Internet Coverage

This section provides you with a list of major indexing & abstracting services and other tools for bibliographic access. That is to say, each service began covering this periodical during the year noted in the right column. Most Websites which are listed below have indicated that they will either post, disseminate, compile, archive, cite or alert their own Website users with research-based content from this work. (This list is as current as the copyright date of this publication.)

Abstracting, Website/Indexing Coverage . . . . Year When Coverage Began

- *AATA Online: Abstracts of International Conservation Literature*
  (formerly Art & Archeology Technical Abstracts)
  <http://aata.getty.edu> 2004

- *Academic Abstracts/CD-ROM* 1993

- *Academic Search: database of 2,000 selected academic serials,*
  updated monthly: EBSCO Publishing 1995

- *Academic Search Elite (EBSCO)* 1993

- *AGRICOLA Database (AGRICultural OnLine Access)*
  A Bibliographic database of citations to the agricultural
  literature created by the National Agricultural Library and its
  cooperators <http://www.natl.usda.gov/ag98> 1991

- *AGRIS <http://www.fao.org/agris/>* 1991

- *Business & Company ProFiles ASAP on CD-ROM*
  <http://www.galegroup.com> 1996

- *Business ASAP* 1994

- *Business ASAP–International <http://www.galegroup.com>* 1984

- *Business International and Company ProFile ASAP*
  <http://www.galegroup.com> 1996

- *Business Source Corporate: coverage of nearly 3,350 quality*
  magazines and journals; designed to meet the diverse information
  needs of corporations; EBSCO Publishing
  <http://www.epnet.com/corporate/bsourcecorp.asp> 1993

(continued)

- *Computer and Information Systems Abstracts*
  <http://www.csa.com> 2004
- *Current Articles on Library Literature and Services (CALLS)* 1992
- *Current Cites [Digital Libraries] [Electronic Publishing]*
  [Multimedia & Hypermedia] [Networks & Networking]
  [General] <http://sunsite.berkeley.edu/CurrentCites/> 2000
- *EBSCOhost Electronic Journals Service (EJS)*
  <http://ejournals.ebsco.com> 2001
- *Educational Administration Abstracts (EAA)* 1991
- *ERIC Database (Education Resource Information Center)*
  <http://www.eric.ed.gov> 2004
- *FRANCIS. INIST/CNRS <http://www.inist.fr>* 1986
- *General BusinessFile ASAP <http://www.galegroup.com>* 1993
- *General BusinessFile ASAP–International*
  <http://www.galegroup.com> 1984
- *General Reference Center GOLD on InfoTrac Web* 1984
- *General Reference Center INTERNATIONAL*
  <http://www.galegroup.com> 1984
- *Getty Conservation Institute (GCI) Project Bibliographies*
  <http://www.getty.edu> 2004
- *Google <http://www.google.com>* 2004
- *Google Scholar <http://scholar.google.com>* 2004
- *Haworth Document Delivery Center*
  <http://www.HaworthPress.com/journals/dds.asp> 1980
- *Higher Education Abstracts, providing the latest in research*
  & theory in more than 140 major topics 1991
- *IBZ International Bibliography of Periodical Literature*
  <http://www.saur.de> 1995
- *Index Guide to College Journals (core list compiled*
  by integrating 48 indexes frequently used to support
  undergraduate programs in small to medium sized libraries) 1999
- *Index to Periodical Articles Related to Law <http://www.law.utexas.edu>* 1989
- *Information Reports & Bibliographies* 1992
- *Information Science & Technology Abstracts: indexes journal*
  articles from more than 450 publications as well as books,
  research reports, and conference proceedings;
  EBSCO Publishing <http://www.epnet.com> 1980
- *Informed Librarian, The <http://www.informedlibrarian.com>* 1993
- *InfoTrac Custom <http://www.galegroup.com>* 1996
- *InfoTrac OneFile <http://www.galegroup.com>* 1984

(continued)

- *INSPEC is the leading English-language bibliographic information service providing access to the world's scientific & technical literature in physics, electrical engineering, electronics, communications, control engineering, computers & computing, and information technology <http://www.iee.org.uk/publish/>* 1986

- *Internationale Bibliographie der geistes- und sozialwissenschaftlichen Zeitschriftenliteratur ... See IBZ <http://www.saur.de>* 1995

- *Journal of Academic Librarianship: Guide to Professional Literature, The* 1996

- *Konyvtari Figyelo (Library Review)* 1995

- *Library & Information Science Abstracts (LISA) <http://www.csa.com>* 1989

- *Library and Information Science Annual (LISCA) <http://www.lu.com>* 1997

- *Library Literature & Information Science <http://www.hwwilson.com>* 1991

- *Magazines for Libraries (Katz) ... (see 2003 edition)* 2003

- *MasterFILE: updated database from EBSCO Publishing* 1995

- *MasterFILE Elite: coverage of nearly 1,200 periodicals covering general reference, business, health, education, general science, multi-cultural issues and much more; EBSCO Publishing <http://www.epnet.com/government/mfelite.asp>* 1993

- *MasterFILE Premier: coverage of more than 1,950 periodicals covering general reference, business, health, education, general science, multi-cultural issues and much more; EBSCO Publishing <http://www.epnet.com/government/mfpremier.asp>* 1993

- *MasterFILE Select: coverage of nearly 770 periodicals covering general reference, business, health, education, general science, multi-cultural issues and much more; EBSCO Publishing <http://www.epnet.com/government/mfselect.asp>* 1993

- *Mathematical Didactics (MATHDI) <http://www.emis.de/MATH/DI.html>* 2004

- *OCLC ArticleFirst <http://www.oclc.org/services/databases/>* 2003

- *OCLC ContentsFirst <http://www.oclc.org/services/databases/>* 2003

- *OCLC Public Affairs Information Service <http://www.pais.org>* 1990

- *PASCAL, c/o Institut de l'Information Scientifique et Technique. Cross-disciplinary electronic database covering the fields of science, technology & medicine. Also available on CD-ROM, and can generate customized retrospective searches <http://www.inist.fr>* 1986

(continued)

- *Referativnyi Zhurnal (Abstracts Journal of the All-Russian Institute of Scientific and Technical Information–in Russian)* <http://www.viniti.ru> 1982

- *SwetsWise* <http://www.swets.com> 2001

- *Trade & Industry Index* 1991

- *zetoc* <http://zetoc.mimas.ac.uk/> 2004

Special Bibliographic Notes related to special journal issues (separates) and indexing/abstracting:

- indexing/abstracting services in this list will also cover material in any "separate" that is co-published simultaneously with Haworth's special thematic journal issue or DocuSerial. Indexing/abstracting usually covers material at the article/chapter level.
- monographic co-editions are intended for either non-subscribers or libraries which intend to purchase a second copy for their circulating collections.
- monographic co-editions are reported to all jobbers/wholesalers/approval plans. The source journal is listed as the "series" to assist the prevention of duplicate purchasing in the same manner utilized for books-in-series.
- to facilitate user/access services all indexing/abstracting services are encouraged to utilize the co-indexing entry note indicated at the bottom of the first page of each article/chapter/contribution.
- this is intended to assist a library user of any reference tool (whether print, electronic, online, or CD-ROM) to locate the monographic version if the library has purchased this version but not a subscription to the source journal.
- individual articles/chapters in any Haworth publication are also available through the Haworth Document Delivery Service (HDDS).

Portals and Libraries

CONTENTS

Acknowledgments   xv

Introduction   1
  Sarah C. Michalak

Chapter 1. The Internet Public Library and the History
  of Library Portals   5
  Susanna L. Davidsen

Chapter 2. MyLibrary@NCState: A Library Portal
  After Five Years   19
  Karen Ciccone

Chapter 3. Portals to the World: A Library of Congress Guide
  to Web Resources on International Topics   37
  Carolyn T. Brown

Chapter 4. The Portal World and the ILS: A Commentary   57
  Sandy Hurd

Chapter 5. If You Build It Will They Come? Services Will
  Make the Difference in a Portal   71
  Ann Marie Breznay
  Leslie M. Haas

Chapter 6. Library Portal Technologies   87
  Krisellen Maloney
  Paul J. Bracke

Chapter 7. Issues in Planning for Portal Implementation:
  Perfection Not Required   113
  Olivia M. A. Madison
  Maureen Hyland-Carver

Chapter 8. Online Catalogs and Library Portals in Today's
    Information Environment   135
      John D. Byrum, Jr.

Chapter 9. Usability Testing, Interface Design, and Portals   155
      Jennifer L. Ward
      Steve Hiller

Chapter 10. Environmentalist Approaches to Portals
    and Course Management Systems   173
      Alison E. Regan
      Sheldon Walcher

Chapter 11. The Association of Research Libraries ARL Scholars
    Portal Working Group Final Report, May 2002   189
      ARL Scholars Portal Working Group

Chapter 12. Looking Ahead: The Future of Portals   205
      Mary E. Jackson

Index   221

ABOUT THE EDITOR

Sarah C. Michalak, MLS, is University Librarian and Associate Provost for University Libraries at the University of North Carolina at Chapel Hill. Previously, she was Director of the J. Willard Marriott Library at the University of Utah. Prior to her appointment as Director of the Marriott Library in September 1995, she held positions at the University of Washington Libraries and the University of California, Riverside.

Ms. Michalak has led initiatives to improve library buildings, to create innovative ways of retrieving information through technology, to improve support for staff and librarians, and to improve library collections and information resources through interlibrary cooperation and through such information technology advancements as the Scholars Portal.

Ms. Michalak has served as a member of the Association of Research Libraries Board of Directors. She has chaired the fifteen-member library Utah Academic Library Consortium which has undertaken numerous cooperative collection purchasing, resource sharing, and automation projects. She has been a member of the Greater Western Library Alliance Executive Committee. GWLA is a consortium of mid-western and western research libraries working together to improve access to library collections and services. She was a founding member of the Scholarly Publications and Academic Resources Coalition (SPARC) and currently serves on the SPARC Steering Committee. The purpose of SPARC, an international coalition of academic libraries, is to introduce competition into the scholarly journal market in order to reduce prices and increase timely access to scholarly information. She currently chairs the Triangle Research Libraries Network executive committee.

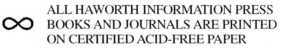

Acknowledgments

To Sul Lee, thank you for the idea for a book about portals and libraries and for recognizing that the goals and philosophies surrounding the portal concept will be central in the coming years to maintaining and improving access to scholarly information and to ensuring that libraries will continue to play a critical role in scholarly research. For me personally, working on this project has been a very important experience and I thank you for giving me the opportunity.

To Mindy Francis, thank you so much for your excellent work as guest editorial assistant. Your thoroughness, attention to detail, and good judgment have added a great deal of value to this compilation.

To Mary Jackson, your good work on the Scholars Portal has advanced the portal concept for all libraries. Library users are in your debt and on their behalf I thank you.

Introduction

When he first heard my proposal for a project to build a new kind of search and retrieval tool, the Marriott Library's assistant director for library computing, Gary Rasmussen, didn't think much of it. To him, it sounded like complicated work that would add to the burdens of an already overworked technology staff. He imagined hard-to-configure software with few instructions, programs that the staff couldn't comprehend, and expenditures for high-priced hardware. We had no Oracle expertise. Our applications programmer was brand new. We ought to spend the money on collections, or professional development, or public workstations.

Less than half a year later Gary changed his mind. "We have to do it–we have no choice." We were discussing participation in the Association of Research Libraries Scholars Portal Project. We were trying to decide whether to sign on as the seventh research library project participant, requiring over three years of work and an expenditure of six figure magnitude in pursuit of an ideal–a powerful search engine that would search the controlled and uncontrolled Web, designated OPACs, and licensed databases all at one time and would return the highest quality academic resources, presorted and de-duplicated, replete with full-text from all of our licensed electronic products, and digital images from the world's great research collections. It would be the dream portal.

What changed his mind? What induced a normally cautious administrator to climb on board for an experiment, one that might culminate in a product far short of our goal? Now in recollection Gary says that he was strongly influenced by Jerry Campbell's August 2000 White Paper

[Haworth co-indexing entry note]: "Introduction." Michalak, Sarah C. Co-published simultaneously in *Journal of Library Administration* (The Haworth Information Press, an imprint of The Haworth Press, Inc.) Vol. 43, No. 1/2, 2005, pp. 1-4; and: *Portals and Libraries* (ed: Sarah C. Michalak) The Haworth Information Press, an imprint of The Haworth Press, Inc., 2005, pp. 1-4. Single or multiple copies of this article are available for a fee from The Haworth Document Delivery Service [1-800-HAWORTH, 9:00 a.m. - 5:00 p.m. (EST). E-mail address: docdelivery@haworthpress.com].

Available online at http://www.haworthpress.com/web/JLA
Digital Object Identifier: 10.1300/J111v43n01_01

making a case for the Scholars Portal.[1] Campbell asserted that librarians are uniquely capable of organizing Web resources in a manner that is consistent with the values of scholarship and that there is now a unique opportunity for the library community to undertake this work for the benefit of our constituencies. Along with Campbell's influence, Gary was motivated by compelling testimonials from reference librarian colleagues regarding the need for a better database searching solution; and by his own instinct that taking a risk on this project as an active partner in a new and important national venture would be challenging professional work that would benefit our users greatly. I remember his vivid comment at the time: "If we don't participate in building a better mousetrap, we really shouldn't complain too much when the old traps don't do quite what we want or when the new traps, developed by others, also miss the mark."

Another factor which contributed to our decision to move ahead was a comprehensive search of the marketplace for a product that would help move academic information seekers away from reliance on commercial Web searching tools to a resource geared especially for academic research. Based on this search we concluded that working with other research libraries to develop such a product, not by programming from scratch, but by assembling modules from a vendor's existing products, might help us to achieve our common goal sooner than waiting for a fully developed commercial product.

With the enthusiastic support of the other two library directors on campus, the health sciences and law librarians, the strong interest and support of the university administration, and the promise of support from our statewide academic library consortium, we signed our Scholars Portal contract.

In the last two years of project participation, we have thought, talked, read, and heard a great deal about portals, and we continue to feel that our vision of a powerful tool for retrieving and organizing scholarly information is soon going to be a requirement, not an option, for academic information seekers. However, we are well aware that other definitions of the portal are thriving. In the belief that examining the spectrum of portals in libraries will be beneficial for anyone wanting to improve information access, I have assembled a volume presenting some of the multiple conceptions of portals.

Before summarizing the themes of the chapters included in this volume, it is appropriate to offer some observations about the use of the word "portal." Librarians often complain that it is an overworked term that does not precisely define the desired new level of access, and some predict that the term will soon fade from use. Perhaps, but for now the term retains its freshness and power. The library and information community continues to be captivated by the idea of a single gateway, a passageway to a more orderly information world. The word portal, while retaining its traditional dictionary definition of "doorway, entrance or gate; an entrance or means of entrance, *a portal of knowledge*," is just flexible enough, just metaphorical enough to permit its attachment to one's own particular vision of the information gateway in a new age.[2] In this volume readers will witness the flexibility of this term.

While the ARL group was thinking of a search platform or search engine (see "super-discovery tool" in the ARL Scholars Portal Project Final Report published in this volume), the innovative Internet Public Library was seeing the portal as a virtual library. Some saw the information gateway as an ordered aggregation of live links to librarian-selected information. Others envisioned an array of resources relating to a particular body of knowledge, for instance, the Library of Congress Portal to the World. Very early thinkers at North Carolina State adapted to the library environment the enterprise or institutional portal emerging in business and higher education, creating MyLibrary@NCState.

Portal terminology continues to remain current. In the 2004 ALA Annual Conference recently held in Orlando, Florida, there was a full-day preconference with eight presenters describing different aspects of portal technology to an audience of eighty. The overall ALA conference offered at least two other portal programs.

The chapters in this volume further demonstrate the continued viability and variability of the portal concept. Here eleven authors discuss different aspects of the portal idea. As you read these chapters I hope you will be impressed by the strong commitment of these authors to improving access to information. Just as impressive is the inventiveness and technical know-how of our librarian colleagues. In one article you will see full comprehension of the technologies that drive complex information systems.

While innovation and technical skill are consistent themes, you will also encounter other important capabilities and understandings. Reflections on library market analysis, useability testing and user feedback analysis, service development, skilled management of a complex software implementation process, and commentary on the successes and failures of various online learning systems also appear impressively among these chapters. Librarians are excellent theoreticians, as readers will once again be reminded in a chapter projecting the relational future of online catalogs and federated search engines (portals). A prediction on the outcome of the portal challenge to the commercial integrated library system and the predicted future development of nine key portal characteristics completes the volume.

Is the portal a fad that will soon join the paper printout of the serials list, the Wang-writer, and the 3 1/2 by 4 inch floppy disk? Is the portal a sort of grail, an ideal of access perfection that can never be achieved? Did my university's library leadership make the right investment in pursuing a portal development project? Here is my prediction after two years of portal implementation here at the University of Utah and after working with the accomplished library practitioners who contributed these chapters: it is probable that the access gateway metaphor will fade from currency. That metaphor suggests a "shape" for information, a recognizable, graspable "place-ness" of the information realm. Our minds grope for a way of understanding the deep space of Web information and the image of a gateway gives the imagination a specific locus from which to begin the search. Very soon, new software and hardware innovations, new receivers and transmitters of information will alter the shape of information in our minds. Even if the name "portal" disappears as a result of some new knowledge transformation, librarians will continue to advance the technology of access, seeking on behalf of our patrons the means of gaining reliable, ordered, comprehensible and applicable information.

Sarah C. Michalak

NOTES

1. Jerry D. Campbell, "The Case for Creating a Scholars Portal to the Web: A White Paper," ARL: A Bimonthly Report on Research Library Issues and Actions from ARL, CNI, and SPARC, no. 211 (August 2000): 1-3, <http://www.arl.org/access/scholarsportal/updates5_24_01.html>.

2. The American Heritage Dictionary, Houghton Milton Company, Boston, 1985, p. 966.

Chapter 1

The Internet Public Library
and the History of Library Portals

Susanna L. Davidsen

SUMMARY. The Internet Public Library at the University of Michigan School of Information was one of the first library portals on the Internet. This chapter covers the history of the IPL and its current manifestation. The IPL's relationship to other important library portals is discussed. *[Article copies available for a fee from The Haworth Document Delivery Service: 1-800-HAWORTH. E-mail address: <docdelivery@haworthpress.com> Website: <http://www.HaworthPress.com> © 2005 by The Haworth Press, Inc. All rights reserved.]*

KEYWORDS. Internet, libraries, portals

Susanna L. Davidsen is Associate Director for Academic Outreach and Practical Engagement Programs, University of Michigan School of Information (E-mail: davidsen@umich.edu). Ms. Davidson also serves as Managing Director of the Internet Public Library, and she created and managed the Michigan Electronic Library for eight years.

[Haworth co-indexing entry note]: "The Internet Public Library and the History of Library Portals." Davidsen, Susanna L. Co-published simultaneously in *Journal of Library Administration* (The Haworth Information Press, an imprint of The Haworth Press, Inc.) Vol. 43, No. 1/2, 2005, pp. 5-18; and: *Portals and Libraries* (ed: Sarah C. Michalak) The Haworth Information Press, an imprint of The Haworth Press, Inc., 2005, pp. 5-18. Single or multiple copies of this article are available for a fee from The Haworth Document Delivery Service [1-800-HAWORTH, 9:00 a.m. - 5:00 p.m. (EST). E-mail address: docdelivery@haworthpress.com].

Available online at http://www.haworthpress.com/web/JLA
Digital Object Identifier: 10.1300/J111v43n01_02

The Internet Public Library at the University of Michigan School of Information (www.ipl.org) is one of the first of the library portals on the Internet (see Figure 1). It played a pioneering role in the development of not only library portals, but commercial ones as well including Yahoo! The IPL is considered a portal because it offers a subject directory to quality Internet sites as well as services that are part of a library's mission. This article considers that past and future of the Internet Public Library in the context of other library portals with similar audiences and missions.

Library portals serve as gateways to the Internet. A library portal can take a very narrow point of view or an expansive world view and can be produced by educational institutions, commercial firms, or governments. All of these collect Internet information and organize it to make that information more valuable to a constituent group.

Applying a descriptive name for these portals has been a difficult task. When the Internet Portals Interest Group[1] of ALA's LITA division first met in 2002, there was extensive discussion surrounding the definition of a portal. It was decided to leave the definition broad in order to include more interested people and let it shape itself as the group came together. It could be argued that all portals to Internet information are a form of virtual library. The library portals discussed in this article are primarily those that collect, evaluate, and organize Internet resources into a subject directory and perhaps offer other library services such as access to proprietary databases or virtual reference service.

HISTORY

The Internet Public Library (IPL)[2] began in 1995 as a class at the University of Michigan's School of Information. Faculty member Joe Janes thought it would be interesting and educational to see if a class of aspiring information specialists could create a public library on the Internet.[3] The class created job descriptions for department heads, directors, youth librarians, and all the people associated with running a library. In place of a facilities manager they needed a computer programmer, and they didn't need a circulation clerk. However, the organization would be familiar to librarians in a public library. The students decided what collections there would be, what services the library would offer and even chose a board to oversee the library. When the IPL opened on St. Patrick's Day of 1995, there was a reference section (http://www.ipl.org/div/subject/browse/ref00.00.00), a youth section with

FIGURE 1. The Internet Public Library Home Page

story times, services for professional librarians, a classroom, exhibit hall, and reading room. In 1996, a Multi-user Object Oriented System (MOO)[4] in the library lobby mimicked public space in a bricks and mortar library where people would run into each other and chat about everything and anything: their jobs, books, and poetry. There was even a wind-up duck used to start conversation.

Of the original group of students all were in Library and Information Studies with the exception of two students from the School of Engineering. IPL Meetings ran late into the night when students were at their best and creativity flowed. The course continued every term and each group of students added to the richness and diversity of the IPL collections and experience.[5] When Janes left the School of Information in 1998, the IPL continued under the leadership of David Carter, who had been director of collections. The IPL's public services and courses continue at the school in the form of a three-credit-hour practicum in which students assume the roles of collection specialists, reference administrators, usability testers, and programmers.

MISSION

The IPL has three objectives:

- Provide a teaching environment
- Provide a research environment for faculty
- Provide services to the public

As a teaching environment the IPL has served as a laboratory for over one thousand students within the U.S. and Canada. Reference courses at the University of Michigan, Maryland, Washington, Syracuse University, and others have utilized the IPL's Ask a Question service to train digital reference librarians, while our course here has also allowed students to gain practical experience in digital collection building, interface design, usability testing, database management, and library administration. The School of Information requires that all of our master's students have some practical experience as part of their degree program here at the School. Our Practical Engagement Program includes the Internet Public Library as one of the places students can get such experiences. In the course, students hear from practitioners and theoreticians during seminar time and work on their projects to meld the theory with practice.

The IPL is a rich resource for faculty. There are over eight years of reference questions and answers. Usage statistics await analysis and our Information Economics, Management and Policy faculty are conducting a study of how public goods are funded using the IPL as a testbed. Visiting faculty from Korea are also eager to use the IPL for their research into digital reference. The IPL is currently working with the Tec de Monterrey in Monterrey, Mexico to export this practicum into their library science program to start building a Biblioteca Publica Internet in Spanish.

Providing public services to Internet users is an integral part of our students' learning experience. Although subject to the vagaries of the

Internet, the pool of students in each term's class, and the sometimes too broad audience we intend to serve, some services are consistently available:

- Reference (http://www.ipl.org/div/askus/), collections (http://www. ipl.org/div/subject/),
- Newspaper access (http://www.ipl.org/div/news/),
- KidSpace (http://www.ipl.org/div/kidspace/),
- Teen Space (http://www.ipl.org/div/teen/),
- Literary criticism (http://www.ipl.org/div/litcrit/)

To our own dismay, we cannot always offer the level of service we'd like. When we don't have enough students handling reference, for example, we need to place our reference service less prominently on the pages so as to slow down the number of queries we receive. At other times we have many students in our reference classes and need to boost our business by advertising the service heavily. This serves as yet another real life learning experience for our students who must deal with the waxing and waning of the public's information needs. The IPL's reference questions follow the academic calendar quite closely in that demand rises when students are in mid- to late-term and writing papers, while demand drops around holidays and the beginning of a term. Both K-12 and higher education calendars influence the quantity of questions.

ADMINISTRATION

The Internet Public Library is currently staffed by 2.75 full time equivalent (FTE) information school employees dedicated to the IPL, 13 students at the University of Michigan, 300 students at various institutions around North America, 33 regular reference volunteers around the world, and volunteer time from one faculty member and one staff member. A full time reference coordinator and interface specialist are on board as well as a 30-hour-per-week technology specialist. These positions are internships intended for recent graduates or people new to the field. Associate Professor Maurita Holland serves as faculty advisor and Executive Director of the IPL and the author acts as Managing Director. The Executive Director and Managing Director positions are voluntary and service is in addition to regular duties in the University's School of Information.

A number of recent articles in the library media have discussed the budget problems of the IPL, which have been existent since Mellon funding ended in 1997. In 1995, the school applied for and received a Mellon Grant to support the Internet Public Library. The School of Information has supported the project since the Mellon Funding ended. The faculty's research into public goods funding will test raising funds through various mechanisms such as fund drives, donations, and memberships. The issue of portal funding will be discussed in more detail later in this chapter.

FEATURES

Like the original IPL of opening day 1995, the current IPL features Ask a Question, Reference, Collections, KidSpace, and Exhibits. Other features are:

- collections of literary criticism
- cataloging records for online texts
- Dublin Core compatible metadata for every link in the IPL
- A database and database entry software

Our most popular features are:

- KidSpace
- Ask a Question
- The newspaper collection
- POTUS (Presidents of the United States)
- Stately News
- Science Fair Project Resources

COLLECTION CONTENT

The IPL collections (Figure 2) contain links to and abstracts of what we consider to be the best sites on the Internet in various subject areas based on our collection criteria. These links are contained in a database that searches for and serves up a list whenever a user chooses a subject

FIGURE 2. The Internet Public Library's Collections

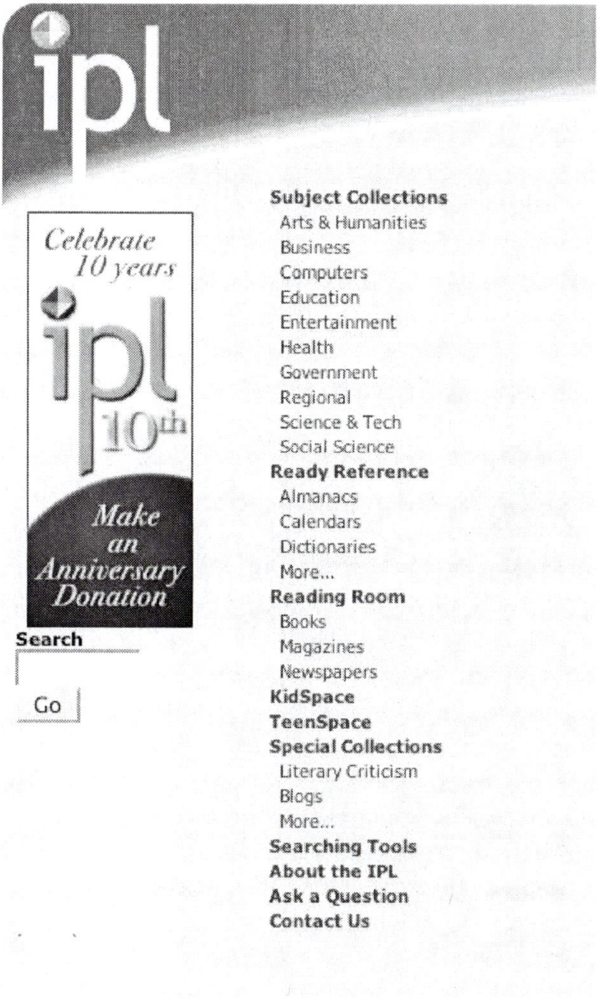

Subject Collections
Arts & Humanities
Business
Computers
Education
Entertainment
Health
Government
Regional
Science & Tech
Social Science
Ready Reference
Almanacs
Calendars
Dictionaries
More...
Reading Room
Books
Magazines
Newspapers
KidSpace
TeenSpace
Special Collections
Literary Criticism
Blogs
More...
Searching Tools
About the IPL
Ask a Question
Contact Us

Celebrate 10 years

Make an Anniversary Donation

Search

Go

area from our menus. Our metadata records for these sites include the basic Dublin Core elements[6] and an abstract. Our goal is to cover all subject areas, but like every other portal trying to do this, we fall short in some areas such as Mental Health and overcompensate in others such as Sports.

OTHER PORTALS

A number of commercial, educational and government portals also meet the definition of a library portal. This is not meant to be an exhaustive nor definitive list, but rather the list of portals that the IPL compares itself to:

- Yahoo!
- The Librarian's Index to the Internet
- Michigan eLibrary
- BUBL Information Service
- InfoMine

Yahoo! began in 1994 as the hobby of two PhD students at Stanford: Jerry Yang and David Filo.[7] The author received a call in 1994 from Jerry Yang asking how the author chose the organizational method for the gopher forerunner to the Michigan Electronic Library, GoMLink. (MLink was a University of Michigan program that created the gopher as an offshoot from a statewide reference service for Michigan.) After a 40-minute conversation about how librarians organize materials, the author was asked if she felt there was any commercial potential for a catalog of the Internet. The answer was that the Internet would never be cataloged completely (nor did it deserve to be) and that there was no money to be made.

GoMLink proved to have a significant influence on the subject directory structure of Yahoo! as well as Yahoo!'s hiring practices. Not long after our conversation, the categories and hierarchy at Yahoo! mirrored those of GoMLink, and Yahoo! began hiring professional librarians to catalog their links. Over time, Yahoo's categories, intended for the general public, and the Michigan Electronic Library's hierarchy, intended for librarians, began to diverge. This was a good thing considering that hierarchies and thesauri should be created for the user of the information not the organizer.

One of the earliest attempts to organize the Internet was made by Carole Leita at the Berkeley Public Library in 1991. She kept an organized list of her gopher bookmarks shortly after the release of gopher software. It became the Web-based Berkeley Public Library's Index to the Internet in 1993. In 1997, the name was changed to Librarians' Index to the Internet,[8] the service was moved to UC Berkeley's SunSITE and began assigning Library of Congress Subject Headings (LCSH) to the entries. The LII is now part of the California Digital Library. The LII's mission is

> to provide a well-organized point of access for reliable, trustworthy, librarian-selected Internet resources, serving California, the nation, and the world.[9]

The Michigan eLibrary[10] was created for public librarians in the state of Michigan to help them use the Internet more easily and efficiently when helping their patrons. In 1992, gopher software was used to create a list of the best sites on the Internet, organized into categories by subject and medium like those of a public library. Funding came from the W. K. Kellogg Foundation and the University of Michigan through a university library program to offer reference services to a statewide network of public library consortia. In 1995, the university library was awarded a grant by the state of Michigan to continue the gopher as a WWW service with the new name of the Michigan Electronic Library. That service was taken into the state library in 2000 when the statewide reference program ended. It has since added access to a number of proprietary databases that are available to all libraries in the state at no cost to the libraries or patrons. More recently some of these databases have been made available for home and office access directly to patrons. The service is now called the Michigan eLibrary and is managed out of the Library of Michigan.

The BUBL Information Service (the **Bu**lletin **B**oard for **L**ibraries), run out of Strathclyde University in the United Kingdom since 1993, provides "Free User-Friendly Access to Selected Internet Resources Covering all Subject Areas, with a Special Focus on Library and Information Science."[11]

BUBL is arranged by Dewey Decimal Classification (DDC) and uses a heavily customized version of the LCSH. BUBL is considered a national resource for members of the higher education community.

The BUBL Mission Statement is:

> To provide value-added access to Internet resources and services of academic, research, and professional significance to the UK Higher Education community by:
>
> • Direct service provision, incorporating subject-based, classified and other organisational routes

- Creating and stimulating the creation of original electronic resources
- Mounting appropriate commercial services
- Providing organised access to other services
- Encouraging and co-ordinating the efforts of information specialists
- Providing associated reference, help, current awareness and training services

To help meet these objectives, BUBL aims to offer fast, easy-to-use and reliable access to selected high-quality resources of academic relevance, both on its own servers and worldwide.[12]

InfoMine is another scholarly portal that covers all subject areas.[13] InfoMine is housed at the University of California Riverside and began as a resource for engineering, science, and math. It now covers all areas of scholarly pursuit and is known for its pioneering efforts on the technical side of portals. The work into iVia, an open source library portal and virtual library system,[14] should prove interesting to all portal sites, especially the work on automated harvesting that will reduce the number of items an evaluator needs to look through.

COMMONALITIES

All of these virtual library portals began early in the history of Internet content utilizing the latest technologies of the time. Forward-looking people, all with library backgrounds (with the exception of Yahoo!), some with technical expertise and others with organizational expertise, took the lead and weren't afraid to experiment.

Another common trait is that they all wanted to bring order out of chaos whether by means of Dewey Decimal Classification (BUBL), Library of Congress Subject Headings (LII) or homegrown hierarchies (IPL, MeL, and Yahoo!). There were no metadata standards when these projects began.

All but Yahoo! evaluate the sites they choose to include and credential the information using library principles and practice in collection development.

Two of the most difficult commonalities to discuss are funding and audience.

AUDIENCE

Although some of the projects such as BUBL and InfoMine state their primary audience is scholars and people in the higher education community, each tried to cover all areas of human endeavor. The Michigan eLibrary and Librarians' Index to the Internet cater to the needs of the citizens of their states, and the Internet Public Library and Yahoo! cater to the needs of all Internet users everywhere. This duplication of effort begs the question as to whether the duplication is valuable or not. On the yes side is that slice of user perspective that makes the Michigan eLibrary and LII and InfoMine successful. Particular attention is paid in the MeL to materials of interest to Michiganders while LII has a strong collection of materials of interest to Californians. InfoMine and BUBL cater to scholars and Yahoo! is all things to all people. If the targeted users of these services are happy, then the purpose has been served.

On the other hand, would the user of LII be just as happy if part of the service was the section of the database from BUBL that covered library and information sciences or the piece of InfoMine devoted to computer software? Could MeL users interested in California be happy with the California-related materials from LII? And could scholarly technology transfer offices be interested in the parts of MeL that cover doing business with Canada? These are intriguing questions that those of us who already run portals have said yes to. Just how this merger could be accomplished, however, is a funding issue.

FUNDING

Funding is the most difficult issue facing all of these portals, with the exception of Yahoo! None of these portal concepts is a new and exciting idea and the major funding providers have grown bored with them, although the aggregated number of monthly visits is in the hundreds of millions. In the state of Michigan, MeL has been accepted by public and academic libraries as a resource for their patrons, leaving local libraries to find and evaluate those Web resources of most interest to their local constituency. The same is true of LII in California. Both projects involved librarians from the outset and were seen as resources rather than competition to public libraries.

The Internet Public Library with its roots in the educational community has more difficulty with this issue and has made more inroads into school libraries where resources are scarce. The name "public library" is also in some ways a difficulty in that it both implies it is the only public library on the Internet and points to the inability of the public library metaphor to extend into funding. "Real" public libraries in the U.S. are funded through local property taxes. The Internet Public Library has no physical property and there is no real estate on the Internet to tax. The constituents include the population of the Internet who, as yet, have not been successfully lobbied to provide funding for something that in most communities is free. Outside of the U.S., the IPL serves a population with limited funding to sustain their own physical needs. And funding will not come from that sector. This leaves the Internet Public Library with trying to meet the needs of the world with funding from no one. Current faculty research aside, the possibility that funding needs will be met by the users of the IPL is slim. The two virtual library portals that have been absorbed by their state governments seemed to have been in a good position until the U.S. economy went into a downturn and states are finding themselves with billion dollar shortfalls. There have been no cuts yet, but that message could come any day. BUBL has some funding from the UK government and may find itself in a similar position during economic hard times. Educational institutions, too, are looking for ways to make up for the lost dollars that come from states and federal governments.

POSSIBLE SOLUTIONS

Life without the library portals would leave users with two options: Yahoo! and Google. What need is there of a library portal with a subject directory if you can simply search for what you want and get it? What need is there if the user can search a database of every Web site on the Internet? As librarians, we know what a simplistic argument these assertions pose. Does the user want (or deserve) whatever comes to the top of the search results or has been entered (even if slipped into its subject category by a librarian) into a non-discriminating database of all Web sites? How do you know who created it? Is it truthful, unbiased, easy to use, and does it meet a dozen other criteria that library portals apply before even showing a user a link? In her upcoming book, Bettina Fabos of the University of Northern Iowa presents her research that addresses the need for non-commercial portals in the classroom.[15] The need for credentialed information is critical until we find a way of turning all Web users into discriminating information seekers. Since that does not look like a likely prospect for the future, the need for what a virtual library portal does to evaluate, organize, and describe Web sites is acute.

A national cooperative effort could help these virtual library portals with funding issues, provide selective, high-quality content to the Internet user, and bring some innovation back into the virtual library portals. There are virtual library portals such as MeL and the IPL with administrative software that could be further developed as joint projects in open source. Sites such as InfoMine are looking at future software needs to help evaluate and cull material in an automated fashion to cut down on the time needed for selectors to spend surfing the Web.[16] Reference services could be integrated with services already extant such 24/7 or the IPL's Ask a Question service. An exchange of records that will bring California's material into the Michigan eLibrary and the ability for a user to switch from public library materials to scholarly no matter which virtual library portal he or she is in would greatly add to the usability of any of these sites.

For those portals that want to begin cooperating, there is a serious concern about maintaining their identities when requesting funding. Identity fuels the current funding of each portal. The state of Michigan would not want to fund the California Electronic Library nor would California care to support the MeL. As each portal grew up within its state or academic setting, the identity of that portal became intertwined with the funder. All of these early groundbreaking portals in some way tied themselves to a state or academic institution upon whom they are now dependent for funding. This is more problematic than may be supposed. How can one co-brand a record in such a way that the originating portal (and funder) is given credit, but the user understands that he or she is in a Michigan portal or California portal paid for by the state? Will the state governments object to the use by other states' citizens of materials paid for by that state?

It may be time for a national virtual library portal or Internet Gateway to bring together the best of virtual library portals already created and still being maintained. As the states of California and Michigan have discovered, a statewide resource shared by all and paid for once has its definite advantages. The requirement to be all things to all people would be eliminated for the contributing virtual library portals and they would then be able to shine where their special talents lie. Some can contribute credentialed content, some laboratory space for training future information professionals, and some software and hardware expertise. There will always be those who choose to go their own ways, but the nation needs to establish a baseline of good content, software and practices to deliver core information to the citizens of the U.S. Should other services, such as BUBL in the UK, wish to contribute their expertise, we would make small steps to a global library (granted, an English global library, but that needn't be true for long!).

CONCLUSION

Virtual library portals are still viable and useful gateways to the Internet that need the expertise of librarians to evaluate and organize high quality information on the Internet. Without them, the only options available will be Yahoo! and search engines like Google, which neither evaluate nor discriminate. A national effort to create a core collection with individual states and academic institutions contributing to special collections would be one way to keep these portals viable and visible. Funding is not the only issue that stands in the way of this type of national effort. Cooperation between libraries, funding agencies, governments, schools, universities, and professional organizations is critical for any of these projects to succeed in the future. As resources become more scarce, cooperation becomes the way to address the need for virtual library portals and yet, paradoxically, it is also the time when many of us look to our own interests first. We need to look beyond ourselves if we want to see the future.

NOTES

1. http://litaipig.ucr.edu/index.php.
2. http://ipl/.org.
3. For the definitive history of the IPL's origins, see Janes, Joseph. "The Internet Public Library: An Intellectual History," *Library Hi Tech.* 1998. Vol. 16, Iss. 2; pg. 55, 15 pgs.
4. Multi-user Object Oriented systems.
5. http://www.ipl.org/div/class/.
6. ISO standard 15836-2003 available at http://www.niso.org/international/SC4/n515.pdf.
7. http://docs.yahoo.com/info/misc/history.html.
8. http://lii.org/.
9. About the LII available at http://lii.org/search/file/about.
10. http://mel.org/.
11. http://bubl.ac.uk/.
12. BUBL Mission Statement quoted from http://bubl.ac.uk/admin/purpose.htm.
13. http://infomine.ucr.edu/.
14. http://infomine.ucr.edu/iVia/.
15. Fabos, Bettina. *A Commercial Highway in Every Classroom.*
16. "Data Fountains: A National, Cooperative Information Utility for Shared Internet Resource Discovery, Metadata Application and Rich, Full-text Harvest of Value to Internet Portals, Virtual Libraries and Library Catalogs with Portal-like Capabilities."

Chapter 2

MyLibrary@NCState:
A Library Portal After Five Years

Karen Ciccone

SUMMARY. The MyLibrary@NCState Web portal was created to help
users reduce "information overload," to allow them to create personal
Web pages containing their most frequently consulted library electronic
resources and services, and to provide a new avenue of communication
between librarians and discipline-specific populations of users. This
chapter will look at each of these goals and discuss how well the current
product has managed to meet them. In doing so, it will also cover the relationships between library portals and course pages, the evolution of
MyLibrary in the context of changes to the Libraries' Web site, and future directions for development. *[Article copies available for a fee from The
Haworth Document Delivery Service: 1-800-HAWORTH. E-mail address:
<docdelivery@haworthpress.com> Website: <http://www.HaworthPress.com>
© 2005 by The Haworth Press, Inc. All rights reserved.]*

KEYWORDS. Portals, personalization, customization, MyLibrary,
MyLibrary@NCState

Karen Ciccone is Head of the Natural Resources Library, North Carolina State University Libraries (E-mail: karen_ciccone@ncsu.edu).

[Haworth co-indexing entry note]: "MyLibrary@NCState: A Library Portal After Five Years." Ciccone,
Karen. Co-published simultaneously in *Journal of Library Administration* (The Haworth Information Press,
an imprint of The Haworth Press, Inc.) Vol. 43, No. 1/2, 2005, pp. 19-35; and: *Portals and Libraries* (ed:
Sarah C. Michalak) The Haworth Information Press, an imprint of The Haworth Press, Inc., 2005, pp. 19-35.
Single or multiple copies of this article are available for a fee from The Haworth Document Delivery Ser-
vice [1-800-HAWORTH, 9:00 a.m. - 5:00 p.m. (EST). E-mail address: docdelivery@ haworthpress.com].

INTRODUCTION

The idea of creating a personalized library portal for NC State users arose as early as 1996, inspired by the advent of such commercial personalized portal services as My Yahoo! and My Excite. Library electronic resources were already proliferating, and it was clear that users were having difficulty navigating the library's information system to access needed information. A personalized presentation of library resources and services seemed a natural way to address this problem. In 1998, focus group interviews conducted by the NCSU Libraries' Digital Library Initiatives department confirmed that users were having trouble finding and choosing from the many electronic resources available. As one participant stated, "We want access to the world's knowledge, but we only want to see one particular part of it at any one particular time." MyLibrary@NCState was created as a means of addressing this "information overload."[1,2]

The primary purposes for which MyLibrary was developed can be summarized as follows:

- To help users reduce "information overload" by providing views of selected ("recommended") library resources and services for particular disciplines;
- To provide a portable, customizable Web page containing a user's most frequently consulted electronic resources and services; and
- To provide an avenue for communication between librarians and discipline-specific populations of users.

While the MyLibrary software has served these purposes, new technological capabilities make possible the development of an improved library portal. This chapter will look at each of the preceding goals and discuss how well the current product has managed to meet them. In doing so, it will also cover the relationships between library portals and course pages, the evolution of MyLibrary in the context of changes to the Libraries' Web site, and future directions for development.

A NOTE ABOUT MyLibrary USAGE

Although the current number of MyLibrary accounts is nearly 5,000 (for an NC State population of approximately 30,000), this statistic includes a large number of inactive accounts. Even at the peak of our marketing efforts, the number of active MyLibrary accounts never reached over approximately five to ten percent of the NC State population. Our statistics have consistently shown that the majority of accounts created are used only rarely, while a small percentage of accounts are very heavily used. We are interested in preserving the features that regular MyLibrary users find useful while increasing the usefulness of the service for the majority of our patrons.

INFORMATION OVERLOAD, CUSTOMIZATION, AND PERSONALIZATION

The problems and issues of MyLibrary are inextricably linked to the broader issue of access to library electronic resources. At the time of MyLibrary's implementation, electronic resources were organized on the NCSU Libraries' Web site into three categories: databases, electronic journals, and "Web sites." Users could choose subjects to retrieve relevant lists of resources in each of those categories. While these lists were manageable in size at first, they quickly became unwieldy in length, resulting in a situation that has been dubbed "information overload." MyLibrary improved upon this situation by presenting users with shorter lists of "recommended" resources for a particular discipline, and by providing users with the ability to customize these lists, choosing resources from multiple disciplines according to need. It also brought users directly to the relevant resources for a particular discipline, circumventing the need to navigate from the Libraries' homepage to the lists of electronic resources for that subject. In these ways, it was a boon to some frequent users of library resources.

MyLibrary is both personalized and customizable, and it is useful to distinguish between those two aspects of the service. When users create new MyLibrary accounts, they profile themselves as belonging to one of 65 "disciplines," terms in a controlled vocabulary based upon the university's course registration system and roughly corresponding to research and teaching programs within the university. This selection enables the software to present users with personalized information, including contact information for subject specialist librarians, links to specialized services and locations (e.g., branch libraries), and lists of selected resources for their disciplines. (See Figure 1.)

Customization, on the other hand, requires greater user interaction with the software. By clicking on any of the many "customize" links on

FIGURE 1. Users select disciplines from the pull-down list in order to receive personalized information. The software also allows the possibility of merging resources from multiple disciplines.

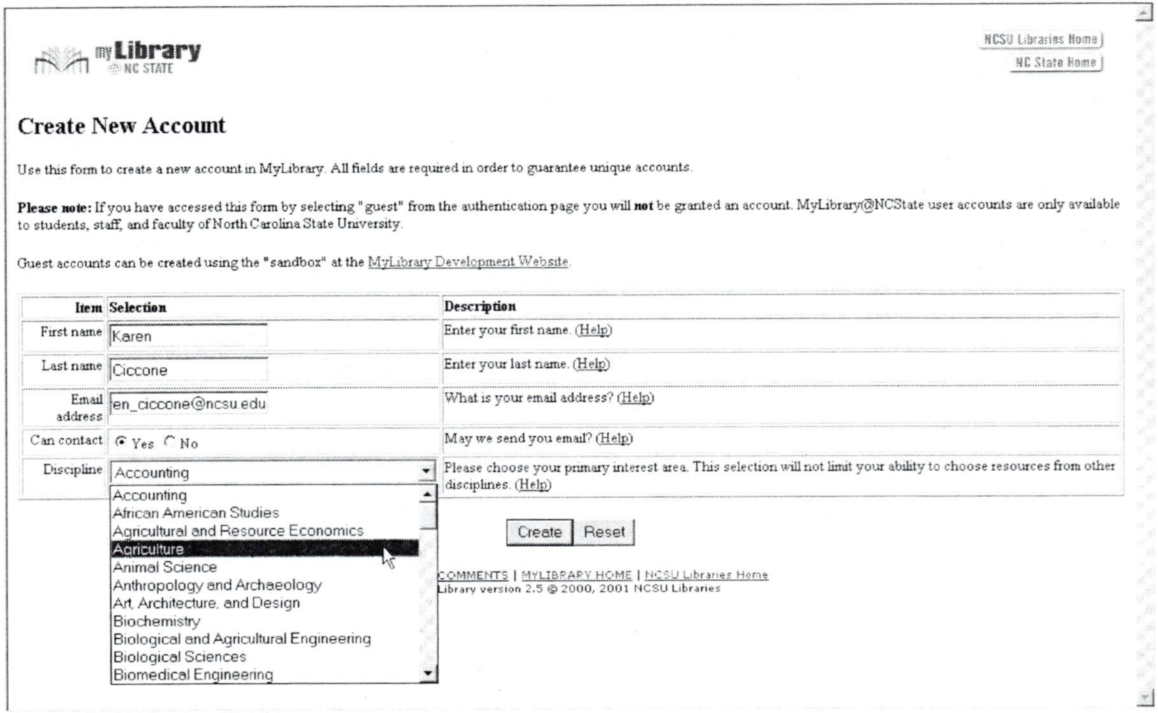

their MyLibrary pages, users can select resources from multiple disciplines and combine them on a single list. Users can also add links to any free resources on the Web, create customized lists of "quick searches" (e.g., a library catalog search, a dictionary search, a Google search of the Web, etc.), and receive customized new book alerts using the "New Titles" feature. They can even customize the layout and style of their pages through the selection of different templates and colors. These features enable users to create Web pages custom-tailored to their research needs. (See Figure 2.)

Whereas customization is integral to the perceived purpose of MyLibrary, it is anecdotally evident that the personalization aspect has been of greater value to many of our users. Rather commonly, a user has requested that a particular resource be added to "MyLibrary," meaning to his or her MyLibrary page. Sometimes this resource is not already in the MyLibrary database, but often it is. In these cases, the response to the user has been to explain how to customize his or her resources lists by clicking on the word "customize" within each category, and then choosing resources from the various lists by discipline. It becomes clear through these conversations that often users are unaware that customization is possible, and that they prefer MyLibrary to the Libraries' Web site simply because it provides them direct access to "just the resources I need." In other words, users are unaware that they can navigate to a similar list of default resources for a particular discipline on the Libraries' Web site. This points out the need for both improved design of the Libraries' Web site, to make it easier to find databases by subject, and of the MyLibrary interface, to make the customization feature more apparent.

It is also the case that users need customization features that take very little time to work through and figure out. Anecdotal evidence indicates that users who are aware of the customization option often find it too cumbersome to be very useful. Users have remarked, for example, that their Internet browser "favorites" or "bookmarks" better serve the same purpose, even though these must be saved to a file for transport from one computer to another. Some libraries with personal portals have responded to the need for easier customization by creating the means for users to select resources by clicking on links in their catalog and/or database lists. The University of Toronto Libraries, for example, includes "add to my.library" links in its catalogue and e-resources lists. An improved library portal would provide customization options in these places where users are likely to encounter library resources, as well as make finding and adding resources within the portal as simple as possible.

FIGURE 2. Users customize their personal pages by selecting resources from alphabetical or discipline-specific lists.

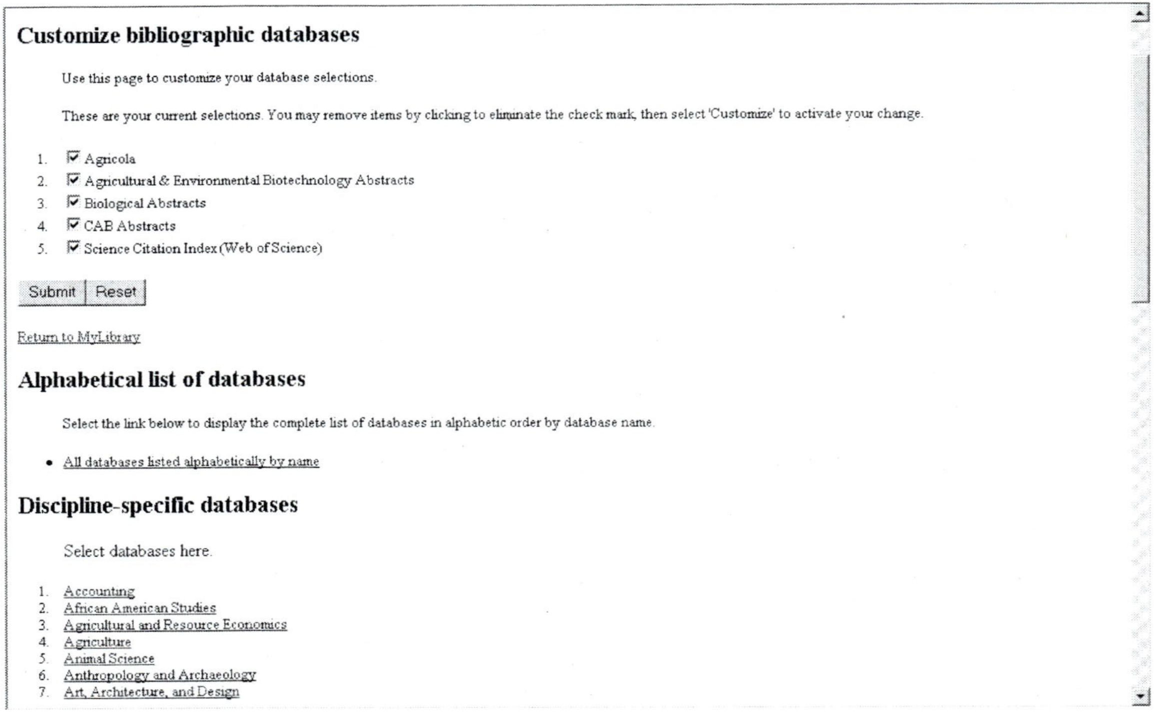

Customize bibliographic databases

Use this page to customize your database selections.

These are your current selections. You may remove items by clicking to eliminate the check mark, then select 'Customize' to activate your change.

1. ☑ Agricola
2. ☑ Agricultural & Environmental Biotechnology Abstracts
3. ☑ Biological Abstracts
4. ☑ CAB Abstracts
5. ☑ Science Citation Index (Web of Science)

[Submit] [Reset]

Return to MyLibrary

Alphabetical list of databases

Select the link below to display the complete list of databases in alphabetic order by database name.

- All databases listed alphabetically by name

Discipline-specific databases

Select databases here.

1. Accounting
2. African American Studies
3. Agricultural and Resource Economics
4. Agriculture
5. Animal Science
6. Anthropology and Archaeology
7. Art, Architecture, and Design

Assuming that users could be made aware, through better design, of how to customize their MyLibrary@NCState pages, and that the customization process could be simplified, there is still the question of whether the current product is flexible enough to allow for a degree of customization that would be useful for many people. Many users have expressed the desire to use MyLibrary as a way to simplify access to resources for their courses and projects, but the software in its current form does not allow users to create these new categories. Resources must be added to the sections already provided on the page. In the NCSU Libraries' instantiation of the software, these are called Library Links, University Links, Karen's (i.e., user's) Links, Quick Searches, Reference Shelf, Indexes and Abstracts, and Electronic Journals. (See Figure 3.) Similarly, users cannot turn off categories, or move them around, or add multiple resource types (e.g., databases AND electronic journals) to the same category. So the product is less useful than it could be for many purposes. This shortcoming is especially apparent for undergraduates, who generally lack a discipline focus and therefore have a difficult time customizing MyLibrary to suit their needs. A product that allowed them to create and populate categories for projects and course work might have more appeal.

The experience of librarians at the University of Toronto with their my.library product supports the assertion that greater flexibility in customization is needed. Unlike MyLibrary@NCState, my.library at the University of Toronto forces users to create a page from scratch, so users are necessarily made aware of the customization option. It also gives users complete flexibility in creating, naming, arranging, and populating categories of resources. Interestingly, this product is quite popular, and the majority of its users are undergraduates.[3] This is quite the opposite of our experience with MyLibrary@NCState, which has seen fairly low usage and seems to be least useful of all to undergraduates. It seems that the ability to create a fully customized page of library resources might indeed be helpful to our users.

COURSE PAGES vs. PERSONALIZED PORTAL

In addition to giving users near-complete freedom in customizing their library resources pages, the University of Toronto my.library software gives users the ability to publish their pages as static Web guides for others to use. Librarians and faculty alike use the product to create customized lists of library resources for specific courses. This is, in fact,

FIGURE 3. There are six MyLibrary layouts available. This one is dubbed "Folder." All contain the same basic sections.

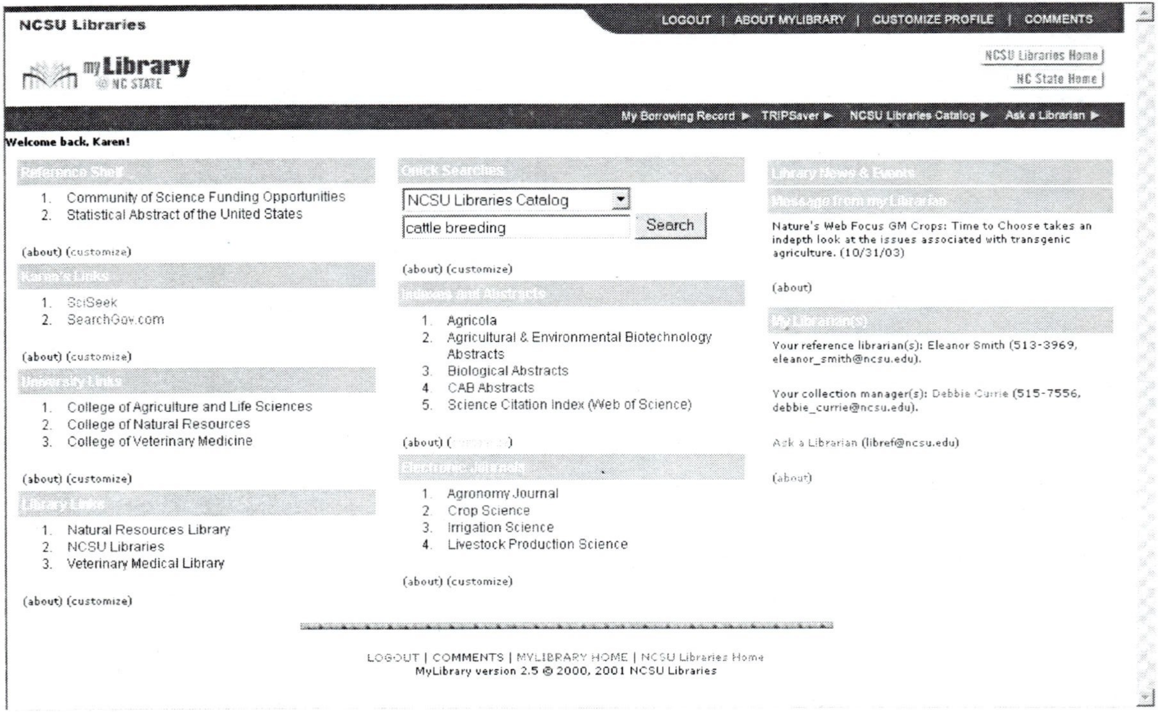

the most popular use of the product. My.library developers are working to further improve functionality for this purpose by adding the ability to link directly to specific articles for course readings.[4]

Librarians at Virginia Commonwealth University have also found the creation of course pages for students to be the most popular use of their My Library software. Dan Ream and Jim Graphery, developers of VCU's My Library, state, "We suspect that students see their needs changing from class to class and semester to semester and thus the content of their My Library page might be too fluid to stay valuable with frequent re-editing. The course-specific page, on the other hand, meets their immediate needs and therein lies its popularity. . . . Our perception is that only regular or frequent users of library resources would [find] any value in a Web shortcut to favorite resources, for they are the only users who have a sense of "favorites" among library tools to begin with."[5]

Librarians at the University of Rochester Library, citing low adoption rates for VCU's and NC State's library portals, chose to develop instead a system for creating course-related library resources pages linked to professors' syllabi and course reserves. By putting library resources where the students were already going, and by connecting them in a meaningful way to their classes, they created a useful and popular service.[6] They are now offering the application they developed, Library Course Builder (LibCB) as open source code. It is available through SourceForge at http://sourceforge.net/projects/libcb/.

Other libraries have integrated library resources into their campus's course management systems to the same end. One successful example is Pennsylvania State University Libraries' adaptation of their campus's ANGEL course management software.[7] Faculty can easily request, and librarians can easily create, course-specific lists of library resources using this software. As with the Rochester approach, librarians are putting library resources where students need them and are likely to use them–in the context of the courses they are taking.

Reflecting a demand for these types of services on the NC State campus is the fact that the MyLibrary feature most often requested by users is the ability to publish personal pages for course use. Librarians would also like to have such a tool, since they currently create and maintain course pages and subject guides by hand. Although the MyLibrary software includes a "publish static page" feature, it again forces resources into the basic categories defined by the software and is therefore not flexible enough for these purposes. One of our goals is to develop a tool to simplify course page creation and better integrate these resources into the online course environment.

An intriguing idea is the possibility of utilizing registration data to provide users with links to relevant course resources within the library portal. While students may not be interested in creating customized lists of "favorite" library resources, they might be very appreciative of being presented with lists of resources or course pages based upon the courses for which they are registered. We plan to explore feasibility of this idea.

MyLibrary AND THE LIBRARIES' WEB SITE

As the Libraries' Web site has become more usable and sophisticated, the advantage of MyLibrary as an easier-to-use interface has diminished to some extent. Additionally, with the creation of new tools such as the NCSU Libraries Database Finder and E-journal Finder, the Libraries' Web site now has functionality not available through MyLibrary. Whereas MyLibrary provides only alphabetized lists of databases for each discipline, Database Finder produces categorized lists with "core" resources at the top, databases covering related or narrower subjects in the middle, and databases including some coverage of the subject at the bottom. For the user who appreciated MyLibrary's ability to provide a personalized list of databases for a particular discipline, the Libraries' Web site can now serve that purpose without the need to create an account.

The NCSU Libraries E-journal Finder allows users to determine whether electronic access to a particular issue of a journal is available, either by subscription or through one of our aggregator databases. Users can search for electronic journals by title, discipline, or publisher. By contrast, MyLibrary does not contain a complete list of journals subscribed to by the Libraries, does not include aggregated titles at all, and does not provide the ability to search for a specific title. As thousands of titles were made available to our users through publisher packages and aggregators, it became impossible for the MyLibrary system to provide access to all of these. Even if a process had been in place to easily import the new titles into the MyLibrary database, the result would have been unmanageably long lists of e-journals for each discipline. Without an easy system for users to search e-journals by title in order to add them to their pages, this would not have been very useful.

Perhaps the most significant piece of functionality missing from MyLibrary is the ability to search across multiple databases at the same time. The NCSU Libraries MultiSearch tool, accessible through the Database Finder, lets users type their searches once and receive results from multiple databases complying with the Z39.50 standard. It also lets them merge and de-duplicate these results. (See Figure 4.) Although links to this tool could in theory be added to the list of Quick Searches available in MyLibrary, these would in effect take users out of the MyLibrary interface and not actually add much to the functionality of that product. Users would not be able, for example, to metasearch across only the selected databases on their MyLibrary pages, as they might reasonably expect to be able to do. A product that could provide metasearching capability as well as the customization features of user-maintained lists of favorite resources, saved results sets and search histories, and article alerts, would be much more useful. We envision enhancing our MultiSearch product to provide this functionality in the future.

There is the potential to migrate other features of MyLibrary to the Web site and catalog in ways that would make them available to a greater number of users. We are currently working to provide an enhanced "New Titles" feature by taking advantage of the capabilities of the Sirsi Unicorn integrated library system. Sirsi's iLink provides custom alerts based on author and subject heading, and this service will eventually be accessible through both the Libraries' catalog and the user's borrower record. A list of recently received titles by call number will also be made available from the Libraries' Web site.

COMMUNICATION

Arguably the most innovative aspect of MyLibrary is the way it connects individual users with librarians. By classifying librarians as belonging to specific disciplines, the software provides users with lists of "their" librarians–collection managers for collections-related requests and reference librarians for general research needs. These librarians also have access to users through the "Message from my Librarian" feature, which lets them post news items of interest to specific user groups to those users' MyLibrary pages. Of equal importance, the software gives librarians the ability to send e-mail messages to all users profiled as belonging to a particular discipline or disciplines.

An obvious limitation of MyLibrary as a means for communication with users is that it requires that users create a MyLibrary account in order to receive information. Another is that, unless the librarian uses the

FIGURE 4. MultiSearch lets users search across all databases for a selected discipline complying with the Z39.50 standard. A separate interface allows for the selection of databases from multiple disciplines.

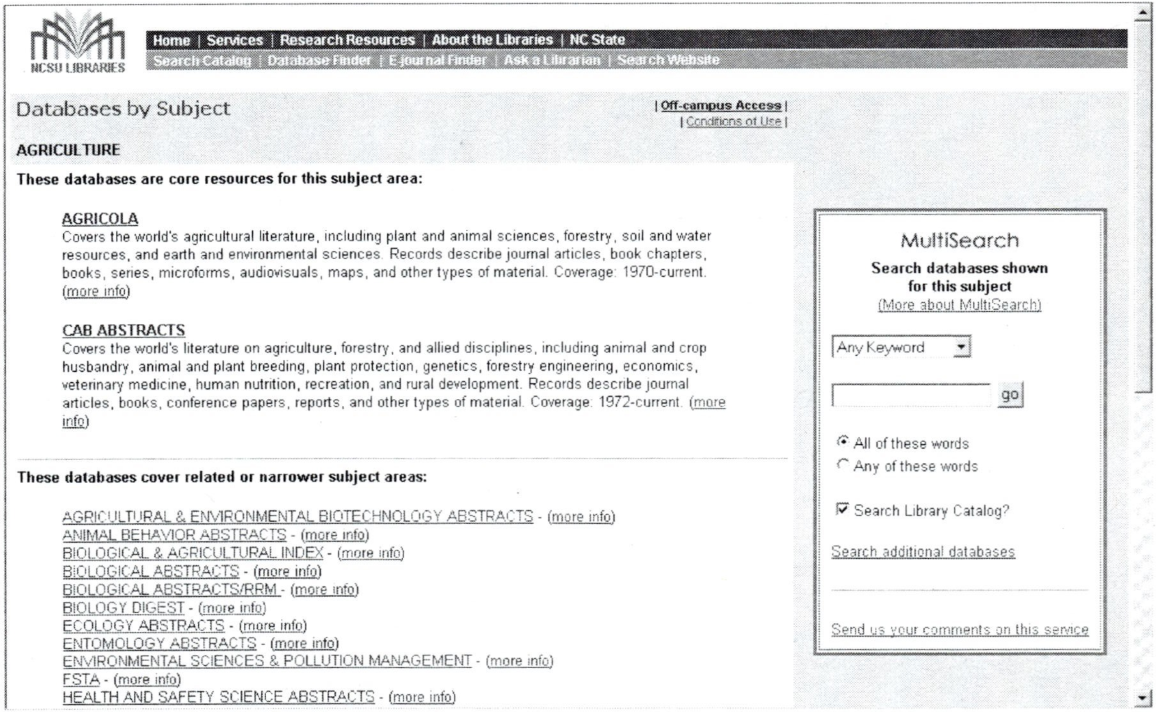

NCSU LIBRARIES

Home | Services | Research Resources | About the Libraries | NC State
Search Catalog | Database Finder | Ejournal Finder | Ask a Librarian | Search Website

Databases by Subject

| Off-campus Access |
| Conditions of Use |

AGRICULTURE

These databases are core resources for this subject area:

AGRICOLA
Covers the world's agricultural literature, including plant and animal sciences, forestry, soil and water resources, and earth and environmental sciences. Records describe journal articles, book chapters, books, series, microforms, audiovisuals, maps, and other types of material. Coverage: 1970-current. (more info)

CAB ABSTRACTS
Covers the world's literature on agriculture, forestry, and allied disciplines, including animal and crop husbandry, animal and plant breeding, plant protection, genetics, forestry engineering, economics, veterinary medicine, human nutrition, recreation, and rural development. Records describe journal articles, books, conference papers, reports, and other types of material. Coverage 1972-current. (more info)

These databases cover related or narrower subject areas:

AGRICULTURAL & ENVIRONMENTAL BIOTECHNOLOGY ABSTRACTS - (more info)
ANIMAL BEHAVIOR ABSTRACTS - (more info)
BIOLOGICAL & AGRICULTURAL INDEX - (more info)
BIOLOGICAL ABSTRACTS - (more info)
BIOLOGICAL ABSTRACTS/RRM - (more info)
BIOLOGY DIGEST - (more info)
ECOLOGY ABSTRACTS - (more info)
ENTOMOLOGY ABSTRACTS - (more info)
ENVIRONMENTAL SCIENCES & POLLUTION MANAGEMENT - (more info)
FSTA - (more info)
HEALTH AND SAFETY SCIENCE ABSTRACTS - (more info)

MultiSearch

Search databases shown for this subject
(More about MultiSearch)

Any Keyword ▼

go

○ All of these words
○ Any of these words

☑ Search Library Catalog?

Search additional databases

Send us your comments on this service

e-mail feature each time she posts a new "message," users must go to their personal pages on a regular basis in order to be kept up to date. Unfortunately, users are unlikely to visit their MyLibrary pages simply to see if a new message from their librarian has been posted there. This is somewhat of a "chicken-and-the-egg" problem, since greater portal functionality would likely bring users to their personal pages more often. It is clear, however, that unless MyLibrary is part of users' daily workflows, this means of communication alone is likely to be ineffective.

MyLibrary contains two types of news—"global" messages, such as library closures and special events, and the discipline-specific messages "from my librarian." Both types of messages could be combined into a newsletter, accessible through the Libraries' Web site as well as available via e-mail to subscribers. Because we want to reach all users, not only those with MyLibrary accounts, we are experimenting in this area. Some of the NCSU Libraries' departments have created online/e-mail newsletters and are also experimenting with Weblog technology to develop library news RSS feeds. (For an example, see the Natural Resources Libraries News at http://www.lib.ncsu.edu/news/nrl.php.) The growing adoption of newsreaders, as well as the potential to syndicate content back to a library portal, makes this communication option worth investigating.

INTEGRATION WITH THE CAMPUS PORTAL

In considering users' workflows, campus portal developments must also be taken into consideration. A library channel on the campus portal could provide general library news as well as an easy customization option for adding additional news feeds on specific subjects. If a campus portal should become an integral part of the NC State community's daily habits, it would be important for the information we want to share to be made readily available there.

Ideally, logging in to the campus portal would also automatically log users in to their personalized and customizable view of the library universe. A tab or link to the library portal would be an integral part of the campus portal design, and a similar link back to the campus portal would appear on the library portal page. Users would need to log in only once to access all of their personal information. At the NCSU Libraries, movement toward making the campus computer login the login for all library services is bringing this integration closer to a reality.

An alternative scenario would have the library portal being sub-sumed by the larger campus portal. Conceivably, customizable access to library resources and automatic login to users' library accounts could be accomplished using the campus portal software. An example of an institution taking this approach is Macalester College, whose library portal exists as the "Research" element of their campus portal, named Lester. (Users must still, however, login separately to their library ac-counts. See http://lester.macalester.edu/login.cfm to create a guest ac-count on Lester.) While the final form of the campus portal at NC State, and whether this degree of integration would be possible or desirable, remains unclear, there is general agreement on the importance of a prominent library presence there.

CONCLUSIONS

Some general conclusions can be drawn from the experiences of the NCSU Libraries and others with library portals:

- Users value the personalization aspect of the library portal. They need a simple way to get to just the resources they need, and the process of navigating to needed databases, e-journals, and other resources through a library's Web site can be perceived as too dif-ficult.
- Users need a simple way to customize their personal portal pages, e.g., "add to MyLibrary" links in the catalog and resources lists. If the customization process is cumbersome, users who desire this functionality will use a system of bookmarks or Web pages instead.
- Undergraduates and others who do not have a single discipline fo-cus need a system that is flexible enough to provide a great degree of customization. At a minimum, users should be able to create and name the sections on their personal page and populate these with multiple types of resources.
- Students' needs for library resources change from course to course. Librarians and faculty therefore need a simple way to create pages of library resources for specific courses, and these pages need to be available to students where they already go to get their course in-formation.
- Metasearching functionality should be available within the library portal.

- News and current awareness services need to be integrated into users' workflows. If a portal is not part of these daily workflows, it will not be an effective medium for communication.
- If a campus portal becomes a significant part of users' habits, it is important for library news and content to be made available there. Multiple options exist for integrating campus portal and library portal content.

THE FUTURE

There is evidence to indicate that there is user demand for personalized and customizable views of library resources and communication. Although MyLibrary was partially successful in achieving these goals, its full potential was never realized due to the limitations of the software. The NCSU Libraries is investigating new options for realizing this potential, taking advantage of technological developments and capabilities that did not exist when MyLibrary was developed.

As part of the larger Web site redesign effort, the Libraries has formed a group to create the next generation MyLibrary. Its official charge is to reconceptualize personalization and customization tools and views of library collections and services, to design course-based access to library resources, and to plan migration from the current MyLibrary service to the new MyLibrary.

Key to our vision for the new MyLibrary is a single user login providing access to a whole suite of services, including the user's library account and borrower services, a customized list of databases for metasearching, saved searches and alerts, news services, and a personal page of library resources, easily and completely customizable by the user. Additionally, librarians and users will have available a tool for easily creating static pages of library resources for others to use, made available through the library portal, campus course management software and elsewhere. With the resource management tools that have already been created, and the pieces currently under development, we are on our way toward achieving these goals.

LINKS TO CITED PROJECTS

MyLibrary Development Website–Here you can read documentation and articles, experiment with the MyLibrary "sandbox," and download the software.
<http://dewey.library.nd.edu/mylibrary/>

University of Toronto Libraries my.library–Click on the link at the bottom of the page to see examples. For guest access, click on the link at top of the page (username: 12345, password: guest).
<http://eir.library.utoronto.ca/MyUTL/index.cfm>

Virginia Commonwealth University Libraries My Library–Click on "Create your own library page" and choose "Guest Access."
<http://www.library.vcu.edu/mylibrary/>

University of Rochester River Campus Libraries Course Resources and Reserves.
<http://www.lib.rochester.edu/index.cfm?page=courses>

Library Course Builder, offered through SourceForge.
<http://sourceforge.net/projects/libcb/>

NCSU Libraries Database Finder, E-journal Finder, and MultiSearch.
<http://www.lib.ncsu.edu>

Natural Resources Library News.
<http://www.lib.ncsu.edu/news/nrl.php>

Lester, the Macalester College portal–Click on "create a new account" under "Alumni, Parents, and Others." Library tools and services can be found under the "Research" tab.
<http://lester.macalester.edu/login.cfm>

AUTHOR NOTE

Ms. Ciccone has published on topics including virtual reference and subject access to images. Her paper, "Providing Subject Access to Images: A Study of User Queries" (written under the name Karen Collins, *American Archivist*, 61:1 Spring 1998, 36-55), won the Theodore Calvin Pease award of the Society of American Archivists for 1997.

NOTES

1. Keith Morgan and Tripp Reade, "Pioneering Portals: MyLibrary@NCState," *Information Technology and Libraries* 19, no. 4 (Dec 2000): 191-198.

2. Eric Lease Morgan, "Putting the 'My' in MyLibrary," *Library JournalNetConnect* (10/15/2003), <http://libraryjournal.reviewsnews.com/index.asp?layout=article&articleid=CA323338> (20 October 2003).

3. Marc Lalonde, telephone interview by author, 26 September 2003.

4. Ibid.

5. Jimmy Graphery and Dan Ream, "VCU's My Library: Librarians Love It. . . . Users? Well, Maybe," *Information Technology and Libraries* 19, no. 4 (Dec 2000): 186-190.

6. Susan Gibbons, "Building Upon the MyLibrary Concept to Better Meet the Information Needs of College Students," D-Lib Magazine 9, no. 3 (Mar 2003), <http://www.dlib.org/dlib/march03/gibbons/03gibbons.html> (16 October 2003).

7. Loanne Snavely and Helen Smith, "Bringing the Library to Students: Linking Customized Library Resources Through a Course-Management System," presentation at ACRL Eleventh National Conference, April 10-13, 2003, Charlotte, North Carolina, <http://www.ala.org/Content/NavigationMenu/ACRL/Events_and_Conferences/snavelysmith.PDF> (16 October 2003).

Chapter 3

Portals to the World:
A Library of Congress Guide
to Web Resources on International Topics

Carolyn T. Brown

SUMMARY. Portals to the World (www.loc.gov/rr/international/portals. html) is a Library of Congress guide to Web resources. A product of the unit Area Studies Collections, it provides one-stop shopping and self-service access to information about every nation of the world, organized by broad topical areas, selected and annotated by the reference librarians and area specialists, and provided without charge over the Internet. The chapter outlines the organizational and management factors that moved the project from vision to implementation and describes the content, structure, and technical background of the Portals themselves. Staff and users have benefitted from the project even while quality control and promotion remain ongoing challenges.

KEYWORDS. Area studies, international studies, international Web resources, OCLC Connexion

Carolyn T. Brown is Director for Collections and Services, Library of Congress. Dr. Brown directs the international collections as well as the general collections, special collections, and the collections management unit.

The author would like to express her thanks to Lavonda Broadnax and Everette Larson of the Area Studies Directorate for their assistance in the preparation of this article.

[Haworth co-indexing entry note]: "Portals to the World: A Library of Congress Guide to Web Resources on International Topics." Brown, Carolyn T. Co-published simultaneously in *Journal of Library Administration* (The Haworth Information Press, an imprint of The Haworth Press, Inc.) Vol. 43, No. 1/2, 2005, pp. 37-56; and: *Portals and Libraries* (ed: Sarah C. Michalak) The Haworth Information Press, an imprint of The Haworth Press, Inc., 2005, pp. 37-56.

INTRODUCTION

"I wish there were some place on the Internet where I could send my students for reliable, authoritative sources of information." Every librarian has heard this lament from faculty and others who are searching for ways to help the next generation sift through the unsorted heap of information that makes up the Internet. In response to that need, one of the foreign area specialists at the Library of Congress, Ken Nyirady of the European Division, developed an annotated guide to Web resources for his country of specialization, Hungary. The guide organized resources by subject, such as government and history, and included Web sites originating in the U.S. and Hungary. It even included a Hungarian language search engine. Thus appeared the seed of the idea that has become the Library's Portals to the World project.[1]

Portals to the World provides one stop shopping and self-service access to information about every nation of the world, organized by broad topical areas, selected and annotated by the reference librarians and area specialists, mounted on the Internet, and provided for free to people all over the nation and the world. The project's goal is to guide and direct users to reliable, authoritative, in-depth, consistent information and knowledge that is freely available on the Web.

WHY CREATE A GUIDE
TO INTERNATIONAL WEB RESOURCES?

Several considerations went into the decision to transform a good idea into a major project.

The Vision

The most casual observer of world affairs knows that the destiny of the United States and of each of us who lives here is complexly intertwined with the nations and peoples of the entire globe. The revolution in communications and cross-border flows of money and commerce have ensured heightened awareness. The illusion that "we" are a separate, discrete entity, and "they" are remote and therefore of little interest is crumbling. The United States is embedded in the world, as are other countries, and as such requires knowledge of other nations and cultures if only out of self-interest. The more idealistic among us also enjoy other cultures for their own sake and for the mirror they hold up to our values and assumptions. Recognition of the international factors impinging on our lives has prompted educators at all levels to bring greater international awareness into the curriculum in a large number of subjects. The recent influx of immigrants, who not only inhabit the coasts but have penetrated into the interior of middle America, has also intensified international awareness.

As Americans and others seek to understand more of this world, if they are remote from the information resources of large cities, they are almost by necessity forced to turn to the Internet for information and knowledge. Others just want the convenience of not leaving home. How will they find and judge the quality of what they need?

The Need

There was never any doubt about the value to the general public of responsible, annotated guides to Web resources. Even in 2001 when the project was initiated, the task of wading through the mass of unevaluated information and misinformation on the Internet was staggering and has only grown more daunting in the intervening years. Identifying sites whose information is reasonably reliable and not skewed by deliberate bias, ignorance, or commercial intent will always be difficult for the person initiating an inquiry in an unfamiliar subject area, and especially for someone of limited research experience. Those well versed in a subject can evaluate quality for themselves and, in fact, have likely already identified the Web sites of greatest relevance. They are not the primary audience for Portals to the World, at least not in their areas of specialization. Rather the primary audiences are those new to a subject area, who are looking for guidance in answering simple questions, or who are seeking in-depth guidance in a new area of inquiry. Portals are particularly useful to the general public and to students.

The Capacity

The Library of Congress was particularly well suited to undertake the effort. In fact, it is hard to think of another research library, with perhaps the exception of the New York Public Library, as well positioned. The Library of Congress has a universal collection, with materials gathered from every area of the world. Most research libraries are associated with universities, and these build their collections around the curriculum and faculty research interests. Even those strong in area studies and international affairs usually do not have strength in every region of the globe. Because it must be ready to serve the informational needs of Congress and these often cannot be known in advance, the Library of Congress acquires materials even from the areas of the world least likely to be of Congressional concern. Who, for instance, would have predicted that Afghanistan would rise to the top of the national agenda, and yet it did. So because we already are providing comprehensive international coverage in print resources, expanding the definition of what needs to be on hand to include Web resources was an easy conceptual stretch.

The staff was already in place. As a consequence of building world class print collections, the Library had already assembled staff with reference, subject matter, and language expertise about most of the nations and regions. Staff were already schooled in the Library's collections development policies and so, as a natural outcome of their expertise, were well prepared to evaluate Web resources and to bring to the evaluation the same high quality of professional judgment honed in the print world.

A third factor in the decision was purely bureaucratic: nearly all the staff required to implement the project fell under a single bureaucratic umbrella. Portals to the World was initiated by Area Studies Collections. This directorate has primary responsibility for collections development, reference, and public programming for Africa and the Middle East, which are coupled in one division, Asia, Europe, and the Hispanic world. Responsibility for the Anglo-American world lies in another administrative unit. Nevertheless, most of the world was gathered under my jurisdiction, which meant that the Hungarian pilot could be generalized without long negotiations across administrative lines. Area Studies did invite the extended British world into the project, and they agreed to join. Still the degree of institutional negotiation required was minimal. Once the Area Studies division chiefs were persuaded, the first challenge was met.

The Audience

In most respects, the projected audience for the Portals is roughly equivalent to the patron-group who comes to the Library's reading rooms. They are a varied lot: members of Congress and their staffs, representatives of other government agencies, university faculty and students, independent researchers, embassy personnel, and the general public. The Area Studies Divisions also draw an international demographic. Both recent immigrants and those from abroad are frequent patrons. We do not, however, attract the kinds of patrons who frequent public libraries. They are welcome enough, but the size and complexity of the institution, with its 21 reading rooms, makes the Library of Congress a bit daunting. Current, popular materials are in short supply and, of course, we do not lend materials.

The Portals project was also envisioned as an extension of reading room service to patrons beyond the walls of the Library. The Web sites selected for Portals are chosen for their research value and are substantive and often academic. We omit sites focused on popular culture, such as sports and celebrities, which fall outside of our collections policies and in general have only transient value. Just as the reading rooms serve materials in some 460 languages, the Portals pages link to Web sites from the nations abroad regardless of whether the site is in English or another language. Selection is weighted towards English language sites but not confined to them.

Among the new "electronic patrons" that the Portals project brings to the Library are young people. Typically, the Library's reading rooms do not admit anyone under 16 years of age. However, we have strong evidence that the young set finds Portals particularly valuable for school work. At a recent meeting of the American Association of School Librarians, this segment of the profession greeted the Portals project director with delight at discovering this cost-free product. Among the sites that link to us are homework resource pages.

Portals to the World complements "Ask a Librarian," a feature on all of the Library's reading room pages, which enables patrons visiting the Library's virtual reading rooms, to pose a research question. Reference staff fielding questions on international issues frequently direct patrons to the relevant Portal, confident a reliable answer is there because they, in fact, are the ones who created the resource.

HOW WAS PORTALS TO THE WORLD DEVELOPED?

The Objective

From the beginning, the project was conceived as a Web publication, not as a collection of wonderful but miscellaneous lists of Web resources. The focus needed to rest on the user's needs and expectations. Both format and content would be viewed in this light. "Consistency but not uniformity" was the watchword. Each country page would have a similar "look" and draw from a standard set of subject categories. All URLs were to be annotated to give users a good sense of the content and value of each Web resource cited. Allowance would be made for the differences among countries, and the creators of each page would have considerable autonomy in selecting sites. This was a modest departure from the thinking about most Library pages, even the home pages of the Area Studies Divisions. These were created in accordance with Library of Congress standards, which require certain features and layouts, but in contrast to Portals pages they permit more flexibility in the design of content. Portals would place more constraints on the creators of each page.

With the decision made, I formed the Portals Committee comprising primarily representatives from each of the six Area Studies Divisions. These are the four regional divisions, noted earlier, as well as the other two Area Studies Divisions, the Federal Research Division, which does research–much of it on international issues–for other federal agencies, and the Office of Scholarly Programs, which manages the Library's center for advanced research. Subsequently, we added a coordinator from the Area Studies Office, Lavonda Broadnax, who in time became the project director, and a representative from the Humanities and Social Sciences Division (HSS), a unit outside of the Area Studies Directorate which has responsibility for the United Kingdom, Ireland, Canada, Australia, and New Zealand.

The Portals Committee met several times and established guidelines for format and for content. During the process they conferred as needed with members of their own divisions. The guidelines they created were accepted by the division chiefs virtually unchanged and inscribed in a document that continues to guide the creation and evaluation of the Portals. The final aesthetic design, now in its second iteration, was created in conversation with another office that has responsibility for monitoring and implementing the Library's Web presentations. That design works in wonderful visual harmony with the Library's broader international page, on which the Area Studies Directorate's other Web publications reside.

Selection Criteria

The committee articulated a general design concept:

> We have attempted to design pages that would ensure comprehensive yet selective coverage of a country, pages with consistency but not uniformity, ones that are easy to understand and use, can easily accept additional resources, can be easily loaded on less than state-of-the-art equipment, and convenient to update. Links to LC resources can be included within the subject/format categories, although the main focus of these pages is links external to LC.[2]

In general, the guidelines call for selecting Internet resources of reference value to researchers in the humanities, social sciences, and science and technology. In establishing criteria, the Committee drew on existing work, recommending that selectors generally follow the Library's current selection policies as outlined in the "LC Collections Policy Statements" and as summarized in the document "Selection Criteria for Resources to be included in the BEOnline+ Project" <http://lcweb.loc.gov/rr/business/beonline/beonel.html>. Thus a primary consideration is whether we would have wanted the item if it had appeared in print. We would look for materials that provide substantial information on topics for which the reference staff receive frequent questions or which provide comprehensive referrals to sources of such information. Sites selected include those of interest both to scholars and the general public. Selectors are urged to avoid private, that is non-institutional links, since they can be highly biased and may disappear without warning. Caution is required with respect to commercial sites so that the Library of Congress does not appear to be endorsing products or services. Provision is made for users to recommend additional links.

In general, Portals links are to large sites that provide substantial content. Specific considerations include issues of accessibility, authority, content, and user interface or navigability.

Among considerations included under accessibility are whether the site has restrictions on its use. Is it generally up and available? We are also concerned about whether the patron without high end equipment would be able to use the site, so we tend to avoid sites that are "graphics" heavy and slow loading. Another concern is whether a site requires plug-ins and whether these are readily available.

Sites selected need to be authoritative. We prefer sites that identify their creators and have creators who clearly speak with authority on the subject of the site. If we are unfamiliar with the organization, then we look to see whether the site provides information about its history and purpose. We look for contact information so that users can report problems, ask questions, or verify information on the site. Needless to say, since the U.S. Copyright Office is an integral part of the Library of Congress, we are interested in whether the producers of the site have the legal right to use the material displayed or, alternately whether it indicates that the materials are posted with permission.

In evaluating content we look for obvious biases or advocacy. We think about whether the site is clear about its audience, whether it is complete and provides appropriate coverage of the subject matter, and whether its quality and depth compare favorably with that of other sources. When was the site last updated? Is it current? Does it offer unique information?

Other issues of concern reflect on the user interface. Is it free of errors in grammar and spelling? Is there a way to search the site? Is there an index? Does it follow accepted design features?

We are well aware that these selection criteria weed out many interesting and important ephemeral sites produced by NGOs, small political parties, and fringe groups. These are the electronic versions of pamphlets and other kinds of transient materials which the Library does sample in the print domain. Sites carrying ephemeral material would escalate maintenance requirements. Thus Portals is inevitably biased towards the established and the mainstream. There was nothing to be done about this. The project already imposes an additional workload on an already busy staff.

Community Participation

The six Area Studies Divisions together with HSS had sufficient expertise to provide comprehensive coverage and execute the project. Their knowledge and experience in making the selections and writing the annotations provided the value added.

Yet certainly the project would have benefitted from the studied contributions of specialists from research libraries across the United States. We thought briefly about establishing the project as a broadly collaborative enterprise and inviting libraries and other entities to join in planning and development. However, how to engage that national expertise quickly and efficiently was not self-evident and would have substantially delayed the project. So we initiated it as an in-house project but constructed it so as to build on the excellent work of other colleagues and to provide a means for the research, library, and other communities to offer suggestions and improvements, and we rested the project on a shared OCLC database.

HOW ARE THE PORTALS STRUCTURED?

The Framework

Portals to the World is organized hierarchically. The first level provides a menu listing all the nations of the world. Level two, the country page, lists a range of subjects relevant to that particular country. The third level provides an annotated list of selected Web sites. The easiest way to understand the structure is to view three sample pages (www. loc.gov/rr/international/portals.html). (See Illustrations 1, 2, and 3.)

The Library of Congress is an agency of the federal government, and as such we follow the State Department's list of official nations. When the project is completed, scheduled for early 2004, the menu page will include every nation on that list, whether or not the United States maintains diplomatic relations with that nation. Thus, for example, the menu page includes Cuba. Further, staff may also choose to create additional pages for regions or other entities if they anticipate that this will assist the user. So, for instance, Tibet and the Galapagos Islands have their own separate portal, and of course are cross listed under China and Ecuador respectively. Comprehensive global coverage is a boon to the user who, after one visit, knows that returning for information on any other nation is an easy option.

We briefly considered creating thematic portals. One can imagine, for example, that a portal on environment issues would draw an enormous international constituency. In fact, we have constructed a portal

ILLUSTRATION 1. Level 1–Menu Page

ILLUSTRATION 2. Level 2–Country Page

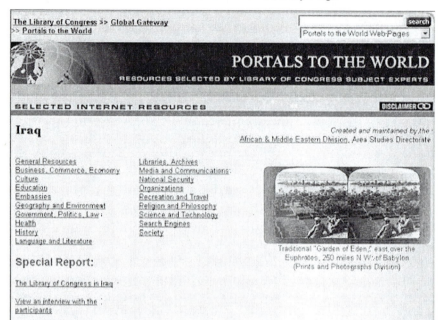

on "Terrorism," but this is the exception. Resources were insufficient to create both geographic and thematic portals. We elected to organize geographically for several reasons. Geography as an organizing principle is more stable than one premised on research trends or popular interests. It is also easier to manage administratively. The languages of library materials, as well as the nature of international publishing, strongly encourage a geographical principle of organization. The area specialists' knowledge is shaped primarily by region, not by subject. There was no compelling reason to work counter to institutional structure and many reasons to stay aligned with it.

The second level of Portals to the World, that of the country page, provides subject access. Most country pages will include subjects such as general resources; business, commerce, economy; government, politics, law; and history. Many add education, culture, and society. Nations that are large or whose international positions are particular pivotal may have categories such as national security or science and technology.

ILLUSTRATION 3. Level 3–Subject Page

PORTALS TO THE WORLD
RESOURCES SELECTED BY LIBRARY OF CONGRESS SUBJECT EXPERTS

Media and Communications: Iraq

Iraq's high literacy rate is responsible for the country's wide variety of print and broadcast news. Although Baghdad is considered one of the region's largest media centers, areas outside the capital which lack strong economic support, are not as well developed. Most daily broadcast programs are in Arabic with a few in English and French.

During Sadam's regime, all media had strong political and religious affiliations with the government. Muhammad Said al-Sabhaf, former Minister of Information, directed the media during the first stage of the war. The public commentary was eagerly followed by Iraqis and throughout the neighboring Arab countries.

The collapse of the Iraqi regime changed the country's public image. The media started to focus on Iraq's economic, political, military and strategic sectors. In response to the American influence, broadcasts began emphasizing the liberation of Iraq and its neighbors from the former oppressive regime.

DISCLAIMER

Index to Page: Broadcast Media   Print Media   General Communication Resources

Broadcast Media
The following provide resources for the rapid dissemination of information about Iraq.

Iraq Media Dossier - Media Networks (http://www.rnw.nl/realradio/features.html/media020715.html)
Provides up-to-date news and press reviews. Partners with over 5000 global organizations. Items credited to BBC Monitoring.

Radio Free Iraq Service (http://www.rferl.org/bd-iq/index.html)
Radio Free Iraq Services Broadcasting. Provides analysis and features about Iraq by the staff of Radio Free Europe/Radio Liberty.

Clandestine Radio Intel Web (http://www.clandestineradio.com/intel/)
Includes essays and specific information about non-government sponsored radio stations and related web sites.

Aljazeera.Net (http://english.aljazeera.net/homepage)
An important English language website, headquartered in Doha, Qatar. Includes international news and analysis. Offers continuous coverage of issues impacting the Arab World and the world in general.

The specialist who constructs the portal has the discretion to determine which subjects are most appropriate to that particular country.

The top of the page at the third level briefly defines the parameters of the page and provides pathfinders, the selected, annotated list of selected Web pages with their URLs. Based on a set of jointly established criteria and individual professional judgment, each staff creator reviews sites, determines what to include, and writes the annotations. This page is the primary point at which "value is added," the level at which professional knowledge and judgment find clearest expression. Site selection is extremely important, as is the annotation, which is a brief interpretative statement of what is special about this link.

Experience has demonstrated the need for a further refinement. Normally the sites listed under any given pathfinder are presented in alphabetical order. We have discovered that some pathfinders point to a rich plethora of sites. Providing sub-groupings under the subject heading would make the page more useable. So we decided that when the number of important sites for any subject category exceeds about 15-20, they will be grouped under subcategories. By the time that this article goes to press, some but probably not all of the largest third level pathfinders will have adopted this refinement.

The Technical Structure

The general menu page and country pages are created with the HTML editor Dreamweaver and reside on a Library of Congress server. The pathfinders themselves were originally created using CORC, an OCLC product that later merged into OCLC Connexion. Approximately 130 libraries and institutions contribute to the resource catalog of OCLC Connexion, and this is the database from which individual pathfinders are created. The Portals Committee adopted this system for several reasons: it is easy to execute without learning HTML; it automatically populates MARC fields by just activating a URL; and it has the potential for broadly sharing the repair of broken links, a major headache in maintaining any collection of URLs.

So far this strategy seems not to have yielded the level of assistance in maintaining links that we had hoped. Of the approximately 5,400 pathfinders in OCLC Connexion, about 4,000 were created by the Library of Congress, most of these by the Portals project. Nevertheless, when several of the Library of Congress's portals link to the same URL, which may be the case for sites with information on multiple nations, then if one Area Studies specialist corrects a link, all Portals pathfinders are automatically updated.

Creating pathfinders in the OCLC Connexion Resource Catalog is a straightforward process requiring only a few minor steps. Once the staff member identifies an appropriate Web site, he/she copies the URL. Connexion then populates a MARC-based form which, after it is edited by the creator, is saved in the Resource Catalog of Connexion and creates a record. Before Connexion populates the fields, it searches the Resource Catalog for the selected record. Instead of entering a URL, one may also search the Resource Catalog for appropriate Web sites entered by others. In either case, once the record is available in the Resource Catalog, the staff member flags the record and automatically pulls it into the appropriate subject pathfinder. These pathfinders are located in a different part of the OCLC system and can be edited to include printed records as well as electronic records. These pathfinders are then linked to the Dreamweaver country page on the Library of Congress server. This is a relatively simple process, easily mastered with a little training and experience.

WHAT ABOUT QUALITY CONTROL?

Over the generations the Library of Congress has developed a reputation for quality products, and so the project has had the advantage of instant credibility. This is the good news. The bad news is that the great responsibility of living up to the image raises quality control to a particularly high level of importance. The literature on subject portals has pointed out the challenges of creating and maintaining quality.[3]

Links

We had anticipated that broken links would be a challenge. This has not been completely solved. In the press to get the country pages mounted by the targeted deadlines, staff, who usually have responsibility for more than one site, focused on mounting new sites, not on maintaining the old. OCLC Connexion provides information on broken links on a continuing basis, but staff still have to take the time to look these up and make the corrections. Many staff have either not learned how to do this or, in the press of other tasks, give it insufficient priority. Sustaining frequent, persistent updating will undoubtedly always be a challenge.

A related issue is the level at which the link is created. The specialist may link to a Web site with information about an entire region, for example sub-Saharan Africa. The selector may decide that the regional information is sufficiently pertinent to create a link at that level or, if that particular site organizes itself by country, may prefer to link directly to the country, not to the general portion of the site. This should be a matter of professional judgment. In the real world, again, pressed for time, the area specialist may simply link to the generic, regional level of the site and use the same link for multiple countries. Yet this may not be best for the user. There is no absolute rule on this issue.

Political Changes

Another issue did surprise us, although in retrospect it should not have. Political turmoil creates havoc with Web sites. Governments come, governments go. Parties come, parties go. Political Web sites come, and they go, but the work to keep them current keeps coming. Every time a government changes, the specialist needs to check and usually change the political links. One very conscientious Portals staffer, Everette

Larson, tore his hair out trying to keep abreast of the Venezuelan attempt to oust the President, Hugo Chavez, on Friday, April 12, 2003. Larson went home on the weekend, redid the site to update it after the political coup, only to have to restore the site more or less to its original formulation by Sunday afternoon when Chavez was returned to power.

Not all specialists are similarly computer savvy and so may not be able to update URLs without technical assistance. This makes rapid response to changing international conditions that much harder. Others have not yet fully come to terms with the fact that every change of government requires a revision of perhaps several parts of the overall country page.

Editorial Authority

Fairly early in the project, we appointed a project coordinator, with the power to convene and persuade, but someone who was not envisioned as an enforcer. We have found that we need a stronger hand with full authority to demand quality, someone responsible for reviewing pages at all three levels to ensure that they in fact are following the established guidelines, and to confirm that any particular pathfinder is sufficiently well developed with high quality annotations before it can be mounted. Each country "belongs" to a single specialist, who typically has responsibility for several countries. Thus it is easy to identify who has created the most outstanding pages and, of course, the reverse. The staff member's name is not visible to the public, but responsibility is easy to track internally. Initially quality control was designated to the division chief, who as the supervisor of record, is in the best position to evaluate the staff member's overall performance. However, given all of the other work that chiefs must execute, in the end they have generally been ill equipped to provide an ideal level of on-going scrutiny. Giving the project director greater authority goes far to resolve the problem.

In general we are confident that the quality is very good but, of course, there is always room for improvement.

IS PORTALS TO THE WORLD A SUCCESS STORY?

There are at least two ways to answer this question. In terms of benefits to the staff, the project is a success. On the primary measure, value to patrons, they are the ultimate judges. Certainly the project has been well received.

Staff Development

The Chiefs of the Area Studies divisions were enthusiastic about implementing the project. So too was the Portals Committee, which inevitably had comprised those who already appreciated the great value of Web-based resources. However, not everyone was convinced.

The Library of Congress staff is no longer young. Within the Area Studies Directorate, as of April 2003, 63% were eligible for retirement by 2007. This is the highest percentage of eligibility in any part of Library Services, which is the part of the Library that performs most of the traditional library functions. (The primary responsibilities of other major units, the Congressional Research Service, the Copyright Office, the Law Library, the Office of Strategic Initiatives, and those that provide the infrastructure, are quite different.) Of the Library Services staff, "only" 50% are eligible to retire by 2007. Clearly, then, a significant majority had come into the profession well before ubiquitous desktop computing. Some had embraced it; others had greeted it with some reservations; and a few had tried to avoid it altogether.

Because nearly every member of the Area Studies reference staff had to create at least one portal, staff were forced to explore the Internet. To the extent possible, we supplied support. In some cases, the Portals representative from each division took on the technical task of creating the pathfinder. In other cases, through an internship program that Area Studies runs with a local community college, we were able to provide technical assistance from students, who often had language expertise as well. Nevertheless, the subject specialists still had responsibility for identifying the sites. Invariably when they did the hard work, they were gratified to discover the great wealth of unsuspected resources that helped them do their work. Having created pathfinders, they also discovered how useful they are for answering straightforward reference questions. As the volume of questions increased as the result of the Library's e-reference service, Ask a Librarian, and general e-mail, the country portals enabled them to respond quickly and efficiently to the increased volume.

I wish I could claim that this was a cleverly designed strategy and that all along I had anticipated its positive contribution to professional development. Alas, this was not the case. I am neither a Luddite, nor an "early adapter." Thus I had assumed, incorrectly, that what was apparent to me was equally apparent to staff: that there was a huge amount of incredibly valuable information on the Internet, much of it not in English and much originating from the non-English-speaking world. I expected that the reference staff, knowing this, would have been scooping up Web resources to use in the conduct of their work. Not so. The project demanded that they acquire these skills. Happily, most now have greater respect, in fact enthusiasm, for Web resources. Several have admitted that although they initially dreaded the task, they learned a great deal from it.

Community Reception

In September 2003, Portals to the World received 120,000 hits. There appear to be no huge disparities in the level of interest between world regions, noting again that statistics for Africa and the Middle East are grouped together. We hope to see an increase in this number as all of the Portals are completed and we focus on refinements to the content and promotion to potential users.

Shortly after being launched, the Project received strong accolades. It was named among "Yahoo! Picks," *yahoo.com* (November 26, 2001), "Useful Site of the Week," by *usatoday.com* (November 26, 2001), "Cool Feds Sites," *fedgate.org* (2001), and "Featured Research Web Site," Charles J. Keffer Library, *stthomas.edu* (2001). There have been other accolades, including "Website of the Month," by New York State, nysl.gov (January 2003), and "Site of the Week," by the International Association of School Librarianship, *iasl-slo.org* (July 2002). *SearchEngineWatch.com* said on June 27, 2002,

> Some of the best search tools on the web aren't search engines at all. Portals of [*sic*] the World, a compilation of web sites created by the U.S. Library of Congress is an example of such an outstanding search resource.

Of great interest, perhaps, is the evidence from the sites that link to Portals to the World. As of November 2003, there were approximately 1,300 such sites. An unscientific sample of links suggests the following. The largest proportion of links come from academic libraries, individual college and university courses, and law libraries. These include some of the nation's most elite universities. Several links have been drawn to us because of the excellent Country Study series, handbooks written initially for the U.S. military that provide complete profiles of individual nations, many of them among those least understood by Americans. Surprisingly, at least to us, law libraries are heavy users. One of the subjects available on most country pages in Portals is "Government, Politics, Law." The Law Library of the Library of Congress has a Web page entitled "Guide to Law Online" which provides links to every nation's constitutions, treaties, laws, judicial systems, and other legal information. Users find Portals a good link to that resource as well as to other legal materials.

We also had not anticipated the international interest in the Project. Libraries, directories, and embassies link to us. For example, the Chilean embassy "grabbed" the whole Chilean Culture portal for the culture section of their own Web site. That was high praise. In addition, some U.S. embassies abroad link to Portals on the embassy's Web site, as do foreign libraries and universities.

A third major audience comprises elementary and high schools. As noted earlier we are mentioned on homework resource pages and resources marked for teachers. We have anecdotal evidence that Library of Congress staff members send their children to Portals for school assignments. Other uses include public and state libraries, business, trade, and economic organizations, Internet directories, and even genealogy sites.

An anecdote: patrons are often surprised by what they find. A group of librarians from Central America who were visiting the Library of Congress were shown their country's portal. One visitor said it was certainly impressive that the political parties' Web sites for their country were listed but queried why we had omitted that of the party which had won the recent election. One might draw the conclusion that maintaining currency is a daunting task. In this case, however, the visitors had themselves overlooked the fact that the winning party's Web site had become that of the newly elected president.

Anecdotal evidence is interesting but not convincing unless your institution's primary funders find the project useful. The Library of Congress is part of the legislative branch and supported by the United States Congress. Thus we were particularly gratified when a member of Congress reported that the Kyzgyzstan portal was useful in preparation for an official trip. The Library's Congressional Relations Office similarly reports that they have used Portals to assist members of Congress.

Marketing, Access, and Use

The Library of Congress's main home page has repeatedly won awards for its extraordinarily rich, extremely reliable content. In 2002, the page received close to 2 billion hits. Prominent on this page is a link to the international page. Portals occupies a visible spot on this international page. This places the menu page of Portals to the World at the third level on one of the world's busiest home pages. Over time this happy location should also encourage greater traffic.

To the extent that we have promoted Portals to the World in particular, we have relied primarily on Internet marketing. We have sent notices to Web directories frequented by librarians. Several now link to Portals. The Internet Public Library *www.ipl.org* is a popular, eight-year-old product of the University of Michigan School of Information that mintains a comprehensive list of selected Web resources. The Librarians' Index to the Internet *www.lii.org* is a searchable, annotated subject directory of more than 12,000 Internet resources evaluated by librarians. The Open Project Directory *www.moz.org*, which claims to be the largest, most comprehensive human-edited directory of the Web, relies on a global community of volunteer editors, and serves as the core directory service for Google, Netscape Search, AOL Search, and many others.

In addition, as resources permit we use other, more labor intensive strategies. Portals Committee members give presentations at conferences. At the mid-winter and annual meetings of the American Library Association, Everette Larson has regularly given a power point slide show in the small theater that is part of Library of Congress's exhibit booth. Early in the project, Everette Larson, Kenneth Nyirady, and Lavonda Broadnax offered a demonstration at the Queens Borough Public Library. In the spring of 2003, we hosted a demonstration here at the Library for the Washington International Library Group and the Metropolitan Public Libraries. Two staff members from the Hispanic Division, Carlos J. Olave and Jesus Alonso Regalado, gave the first international presentation at the 48th SALALM Conference in May 2003 in Cartagena, Colombia. Library of Congress publications have carried articles. We created attractive bookmarks that we hand out at various events, place with other public information in the Area Studies reading rooms, and distribute in the Library's Visitors' Center, which sees about one million tourists each year. In short, we take advantage of opportunities as they arise.

Our intent is to further strengthen the connections between the Portals and other Library of Congress online and print information. We are linking each country page and eventually each of the subject headings under each country page to the Library of Congress's online catalog. At the level of individual countries, the Portals already link to the home pages for the Area Studies Divisions. Over time, and workload permitting, we hope that each divisional page will provide a full overview of the collections and databases of likely interest to their patrons that are available only on-site at the Library. Thus the Portals will promote the Library as a physical location where even more wonderful material can be found, and those seeking information about our on-site resources will more easily grow aware of what the Internet can provide. In short, a busy two-way street.

CONCLUSION:
LOOKING TOWARDS THE FUTURE

One of the open questions for Portals to the World is whether it will remain a discrete project, with a beginning, a middle, and an end, or whether it will serve as the groundwork for some unfolding, yet unseen future.

As a project, Portals to the World will always require maintenance, which, as noted, is not a small issue. And we will always be envisioning improvements, such as the further breakdown of subject categories for each country and using the Portals to inform patrons about on-site resources. We will always want to add new Web sites, as excellent new pages emerge. Doing so is a logical part of the reference staff's work. We will continue to welcome suggestions from the library and scholarly communities, here and abroad, for improvements in the site, small changes such as "must have" URLs or even major proposals for re-conceiving the site in some way. We will always be especially interested in frank feedback from colleagues abroad about our selection of sites from their countries. If it ever happens that greater resources are available, we may well want to initiate subject portals for cross-global issues such as HIV/AIDS and global warming. All of these are refinements that would improve the project without fundamentally altering its nature.

A more expansive notion of the future might include other kinds of initiatives. Having identified important Web sites, Portals could become the basis for decisions about which Web sites we might seek to archive and to catalog for long term retention. Area Studies Collections is in the early stages of proposing an approach to archiving foreign sites within the context of the Library of Congress's policy on archiving. We might, perhaps, redefine Portals as a framework into which others throughout the world would proactively be enlisted to help shape the Portals content so that as a product it becomes less American and more international in its perspective. It is not clear how this would be accomplished or whether, in fact, it is desirable. Finally, as the technology storms into the future, more efficient, automated ways of identifying valuable, content rich Web sites may emerge. In time, the semantic Web may produce opportunities. At this point it is hard to imagine how computers will ever be able to replace the qualities of human judgment that Portals enshrines. But in the current climate of innovation, we can imagine the future but not predict it with any certainty. We knew enough to never say "never."

For the moment, Portals remains a reasonable solution to the need for human intermediaries to provide guidance to the vast quantities of unsorted "stuff." As long as the project serves a valuable purpose, maintaining it will be a high priority.

AUTHOR NOTE

Prior to joining the Library of Congress, Dr. Brown served on the faculty and in the administration of Howard University. At the Library of Congress, she has held several positions in the area of education, culture and research. She developed the visitors' center and the volunteer program that staffs it, and initiated the Library's Islamic Studies Program. She sits on the executive committee of the John W. Kluge Center for advanced research, and directs the Global Gateway Projects, collaborative digitization projects with national libraries and cultural institutions across the world.

NOTES

1. Portals to the World was named at a time when the term "portal" had a somewhat different meaning from what it commonly means today.

2. "Area Studies Portals to the World, Guidelines prepared by the Portals Planning Committee."

3. I am indebted to Louis Pitschmann's very valuable assessment of issues related to the collection of Web resources in his *Building Sustainable Collections of Third-Party Web Resources*, Washington, D.C.: Digital Library Federation, Council on Library and Information Resources (June 2001). I read his report cover to cover before we embarked on this project.

Chapter 4

The Portal World and the ILS: A Commentary

Sandy Hurd

SUMMARY. Will integrated library systems become more portal-like in the future? Will they need to evolve towards being portals in order to retain and even enhance the vital role they play today? This chapter addresses these questions, discusses portal functionality in the corporate world, and speculates whether such functionality also belongs in the library world. *[Article copies available for a fee from The Haworth Document Delivery Service: 1-800-HAWORTH. E-mail address: <docdelivery@haworthpress.com> Website: <http://www.HaworthPress.com> © 2005 by The Haworth Press, Inc. All rights reserved.]*

KEYWORDS. Portal, integrated library system, ILS, search engine, federated search, collaboration, usability

HOW DO INTEGRATED LIBRARY SYSTEMS FIGURE INTO THE PORTAL EQUATION?

The concept of "portal" has become widespread in our library community and has taken on a life of its own. In its simplest incarnation, a

---

Sandy Hurd is Director of Sales, Digital Solutions, Innovative Interfaces, Inc., 7 Wintergreen Lane, Groton, MA 01450 (E-mail: shurd@iii.com).

[Haworth co-indexing entry note]: "The Portal World and the ILS: A Commentary." Hurd, Sandy. Co-published simultaneously in *Journal of Library Administration* (The Haworth Information Press, an imprint of The Haworth Press, Inc.) Vol. 43, No. 1/2, 2005, pp. 57-70; and: *Portals and Libraries* (ed: Sarah C. Michalak) The Haworth Information Press, an imprint of The Haworth Press, Inc., 2005, pp. 57-70. Single or multiple copies of this article are available for a fee from The Haworth Document Delivery Service [1-800-HAWORTH, 9:00 a.m. - 5:00 p.m. (EST). E-mail address: docdelivery@haworthpress.com].

Digital Object Identifier: 10.1300/J111v43n01_05

portal is a door or an entryway into a place or an environment. We have come to define a portal as a means for searching and retrieving information, or as a place where search and retrieval occurs and where electronic resources, including the library's descriptive catalog, are accessed. At some institutions, portal teams from the library in collaboration with staff from the academic computing department work towards the incorporation into a portal of campus-wide resources such as student information services, course registration facilities, and full library services access and authentication for local and remote users. At others, the library is developing an information access portal apart from the activities of the campus at large.

Much has been written about portals in academia, their conceptualization, and implementation. The Association of Research Libraries' Scholars Portal Initiative, well documented in the literature, continues to be a most visible and laudable portal application. It remains to be seen whether the particular methodology and feature set inherent in this initiative will spread throughout the academic community or whether libraries will seek other paths towards total integration of information resources within their own environments. History tells us the latter is inevitable. Librarians have strong ideas about what is appropriate for their own institution and they have equally strong opinions about the vendors with whom they choose to work.

Because we are fortunate to have choices, we can make of the portal world what we like. We can offer straightforward "A to Z" lists of electronic resources and a basic search of our catalogs; we can present advanced searching options within the integrated library system (ILS) separate from or combined with metasearch of all or part of our electronic resources. We can organize our resources alphabetically or by subject; we can offer all or part of our resources to all or part of our constituents–simultaneously. In effect, the sky's the limit when it comes to technology and our imaginations. We really can have just about anything we want. In reality, however, budgets and available human resources, whether internal or external, frame the limitations of our projects and therefore of our offerings.

What, then, is the role of the ILS in today's library environment? Almost all libraries have an ILS, but what makes the true difference is how we choose to use and expand upon that which we have. A typical, fully featured library system includes modules that allow libraries to manage their collections and to display those collections to users. An ILS is that simple. Yet in order to attain such apparent simplicity, millions of lines of programming code must mesh and mesh well. To use a construction analogy, the catalog database is the foundation and the framing. The online public access catalog (OPAC) is the display in the main front window. Circulation brings in the people and distributes the materials. Acquisitions, serials control, and electronic resources management software supply the building materials, manage the project, and communicate status. There are rooms for reserves, media management, XML serving and harvesting, interlibrary loan, and many other functions. A complex floor plan is possible and overall expenses vary depending on materials used. Excellent code holds it all together and makes it work; standards support the construction.

Functionality is the key. The ILS must perform well and be usable by staff and users. If there is weakness in a key module, staff will spend time, and therefore "invisible" dollars, creating, even perfecting, work-arounds. Those work-arounds are difficult to displace when staff become attached to them. The consequence, however, is that productivity suffers. If the inadequate module's failings impact the overall usability of the system as a whole, expenses increase, satisfaction deteriorates, and the library is less likely to desire that the ILS be a centerpiece of a broader information offering–a portal.

Perhaps a brief word here about usability is in order. Web experts at Diamond Bullet Designs in Ann Arbor, Michigan operate a group called Usability First that specializes in usability consulting and Web site design (http://www.diamondbullet.com). They list ways to improve usability as:

- Shortening the time to accomplish tasks
- Reducing the number of mistakes made
- Reducing learning time
- Improving people's satisfaction with a system[1]

It seems obvious that usability evaluation is a good thing for staff and users both. Libraries must get the best possible functionality for their dollars and must have a foundation on which to build. To return to the earlier construction analogy, a building needs a firm foundation and correct framing in order to bear the weight of upper levels. The point is that if the ILS does not perform optimally, it would be difficult to add services provided by other sources or to have the system be a core of sophisticated or expanded offerings. It would be truly unfortunate should the ILS be marginalized because of a structural failing.

Why should the ILS continue to be core functionality? We know that the OPAC is the principal discovery and display tool used in our libraries to find materials and we should preserve that role. Yet the importance of electronic resources is increasing. A recent article by Deanna B. Marcum and Gerald George provides statistics that confirm this assumption. They found that 96.6 percent of faculty and graduate students use printed books in their research and that 93.3 percent of graduate and undergraduate students do so.[2]

> Almost everyone doing sophisticated research continues to use printed books and journals, but, at the same time, nearly three-fourths of faculty and graduate students said that they use e-journals, and nearly one-fifth reported using e-books. Moreover, though some variation exists by field, more faculty and graduate students overall use online abstracts and indexes in research than use print abstracts and indexes; and slightly more use online databases, data sets, or data sources than use manuscripts and other primary source documents. Patterns are similar for coursework.[3]

The ILS increasingly plays a role in managing electronic resources. At least one library system makes that possible today, and others may follow. Library staff has heretofore developed homegrown solutions in Excel or Access or with other database tools to meet the challenges inherent in the control and tracking of what are frequently inconsistent and difficult license agreements. Software exists that makes it possible for library staff to manage these resources within the medium of the library system.

INFORMATION INTERRELATIONSHIPS

In our minds the library occupies a central role in the life of the whole institution; that role should indeed be at the core of academic pursuits. Our challenge is to ensure the veracity of that statement for years to come. If the ILS is in danger of being marginalized in some institutions, can the library itself be marginalized as well? This is a radical question. If we lose sight of the essence of what it is that we do very well, however, and fail to look beyond our core competencies, we are likely to find ourselves in the "back seat." The proliferation of portal technology opens the door to rising demands for increasing numbers of data sources that are accessible with speed and flexibility and are organized in new ways. We should be prepared to meet the challenge.

The following graphic illustrates the interconnectedness of our multiple information environments (see Figure 1). We are becoming adept at looking outside the library by building links to research programs and resources beyond the library. Also, many staff hours are spent crafting and maintaining lists, links, and dedicated search environments for print and electronic resources. There is a valuable tradition of making use of book vendor, serials agent, and library system vendor offerings to enhance or substitute for required or desirable services that might have

FIGURE 1. Information Interrelationships

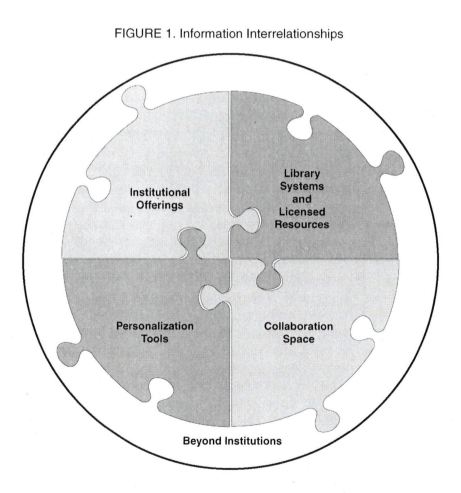

been built in-house if resources permitted, and the library is able to incorporate these features or tools into their total library information system environment. It is in the third and fourth areas–collaboration and personalization–where we will see the most significant impact in years to come, and it remains to be seen who will provide the tools that will make those activities pervasive in academia.

ROLE OF COLLABORATION AND PERSONALIZATION

In an interview, C. David Seuss, chief executive officer of Northern Light Group (http://www.northernlight.com, formerly Northern Light Technology), stated, "There is a realization that most portals do not impact the way people work. The next round of portal development must be more integrated into the workday of people. The current search and portal tools don't really facilitate collaboration, and portal use breaks down as tools either don't exist or fail."[4]

These statements should alert the library community that there is a good deal of conceptualization and technical development still to be done. We need to stretch our collective imagination and think past the satisfaction of having attained a level of information competence and delivery in our current offerings. Of course, it can be argued that certain disciplines within academia do not normally function in a manner conducive to collaboration–the lone scholar concept.[5] But it can also be argued that even people who have never lived in a world without microcomputers, Web access, chat rooms, BlackBerry, and the instant gratification of surfing with a remote control device in hand are likely to demand some level of collaborative work space that we are not yet equipped to provide. Communication will need to flow into and out of a new type of work space that extends beyond the institution and its library, as illustrated in Figure 2.

We should resurrect a term that first came into use roughly a decade ago and then faded away–"groupware." The Usability First site defines groupware as, "Software that enables a group of users to collaborate on a project by means of network communications. Groupware is any type of software designed for groups and for communication."[6] The use of groupware to facilitate Computer Supported Cooperative Work (CSCW) is a field of growing interest within technology circles and may also prove to be useful in the library community. One site that provides information about CSCW is the Association of Computing Machinery's 2002 CSCW Conference site at http://www.acm.org/cscw2002/.

FIGURE 2. The Gap in Portal Functionality

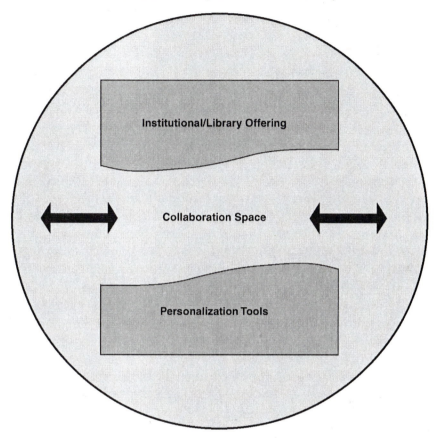

Groupware lives between the bookends of institutional/library offerings and personalization tools/practice; it is what will make possible the sharing of resources and ideas between individuals and groups of individuals. Seuss calls the concept "group-ization, a process that focuses on workflow."[7] He also states that, "Today's end-user, or personalization, tools do not make it effective to share work. Their nature virtually demands the re-invention of the work world by each member of the group and then, still, there is no ease of collaboration."[8] Thus, there is a continuing, urgent need for an improved tool or suite of tools to enable work and communication among the scholar, the institution, the library, the collaboration space, and the personalized space.

To a certain extent the library community's recent discussions of "institutional" or "disciplinary" repositories overlap with the concept of groupware, but the repository also has unique characteristics that distance it from collaboration and personalization. Depending upon the institution, a repository might be used as a work space, but it is more frequently associated with a desire to "capture and preserve scholarship, to push the envelope on the scholarly communication model, and to provide a link to instruction that would allow the faculty to create a linkage to e-learning for the creation of research and teaching."[9] The repository space could very well include search boxes and/or links to take users to the ILS or to other search and research resources.

ROLE OF SEARCH

The importance of potent search and retrieval tools is paramount for obvious reasons. Without superior search tools, much of what we create and store individually or through collaboration will be lost. We can list important themes in the manipulation of data and the use of software in an information rich environment:

- *More effective/productive search*–a search engine must accurately and efficiently retrieve appropriate results in an appropriate order using multiple techniques such as keyword, Boolean, natural language, and phrase searching. Recall and precision are paramount: recall indicates the number of documents retrieved; precision indicates the number of documents that satisfy the query.
- *Scalability to millions of pages*–we must be prepared to wrestle with the need to house and search many thousands of documents containing millions of pages. A search engine that slows or breaks is inherently inadequate to the cause. Of particular concern are the numerous institutional and disciplinary repositories springing up throughout academia. Hastily installed or inadequate search platforms or browsing tools will quickly nullify benefits to be derived from these important repositories.
- *Vertical search*–it is likely to become increasingly desirable for search tools to be able to search against a pre-designated slice of a given database. When users indicate that they want a search to be run against a certain topic or type of material, they are performing a vertical search. For example, a search might retrieve only those

documents classified as pertaining to biology or industrial toxicology or only those documents from journals or news sources.

- *Classification*–a uniform taxonomy applied universally or in specialized, vertical, segments.
- *Robust relevancy ranking based on multiple criteria*–a great deal has been written about ranking results based on link popularity, but in a sophisticated search environment, popularity is often the least valuable criteria to be considered. Among the many possible criteria are: number of occurrences of query terms in the document, the length of the document, location of the terms in the document, and case sensitivity.
- *Sophisticated alerting*–users should be able to request alerts that notify them of new content on a schedule they can set up and edit at will. Alerts should be able to run against an entire file or against a vertical slice.

Librarians must demand the highest quality search functionality from their vendors; there is no technical reason why they cannot have it. Judy Luther recently published a comprehensive article in *Library Journal* titled "Trumping Google? Metasearching's Promise" in which she states,

> Like it or not, Google and its competitor search engines have created a model that librarians, as information providers, must meet head on. The question is, will librarians, (who are Google users themselves) embrace the new technology to simplify access to their own resources? Metasearch technology, also known as federated or broadcast search, creates a portal that could allow the library to become the one-stop shop their users and potential users find so attractive.[10]

Let us briefly examine the concept of metasearch from another perspective. For the most part, the terms "broadcast search" and "federated search" are used interchangeably, as Luther maintains. For the purposes of this chapter, however, let us identify important distinctions in the nature and construction of search environments. We can think of broadcast searching as the "buckshot" approach in which a search query is sent simultaneously to multiple data sources resident in multiple locations. From the user's perspective, the search runs against one database. Search results are returned (depending on the vendor) in various ways into a single user interface. One approach displays results separated by data source where the user checks each source for results; another approach displays results as they are returned from the source and in the order they are returned (that order is governed by the policies of the information provider); another method could be to separate results by type of material. Examples of broadcast search can be seen in numerous products available from the principal ILS vendors. It is frequently difficult to apply sophisticated relevancy ranking and sorting algorithms to results obtained from a broadcast search, but vendors are working hard to achieve this capability.

Paula J. Hane succinctly presents five principal misconceptions about broadcast/federated searching in a brief piece titled "The Truth About Federated Searching."

- Federated search engines leave no stone unturned. [Authentication is critical, particularly for remote users.]
- De-dupe really works. [A completely accurate de-dupe is "virtually impossible."]
- Relevancy rankings are totally relevant. [Ranking is a moving target in the broadcast world.]
- Federated searching is software. [The author maintains it is a service.]
- We don't make your search engine. We make your search engine better. Reality: You can't get better results with a federated search engine than you can with the native database search.[11]

These are vital points. Librarians must be cognizant of the pros and cons of the technologies and products they embrace and be prepared to educate and manage users' expectations as services are moved into general use.

In contrast to the commonly styled broadcast/federated model already discussed, there is another search environment that should not be ignored. We can think of this as the "bucket" approach to search where multiple data sets from multiple sources originating in multiple formats are processed and combined into one large physical database resident in one location. It is no longer necessary to support a massive array of hardware in order to store massive amounts of data. Recent advances in compression technology make this possible. The ability to update and manipulate data stored in one physical database enables high quality and uniform relevancy ranking, sorting, classification, and application of taxonomy to occur. There is a single user interface. User satisfaction is often quite high. A simple example of this search in use in libraries today is the catalog database. Many incoming data sources in many formats populate catalogs every day. A more complex example would be a host aggregator who loads and processes data from multiple publishers in order to apply uniform processes.

Neither one environment nor the other is the only way search should happen, nor is it practical to believe that this will ever be the case. The application should determine the method. As databases grow and demands increase for the inclusion of locally produced data sets within the specialized/vertical search environments or within the larger search framework, and as some commercial information providers continue to insist on the need to house their data separately, we may ultimately see a combination of both methods where some data is poured into a large bucket and other sets must be searched simultaneously with buckshot. Whatever the outcome, none of us should take search methodology for granted. Some librarians believe that the choice of search software is a "make-or-break" decision. It is probable that both search models will function side-by-side in a transparent manner within a library's information system environment.

PORTALS IN THE CORPORATE WORLD

Search and complex portal environments are common in the corporate world. An article by James Watson and Joe Fenner appeared in *Information Management World* in July 2000 that, although now somewhat dated given the Internet economy bust that was just beginning at that time, does give us a thorough outline of what a portal is intended to do and what features are most important. Watson and Fenner define a portal as "a single window or jumping-off point for users"[12] and state that companies are looking for two main benefits: "(1) a means for gathering information from disparate data sources and for making it available to users, and (2) a common browser-based interface that allows users to do whatever they need–whether that means searching, accessing documents, or interacting with other users."[13] Librarians will find these goals familiar territory.

Just like libraries, corporations often must support multiple layers of users with their portal offerings. The publicly available Internet is usually accessible by all employees and the company mounts a public Web presence through a site. The company frequently also supports an Intranet consisting of sites and documents limited to use by authorized employees, some of which may be mounted in secure areas. And, companies mount Extranets for the exclusive use of their customers.

An Extranet contains material that can be accessed by customers for the purpose of conducting business with the company and may include special information areas and business-to-business commerce areas. Extranets are almost always password protected. Library system vendors have adopted this model to provide sophisticated customer service via a secure Web environment.

Watson and Fenner's list of important features for corporate portals follows:

- Information gathering [access and gather information from disparate data sources]
- Categorization and organization [manual or automatic indexing, support taxonomy]
- Collaboration [interactive features, sharing, communication]
- Search [full text and fielded]
- Distribution and publishing [Web distribution, many formats]
- Personalization [modify interfaces, specify preferences, dynamic delivery of data]
- Life cycle management [records management and institutional repository]
- Auditing [track usage, reporting]
- Analysis [refine and filter, data mining]
- Determine expertise [individuals declare or portals infer expertise]
- Locate individual experts [look for experts or knowledge within the organization][14]

Librarians will recognize the parallels of each area to their individual situation and will also recognize that the ILS and portals need to be linked. We have already done so much to describe, organize, and present an electronic face to the body of work built over time that we must take advantage of what has gone before and what continues to grow in our catalogs, processes, and new repositories. It is a natural link from information housed in our libraries to the wider body of work being created by those who also happen to use our physical library buildings. The information interrelationships to be fostered can expand well beyond our imaginations.

CONCLUSION

Integrated library systems may increasingly assume more portal-like characteristics; however, they must retain their central role of organizing and providing access to all library collections whether they are print or electronic. It is critical that strong technical service functionality be preserved for the management of print and digital resources. Public service functionality must expand to incorporate the broader expectations of varied types of users. Will the ILS vendor have a role in building portals as they can be? Yes, absolutely. Any ILS vendor that does not continue to enhance metasearch functionality will not prosper. Any ILS vendor that does not keep system/portal functionality in mind is doomed to have a backwater system. Happily, it is clear that vendors taking notice of needed interrelationships will be able to bring great benefits to libraries by maximizing already large investments in their integrated library systems.

AUTHOR NOTE

Ms. Hurd is a Member of the American Library Association, New England Library Association, North American Serials Interest Group, and Beta Phi Mu. The author has extensive experience in the library industry. At Innovative Interfaces her principal responsibilities are the launch of their Electronic Resources Management software and marketing strategy. Before joining Innovative, she worked for three years as senior manager of library information services at Northern Light Technology where she was responsible for the introduction of the Northern Light Alumni Content Portal. Prior to that, she spent over seven years as assistant vice president and director of library automation at EBSCO Subscription Services. An active member of the standards community, she was chair of the Serials Industry Systems Advisory Committee (SISAC) for over two years and also represented the company at International Committee for EDI for Serials (ICEDIS) meetings. She has spoken extensively on EDI, the serials world, and portals. Ms. Hurd has also held management positions at The H. W. Wilson Company and Entree Corporation where, as Director and Editor of abstracting services, she was heavily involved in bringing to market the abstracted version of Wilson's *Reader's Guide to Periodical Literature.*

NOTES

1. See: http://www.usabilityfirst.com/index.txl.
2. Deanna B. Marcum and Gerald George, "Who Uses What? Report on a National Survey of Information Users in Colleges and Universities," *D-Lib Magazine, 9,* no. 10 (October 2003). See: http://www.dlib.org/dlib/october03/george/10george.html.
3. Ibid.
4. Conversation with C. David Seuss, chief executive officer, Northern Light Group, LLC, September 16, 2003.
5. Conversation with Bernie Hurley, director of library technologies, University of California, Berkeley, Library, November 4, 2003.
6. See: http://www.usabilityfirst.com/groupware/.

7. Seuss conversation.

8. Ibid.

9. Hurley conversation.

10. Judy Luther, "Trumping Google? Metasearching's Promise," *Library Journal*, October 1, 2003. See: http://libraryjournal.reviewsnews.com/index.asp?layout=article&articleId=CA322627&display=searchResults&stt=001&text=judy+luther.

11. "The Truth About Federated Searching," *InformationToday*, Nov./Dec., 2003. Source: WebFeat (http://www.webfeat.org). See: http://www.infotoday.com/it/oct03/hane1.shtml.

12. James Watson and Joe Fenner, "Understanding Portals: At the Core," *Information Management Journal, 34,* no. 3 (July 2000). Source: EBSCO Academic Search Elite database.

13. Ibid.

14. Ibid.

Chapter 5

If You Build It Will They Come?
Services Will Make the Difference
in a Portal

Ann Marie Breznay
Leslie M. Haas

SUMMARY. Identifying and adding services to a library portal will add to its long term success in a market that pits libraries against commercial vendors such as Google and Amazon.com. The current focus on portals has been on selecting collections and developing the basic functionality of the Web site. We look at the added features needed in order to make this a product that is attractive to today's researcher. *[Article copies available for a fee from The Haworth Document Delivery Service: 1-800-HAWORTH. E-mail address: <docdelivery@haworthpress.com> Website: <http://www.HaworthPress.com> © 2005 by The Haworth Press, Inc. All rights reserved.]*

Ann Marie Breznay is Electronic Resources Librarian (E-mail: annmarie.breznay@library.utah.edu); and Leslie M. Haas is Head of General Reference (E-mail: leslie.haas@library.utah.edu), both at the Marriott Library, University of Utah.

The authors would like to thank Margaret Landesman and Ceres Birkhead for their assistance.

[Haworth co-indexing entry note]: "If You Build It Will They Come? Services Will Make the Difference in a Portal." Breznay, Ann Marie, and Leslie M. Haas. Co-published simultaneously in *Journal of Library Administration* (The Haworth Information Press, an imprint of The Haworth Press, Inc.) Vol. 43, No. 1/2, 2005, pp. 71-86; and: *Portals and Libraries* (ed: Sarah C. Michalak) The Haworth Information Press, an imprint of The Haworth Press, Inc., 2005, pp. 71-86. Single or multiple copies of this article are available for a fee from The Haworth Document Delivery Service [1-800-HAWORTH, 9:00 a.m. - 5:00 p.m. (EST). E-mail address: docdelivery@haworthpress.com].

Available online at http://www.haworthpress.com/web/JLA
© 2005 by The Haworth Press, Inc. All rights reserved.
Digital Object Identifier: 10.1300/J111v43n01_06

KEYWORDS. Services, portals, Web design, functionality, customization

Why all the interest in portals? Bluntly put, our users find our collections too confusing and intimidating and want us to do something to help them. Portals offer libraries the opportunity to vastly simplify our highly complex collections and to enhance that access with a variety of services.

What do Yahoo, your local bank and SilverPlatter have in common? They demonstrate that it is no longer enough to have a product; today users want personalized service. Libraries are not immune from this expectation. Librarians long have been aware that the size and complexity of research collections puts some users off and have developed a variety of approaches to make access to information in the collections easier. However, users continue to hope for something simpler than any of the traditional means librarians have devised. We have reminded users that we are here to help them find and interpret material.

After centuries of building collections of research material and making them available to our users, ironically, recent research suggests that user reluctance may be, in fact, due to too much choice. Barry Schwartz reported research showing that as the number of possibilities increased, satisfaction went down. He continued, "Similarly, an abundance of options raises people's expectations about how good the option they have chosen will be" (Schwartz, 2004). Users of libraries today find the number of databases overwhelming, the search interfaces complicated, and the service options confusing. They want to be able to ask a question in a single interface and see the results, they want to arrange for document delivery of articles and ask questions of experts in the field when necessary. Some academic libraries are responding by developing scholar's portals.

What is a portal? Marketingterms.com defines it as "a site featuring a suite of commonly used services, serving as a starting point and frequent gateway to the Web (Web portal) or a niche topic (vertical portal)." The new Oxford English Dictionary includes a definition in this sense, as "Originally: a server or web site that provides Internet access. Later also: a web site or service that provides access to a number of sources of information and facilities, such as a directory of links to other web sites, search engines, e-mail, online shopping, etc." (Oxford English Dictionary, 1989).

Typically, the difference between a Web site and a portal is that, while both offer a set of Web pages and links, a portal additionally can be personalized and customized, it is role based (the resources and services presented to you depend on your "role," as a student, a faculty member, a community user), and it provides for user authentication for access to licensed content.

The strength of the portal lies in its ability to offer added services to patrons. Libraries historically have looked for ways to make collections more accessible. We have been early adopters of technology, computerizing catalogs and databases, and creating–from the beginning–highly structured MARC records that have been adaptable in multiple ways. More recently, we have invested in the development and use of online chat software, and have implemented federated search engines and portals to try to make users' research lives even easier. We have built large collections of electronic serials and books, and have digitized rare collections. Interfaces have long allowed cross-database searches within a single vendor's software; new federated search engines provide the ability to search across databases and indexes from multiple vendors and multiple interfaces. Portals take these technological advances a step further by including not only a wide range of search options, but also the ability to personalize, to customize, and to authenticate.

As librarians evaluate what services to offer within the portal environment, a look at two typical yet disparate users helps to highlight the features and functionality users might find most appealing.

WHO ARE OUR USERS?

In 2002, the Pew Internet and American Life project released a study titled *The Internet Goes to College*. The study examined the impact of the Internet on the daily lives of college students. Not surprisingly, college students use the Internet heavily as part of their daily routine. Students rely on the Internet to communicate with each other and they turn to it regularly when assigned research for their classes. Approximately 73% of the students surveyed said that they use the Internet more than they do the library; and 68% subscribe to academic discussion lists related to their classes or majors (Jones, 2002). With this data as a background, let us look at two students currently enrolled in college.

George, an undergraduate, needs to use a variety of resources to complete his twenty-page term paper in history. George is typical of many students: his paper is due soon; he is unfamiliar with library research, and he wants, quickly, to get full-text articles, not just citations. George has never taken a library orientation class, so he finds it frustrating to do research in his academic library. He doesn't even think about asking one of the librarians at the reference desk for help; in fact, he does much of his research at one of the many computer labs on campus. He is confused by the number of databases and does not know how to select the right database or how to prepare a search statement appropriate to the interface presented. He is not sure how to get the actual articles, and he has to prepare a bibliography of sources used.

It is not atypical for students to consult several databases in their search for the right article(s). Depending on how the library's indexes are arranged, George may be able to find a history database, but once he is connected he may not be able to figure out how to construct a search statement to find what he needs and if the database does not supply full text, then George will hunt around until he finds a database, any database, that has full text available. When the full text is not available in the database, he needs to know that he has to search his library catalog or electronic journal list to find out if the journal is available in the library or, even better, online. If he is not easily able to find articles that will help him with his paper, he likely will turn to a Web site that has served him well in the past, Google. With the entry of a simple search statement, and no need to worry about Boolean operators, George will have at his fingertips hundreds if not thousands of "hits" directing him to information on his topic. Is it good information? Is it scholarly? George does not care. He got the results he wanted in a matter of minutes, instead of spending hours to learn how to do research at the library.

Our second "scholar" is a graduate student, working on her dissertation in anthropology. Sarah is a skilled library user and is away from her home institution doing fieldwork. She is familiar with the resources available to her at her home institution and if she is lucky, she knows how to enable off-campus access and can get to her home library's databases from her computer. Sarah may have some privileges at a nearby university, but they may not include off-campus access. The library she's visiting may not subscribe to the resources she needs and they may not allow her to use Interlibrary Loans. Sarah needs easy access to library materials and, ideally, wants them delivered to her desktop. In addition, she would like access to bibliographic management software to manage the many citations she has amassed for her research.

The difference between these two users is the degree of familiarity they bring to the overall library research process. George, as a novice, needs a Web site that does not overwhelm him with the number of choices available on a chosen topic. Instead it allows him to enter his search statement and retrieve results containing both full text and citations. He should be given the option of getting additional assistance and more databases if he so desires. Sarah, as an experienced researcher, needs easy access to library tools off campus and additional resources that allow her to manipulate, deliver, or save the results of her long-term research. Both Sarah and George would benefit from a portal and the services it provides.

Before we look further into the world of portals, let us take a look at telephones and the Internet and how they have developed in the last 100 years. Why? Because their development in many ways reflects the journey we are currently undertaking in the development of federated search engines and portals.

A HISTORICAL PERSPECTIVE

Alexander Graham Bell invented the telephone in 1876. It took a hundred years to get to today's environment where we have confidence that when we pick up the receiver, we will have a dial tone, it will be stable, and we will be able to use the system to call anywhere in the world we choose.

ARPANET linked four sites in 1969 (UCLA, Stanford Research Institute [SRI], UC Santa Barbara, and the University of Utah). In 34 years, a third of the time it took for the phone system to mature, we have seen growth from 4 connections to 19.5 million. Technology is continuing to grow, develop, and move, sometimes slowly, sometimes fast, toward stability. We were happy in 1876 just to make the connection, while today's phone users expect services ranging from answering machines to Caller ID to cell phones to complete mobility and ubiquity.

In parallel, computer users once were happy with 300 baud dial up connections; we now demand "always on" Internet connections, delivering content plus a growing array of services. We shop, we communicate, we play games, and we sometimes even do work. Our students have grown up using computers and expect quick connections, rich content, and a variety of services. How do libraries provide that?

Librarians are hampered by the costs of developing online versions of traditional services. It is hard to compete with the rich features of, say, an Amazon.com, when we lack the millions of dollars that such commercial sites spend on programming and development. On the other hand, a 2003 report from OCLC, "Libraries: How they stack up," points out that U.S. public library cardholders outnumber Amazon customers by almost 5 to 1 and each day, U.S. libraries circulate nearly 4 times more items than Amazon handles (OCLC, 2003). We can be optimistic that when a hundred years have passed in the computing development timeline, we will have fixed the software, resolved the technical issues, and created the services as did telephony in its comparable century.

What libraries have to their benefit, however, is a long history of cooperation. We form coalitions, consortia, partnerships, and project groups and work together to develop strategies and services that benefit us collectively.

Ironically, recent research suggests that our problem may be "too much choice." Barry Schwartz presents research evidence to suggest that "for many people, increased choice can lead to a decrease in satisfaction. Too many options can result in paralysis, not liberation" (Schwartz, 2004). The single-entry Google search box becomes attractive, then, in part because it reduces the choices a person must make among dozens of databases and Web pages. Libraries actually have attempted to deal with this problem. Whether we have articulated it in the same way as Schwartz and his fellow researchers, we have been aware, especially in large academic libraries, that our collections can be intimidating. We have addressed this by creating smaller subject-based libraries (the science library, the documents library, the undergraduate library) or focused collections (the browsing collection of contemporary fiction).

WHAT CAN LIBRARIES DO?

In the last several years, librarians have begun to talk about "portals" or, more accurately, federated search engines, usually understood as systems which allow a single search executed across a number of databases or indexes. While federated search engines allow searching across disparate databases, portals imply an additional layer that adds personalization, customization, and authentication. Portals aim to offer users a level of service they are used to seeing in the commercial sites they visit regularly on the Internet.

Academic librarians face challenging questions. Do we integrate software and services at the campus level? Should the campus portal–a role-based, personalizable, customizable, authenticated portable desktop–be the main point of contact through which we provide library services in addition to campus services? Or should the library itself provide such an access point?

The current array of services offered divides the tools users need into subject (or other) categories, but for the most part they will need to search each one individually. The portal makes the same information available, but rather than repeating a search several times, users select the databases and enter searches one time. In addition to the single search across multiple databases, federated search systems typically offer de-duplication of results, links to full text, and the ability to create a customized list of databases to be searched that match the researcher's needs.

THE NEXT STEP:
SERVICES

Other sources have described the ideal federated search system. It can connect to all library electronic resources, offer high-level search functionality (Boolean searches, de-duplication of results) and connections to full-text sources. This chapter focuses on the services in either a portal or a federated search engine that ought to be available.

As Jakob Neilsen has pointed out, portals ought to know a lot about their users without the users having to describe themselves. He was talking about corporate intranets, but in a college setting, we also know a lot about our users. Before users begin any kind of personalization, especially in portals integrated at the campus level, those who create and manage portals can determine the status or role of the person (student, faculty), know what courses they are taking or teaching, what reserve readings are available to them, and what subject areas they are interested in–all based on their public identities (Neilsen, 2003). We can start to create services that are tailored to the users, available at point of need, and offer genuine assistance in navigating through multiple sources.

It is easy to see how helpful Amazon.com-type services might be in a library setting. In some cases, they are services we already offer, but libraries tend to present them in "library-ese." Patrons don't grasp the library terminology as readily. "Look for similar books by subject" makes sense. Clicking on the subject heading link in the catalog accomplishes the same thing, but is not always intuitive. Libraries need to be more sensitive to marketing services in language that resonates with users, so that they are clear about what service they can expect when they click.

ADAPTING AMAZON-LIKE FUNCTIONS
TO LIBRARY OPERATIONS

Looking at Amazon.com's services suggests ways existing library services could be made more intuitive and friendly. As mentioned in the previous paragraph, libraries offer many of these services, it is just not apparent to the user. We are not advocating that we turn completely away from traditional library services, but that we consider ways to attract users back to libraries again and again. Nor is it necessary to implement a portal in order to think about new ways of presenting services to users. Amazon's structure is relevant in part because both Amazon and libraries work toward, as Ranganathan once said, matching every reader to his or her book.

Below are some ideas which take Amazon.com's current list of services and suggest ways those services can be adapted to the library environment.

- *Recently Viewed Items:* Helpful to people doing extensive research in catalogs, indexes, or databases as a tracking device.
- *The Page You Made:* An online "data locker" where people can keep notes, citations, favorite URLs, downloaded copies of articles and more.
- *See What's New for You:* New books, journals, articles, alerting service requests.
- *Where's My Stuff?* Items checked out, my recalls, the ILL articles I've just received electronically.
- *E-mail notifications:* Books are available to pick up, a class is being held on a database of interest, the subject librarian is teaching a short class on a database today.
- *Recommendations:* Subject librarians could create recommendations of new books, journals, important articles, new services.
- *Personal Information:* A place to record or change e-mail and regular mail addresses, passwords, subject areas of interest, etc.
- *Customers who bought this also bought:* "People who checked this out also checked out. . . ."
- *Product Details:* Help files, of course. Title lists and content descriptions.
- *Our Customers' Advice:* In Amazon, what customers recommend in addition to the item selected; in a library context, parallels the recommendations section–librarians make the recommendations, users provide the advice to their fellow readers.

- *Listmania!* User-contributed best books/best resources lists both for scholarly study and for recreational reading.
- *Look for similar books by subject:* Enhanced subject heading links.
- *Editorial Reviews:* Direct links to online review content from other sources.
- *Customer Reviews:* As in Amazon's site, links to comments by readers on library resources, providing a level of user feedback we may not have seen before.

Without advocating that we re-make our portals in Amazon's image, studying the services provided and adapting them to libraries, as appropriate, is a way to repackage or reshape activities libraries long have performed. People return to Amazon time and time again. What is it that people find so attractive? Is it the price? Reviews? Lists? What can librarians learn from Amazon.com and similar commercial sites that could apply to the development of portals?

We also–and this is not an effort unique to portals–must identify and remove barriers to user success (Souza, 2001). More and more libraries are actively seeking user feedback, asking them for ideas on how the library can better meet their needs. The most progressive organizations are willing to rethink administrative and technological operations that have become barriers to library use.

SEARCHING

One of the strengths of the portal is the simplicity of its interface. Ideally, patrons can use one search interface to search multiple sources at one time. However, this can also be one of its "weaknesses" if good interface design practices are not followed. For the portal to be successful, it has to be very easy for patrons to identify the types of databases they need to search for their topic. Subject groupings should be kept to a minimum and the databases in each carefully chosen. The criteria for inclusion will vary, but patrons want to know at least two things about each database beyond the topic it covers: Is it full text? Is it popular or scholarly? The groups also should be arranged so that patrons can pick out the type of material being searched: digitized collections, images, books, reference tools, articles, and so on.

Users should be able to personalize the portal. Without this capability, users will see no difference between it and other databases that libraries now subscribe to. They may find it even less useful if they cannot combine databases and other tools in order to do their research.

Similar to the "My Library" concept, users should be able to either personalize a pre-existing subject group, adding and deleting databases or Web sites to better suit their needs or build a subject set from scratch, selecting their resources from a list of available databases and building a "favorites" list of Web sites.

A further search tool beneficial to patrons is a "411" (or information) search, named after the telephone company's directory information service number. This type of search was and is one of the strengths of the Dialog search system, whose file number for this service (DIALINDEX®) is indeed 411. Users can see possible databases for a topic and see the number of retrievals available from the databases chosen. This allows users to focus their efforts on the databases with the higher number of "hits." While this is not foolproof, it does allow the patron to quickly eliminate databases that are not promising. Anything that can be done to allow the patron to move quickly and efficiently through the search process will keep them coming back again and again.

Natural language searching, while not perfect, is a style that patrons frequently request and automatically do when searching a database. Undergraduates type in a topic sentence without much thought. They are frustrated when expected results don't materialize and don't know how to construct a search statement that will produce the desired results. They often do not understand Boolean searching. Still, while natural language searching may return fewer results, much of the time it satisfies users' needs. Making natural language searching the "basic" default in the portal will give students results that most of the time will satisfy their research needs. A link or icon to more advanced search options should be available to those who need the power of the Boolean operators. Many databases include basic and advanced search engines and the natural language search should be the basic option to help novice researchers get started. Too many search rules at the start will be frustrating and overwhelming, and will only cause them to turn to Google where they "know" they can get results.

Once the results have been returned, they need to be processed to remove duplicates and sort as desired. Relevancy ranking is the most useful of the sorting options and should be a staple of a portal from the very beginning. Searching multiple databases retrieves large result sets; often the results are returned based on the fastest response time. For the patron to find results useful, automatic relevancy ranking is necessary. This may slow response time, but will make the system more useful to the researcher. Standard sorting options should also be available, including the ability to sort by document type (article, Web site, book, dissertation, etc.) year of publication, and location (identifying those locally available versus those which must be obtained via ILL). Patrons will return to a service that gives them targeted results and in addition allows them to identify those items that are readily available. While there will be times that a patron will want the item available only via ILL, providing the link to make the request automatic will increase the likelihood that they will actually use the power of ILL.

Searching multiple databases can also be a weakness in a portal. While you gain in the ability to search across databases, you may lose some functionality available in the database's own search engine. One solution is to provide a link to the database that transfers the search statements to the native interface for the user who wants to delve deeper into his or her topic using just one database. This bridge would allow users the benefit of seeing what is in multiple databases, allowing them to take advantage of each database's search engine when necessary, without having to remember and retype their searches.

Microsoft has made office assistant icons available to those customers who want a personalized guide to assist them in using its products. Designing an online advisor to help users focus their research questions and suggest resources would assist them in confronting the overwhelming number of tools. Allowing users to select their online advisors will further personalize the service and if the "advisor" had access to user information, it could be very effective in guiding the user through the necessary steps in developing a good search strategy. Useful information might include: syllabus, reserve readings, lists and subject databases selected by the professor for a class. This advisor could conduct "reference interviews" to help users isolate their questions and make suggestions regarding the direction of their research as well as possibly suggest search statements as a starting point.

Finally, patrons will want a variety of output options beyond the standard e-mail, download or print. More and more citation tools are available via the Web and researchers will want to be able to transfer and save results to their preferred software files. In addition, saving search statements to run at a later date (or better yet, automatically) will be a service desired by the more sophisticated scholar.

DOCUMENT DELIVERY OPTIONS

Adding services to a federated search engine elevates it from a mere search tool to one which is a true research assistant. Alert services already exist within vendors' sites and within specific databases, but the ability of a robot or search assistant to manage a fine-tuned alerting service across multiple databases is needed. Enhancements to traditional e-mail delivery must include delivery to cell phones or PDAs. Patrons will want to set alerts for topics, or for items published in specific journals. Subject specialists will be able to craft subject-oriented alerts, to notify patrons of new materials (items received in the library, selected Web sites, and perhaps even notifications of upcoming speakers or conferences). Users can subscribe to such services and have information pushed to them, again either via e-mail, cell phone, or PDA. It would be helpful (and really cool) if, as you walked into the library with your wireless device, the system would "know" you were there and alert you to items on the new book shelf, talks being given that day, or new issues of journals.

Users will want to know how to get items delivered. Does the library subscribe to the item in an online form? Then a link must be provided to connect to the full text. Is the item in print? Then call numbers or locations and interactive maps to guide the user to the shelf should come into play. Such tools must be integrated into other library systems as well, to determine whether an item is truly on the shelf, is checked out, is in a processing area, in a consortium partner library, or in a local or regional storage facility.

ASSISTANCE

The portal is designed to bring collections together making them easily accessible. However, patrons will still need assistance and it can be assumed that many will not actually be in the library near a reference desk at their time of need. A robust array of online assistance options will be needed and these services need to go beyond the basics of what is currently available. Tutorials, help screens, mouse-overs, e-mail assistance, and 800 numbers are most commonly found today. While these will be available on the portal, user assistance needs to go further. Portals should provide a menu of point-of-use tools that work with the user's preferred mode of learning. (Note: Some of the tools listed are not "aids" in the truest sense, but instead focus on the different ways users can communicate with librarians, scholars, students or instructors.)

Chatrooms, blogs, and bulletin boards are some of the online tools being used more frequently by faculty to allow students a space to ask questions outside of class and carry on discussions with their classmates. Portals can provide space in various subject areas for users to ask questions and talk with scholars about topics in a particular field. Systems should provide a way to examine user behavior while stripping out identifying user data so that librarians and others could monitor these tools to look for areas that are particularly troubling users and use the information to improve the product. Librarians could also hold subject oriented "office hours" to answer questions and assist users with their research. A "hot topics" area would be useful for undergraduates who need to identify current or controversial topics for their papers. This area could include a list of topics, search statement possibilities, opposing viewpoints, print and electronic resources providing popular and scholarly information. Building a favorites list based on professor or librarian suggestions and ideas from fellow students could also be included in this area.

Another tool that could be included is a writing toolkit. It could include links to bibliographic management tools, style guides, and sites on plagiarism. A link to the school's writing center would promote the importance of research to writing and could highlight the interconnection between research and writing and the importance of clear communication in research papers.

ACCESSIBILITY

Early computerized databases were little more than print indexes transferred to computer and mostly searchable, albeit more quickly, in the same author/title/subject manners as the paper indexes. Each generation of computing adoption, certainly in libraries, has seen the following repeating sequence. First, the tool or service itself is exactly reproduced on a computer. In the second phase, more functionality is added, though the structure of the original is retained. Now, abstracts and in some cases even full text are searchable but the structure still is more or less that of a traditional index. In later phases we finally see a movement away from traditional structures and a willingness to look at new ways of searching and presenting information. We saw this pattern played out in library Web pages; early pages had limited information and mirrored libraries' organizational structures. For example, in order for users to find out online whether they had books checked out, they had to know that book check out was a function of the circulation department and first go to the circulation department's Web page. Only in later iterations did libraries finally learn to create pages to provide access to information and services that did not require the user to understand the structure of the library in order to find what they needed.

We need to keep this development pattern in mind as we work with portals, especially when a decision needs to be made about creating a library portal versus integrating library content and services into a campus portal. Do we still require our users to understand the structure of the university in order to find information? Why not create a library channel on a university portal to smoothly provide content and services to students, faculty, and staff? Why create multiple portals requiring multiple authentications? At the very least, library staff should work closely with campus developers as these decisions are being made. There may be reasons why a separate library portal is desirable (which may be contractual or technical) but the decisions should be carefully evaluated by both library and campus portal builders. The best choices will be informed by values that insist on the delivery of clear, understandable content and services, ideally not determined by politics or territoriality.

ADMINISTRATIVE TOOLS

Any kind of portal, whether at the campus-level or at the library, must have a variety of administrative tools to help manage content and delivery of services. Among useful ideas are dynamically-generated Web pages, Web interfaces for adding and removing resources, an easy way to manage user accounts and authentication, and clear tools and rules for maintaining data on individual users in the light of growing privacy and confidentiality concerns. Feedback mechanisms are not just necessary, but vital to the success of the portal. Knowing what our users like and dislike about the portal concept will help us to evolve and respond quickly to the changing technological landscape. User focus groups and other usability testing processes are essential to ensuring that the final product is useful to various constituencies.

CONCLUSION:
GEORGE AND SARAH

Let us return to our two scholars mentioned at the beginning of this chapter. How would they approach their research assignments if they had access to a portal?

George, our intrepid undergraduate student, logs in to his personal university account and on the first page he sees an icon directing him to a link for history research. This link is personalized for his class and is targeted to an undergraduate researcher. As he enters this portal, he is offered the option to either look at a select list of databases to start his research or to click on the online assistant to help him focus his research topic and identify the right database(s) for his research question. George notes that the history librarian and his professor will be online in an hour if he has questions about his research project. George also sees that there is a list of Web sites that students who have taken this class last semester recommend to help him get started with his assignment. George does some preliminary research and is pleased to discover that he can save his search statements and results so he can come back to this later when he has time to do more work on his paper. He also notes the library hours, in case he decides later to look at some reference books, or to speak directly to a reference librarian about his paper when he picks up the books being held for him at the circulation desk.

Sarah, in the portal environment, has authenticated as a university graduate student. Within her university's portal software, her role as a graduate student means she has access to resources and tools from locations outside the library and campus. Even from her remote research location, she can connect to the electronic resources she is accustomed to consulting. She has remote access to a Web-based bibliographic citation manager, so she can document the material she is consulting at her remote research site, whether she has viewed it via her authenticated connection or whether she identifies it at the local library. Even though she is away from her campus, she can connect to her online class Web site and participate in a discussion among the students. In the course of her research, she has a question about the mechanics of a particular database, so she connects to her library's chat reference service and consults the librarian for clarification. She can even store copies of articles in her digital storage locker and work with them later when she returns home.

Campus funding is often dependent on our ability to demonstrate our centrality to the teaching, research, and service missions of our universities. Students vote with their feet and satisfied student users will continue to use our resources and services, turning to us first, before they try general Web surfing or giant Web search engines.

Portals tie together access to online and print collections, functionality, and services, to provide users with a single point of access to a variety of resources. Portals can be integrated with school or campus portals, or can operate as independent library ones. In any scenario, their easy access to online materials and functions will draw users initially, but services will keep them coming back.

REFERENCES

Agustine, Susan and Courtney Greene. 2002. Discovering How Students Search a Library Website: A Usability Case Study. *College & Research Libraries* 63, no. 4:354-365.

Hane, Paula J. 2003. The Truth About Federated Searching. *Information Today* 20, no. 9:24.

Head, Alison J. 2003. Personas: Setting the Stage for Building Usable Information Sites. *Online* 27, no. 4:14-21.

Jones, Steve and Pew Internet & American Life Project. September 15, 2002. The Internet Goes to College: How Students are Living in the Future with Today's Technology. http://www.pewinternet.org/reports/ [cited January 19, 2004].

Karat, Clare-Marie et al. 2003. Personalizing the User Experience at ibm.com. *IBM Systems Journal* 42, no. 4:686-701.

Marketingterms.com Internet Marketing Resources. http://marketingterms.com [cited January 28, 2004].

Neilsen, Jakob. 2003. Intranet Portals: A Tool Metaphor for Corporate Information http://www.useit.com/jakob.ed [cited January 22, 2004].

OCLC. 2003. Libraries: How They Stack Up.

Oxford University Press. Oxford English Dictionary Online. Oxford: New York: Oxford University Press http://www.dictionary.oed.com [cited January 19, 2004].

Ozmutlu, Seda, Huseyin C. Ozmutlu and Amada Spink. 2003. Are People Asking Questions of General Web Search Engines? *Online Information Review* 27, no. 6: 396-406.

Schatz, Bruce et al. 1999. Federated Search of Scientific Literature. *Computer* 32, no. 2:51-59.

Schwartz, Barry. 2004. A Nation of Second Guesses. *New York Times*, 22 January, national edition.

Souza, Randy. 2001. Get ROI from Design. *Forrester Report* 6.

Tenopir, Carol. 2003. What User Studies Tell Us. *Library Journal* 128, no. 14:32.

Wadham, Rachel L. 2004. Federated Searching. *Library Mosaics* 15, no. 1:20.

Wonnacott, Laura. 2000. To Keep Users Happy, Ensure the Search Tool Is Matched to Your Audience's Needs. *Infoworld* 22, no. 19:102.

Chapter 6

Library Portal Technologies

Krisellen Maloney
Paul J. Bracke

SUMMARY. The purpose of the library portal is to enable users to discover relevant information from multiple distributed information resources; to seamlessly, and directly as possible, access related content; and to effectively use the information. The library portal is not a single technology. Rather it is a combination of several systems, standards, and protocols that interoperate to create a unified experience for the user. This chapter describes the various technologies and the relationship among the technologies that combine to enable the user to move seamlessly through the processes related to discovery, access, and use of information. A framework that incorporates many aspects of the JISC Information Environment Architecture (Joint Information Systems 2002) and the IMS Digital Repositories Framework (McLean and Lynch 2003) provides a structure to facilitate the discussion of issues related to each

Krisellen Maloney is Digital Libraries and Information Systems Team Leader, The University of Arizona Library, 1510 East University Boulevard, Tucson, AZ 85721-0055 (E-mail: maloneyk@u.library.arizona.edu).

Paul J. Bracke is Head of Systems and Networking, Arizona Health Sciences Library, University of Arizona, 1501 North Campbell Avenue, Tucson, AZ 85724-5079 (E-mail: paul@ahsl.arizona.edu).

[Haworth co-indexing entry note]: "Library Portal Technologies." Maloney, Krisellen, and Paul J. Bracke. Co-published simultaneously in *Journal of Library Administration* (The Haworth Information Press, an imprint of The Haworth Press, Inc.) Vol. 43, No. 1/2, 2005, pp. 87-112; and: *Portals and Libraries* (ed: Sarah C. Michalak) The Haworth Information Press, an imprint of The Haworth Press, Inc., 2005, pp. 87-112. Single or multiple copies of this article are available for a fee from The Haworth Document Delivery Service [1-800-HAWORTH, 9:00 a.m. - 5:00 p.m. (EST). E-mail address: docdelivery@haworthpress.com].

Available online at http://www.haworthpress.com/web/JLA
Digital Object Identifier: 10.1300/J111v43n01_07

of the many individual components while it depicts the interrelation-ship among the components. *[Article copies available for a fee from The Haworth Document Delivery Service: 1-800-HAWORTH. E-mail address: <docdelivery@haworthpress.com> Website: <http://www.HaworthPress.com> © 2005 by The Haworth Press, Inc. All rights reserved.]*

KEYWORDS. Portals, library technology, systems architecture, systems design

INTRODUCTION

There are several definitions that present similar visions of the library portal. Despite the minor variations between them, there is significant agreement that services that support discovery, access and effective use of information will provide the foundation for the portal (Association of Research Libraries 2001, European Library Automation Group 2002, Joint Information Systems Committee 2002, Butters 2003, and Library of Congress 2003a). Discovery services enable users to identify a range of information sources, regardless of format or location, which are appropriate for their need. In current library portals, discovery is often facilitated through metasearching tools, browsable interfaces, and online reference help. Librarians work behind the scenes selecting resources that are useful for specific user groups (e.g., courses, majors, departments) or purposes (e.g., papers, events). These searchable lists can include heterogeneous information such as commercial or licensed electronic resources, locally developed collections, and finding aids for special collections and archives. Some freely and commercially available library portals provide features that enable users to customize their own lists of resources and save them between sessions. Besides providing appropriate lists of searchable resources, librarians also provide guidance in selecting and effectively using resources by means of online reference and help.

Currently, the result of browsing or searching for information is a list of records from multiple sources. As a possible next step, the user may want to save or print the citations for future use. More likely, the user will want to directly access the content that is described by the citation metadata. This may include links to full-text articles, a link to a museum exhibit, or a request for Interlibrary Loan or document delivery. The discovery and access processes are the functional core of the library portal.

The final goal of the library portal is to provide services that assist the user in managing and using the information. These tools include citation management and other tools that allow the user to organize content effectively. Examples include the ability to create a personal environment (i.e., "MyLibrary" functionality), save search results, save search histories, and create automated alerts of new content. The library portal may also include additional services to further assist the user in accessing content. These services include online reference and the ability to check the user's library circulation record.

As the library portal matures as a hub for user activity, librarian roles will undergo an evolution. Public service roles will expand to include the design and definition of user interfaces and systems. For example, it may be possible at some point to design a library portal component that would assist users with the process of locating a known, physical item in the library. A user looking for a specific book would be able to easily query a system to determine the book's availability, and then receive directions to the item's location in the bookstacks. As directional components of the reference process are automated, librarians will be able to concentrate efforts on in-depth reference questions, instruction, and other sophisticated activities.

There is a wide-range of services and information resources that must be implemented and integrated to create a library portal. The emphasis of this chapter will be on the services related to the discovery and access of information. This chapter will focus on technical issues related to the services provided by commercial portal products currently available, and will discuss future services only in the context of current application.

GENERALIZED ARCHITECTURE

Library portals are composed of many separate software systems. Figure 1 depicts a generalized architecture for a library portal. The architecture incorporates many features of the JISC Information Environment Architecture (Joint Information Systems 2002) and the IMS Digital Repositories Framework (McLean and Lynch 2003), and is not fully realized in any current implementation. The generalized architecture presented here is provided as a framework for integrating the range of functionalities within a library portal. The layers in the diagram show the relationships between different types or classes of functionality. By separating the functional components of the portal into layers that repre-

FIGURE 1. A Generalized Architecture to Support Library Portals

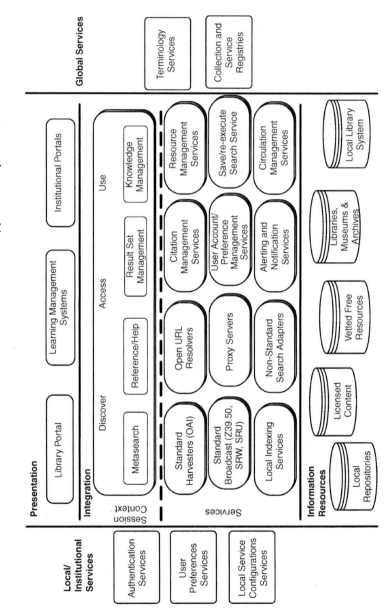

sent classes of services, overall system functionality can be discussed at varying levels of abstraction. For example, the functional requirements of metasearching can be discussed separately from the implementation details of the Z39.50 protocol. Layered, service-based architectures are the trend of the future (Atkins et al. 2003). While it is currently uncommon to find library software that conforms to this type of architecture, it is still useful to conceptualize an ideal, layered architecture.

The upper layer of the diagram depicts the presentation services that render information from various sources into a unified display for the user. This presentation layer is independent of lower, functional layers. This separation of presentation from content and functionality would allow library content to be integrated not just into library portals, but also into other contexts including learning management systems and institutional portals. Presentation configuration provides customized colors, fonts, and screen layouts, and may be performed either by librarians or, in more advanced applications, by end users. In addition, the presentation layer can provide a simple form of functional integration. At this layer, services can be visually integrated so that the user is offered access to available functions that are not integrated at a deeper level. For example, a library portal may provide access to virtual reference services by including an "Ask a Librarian" icon in the portal display. By clicking the icon, the user will initiate a chat session but none of his or her context (e.g., affiliation, previous searches, current searches, etc.) will be available to the virtual reference software. The library portal software and the virtual reference software are not truly integrated but they are made available to a user in an integrated presentation.

The middle layers include the services that provide deeper levels of integration. Library technical infrastructures are rapidly moving away from architectures where a single system, historically the Integrated Library System, provides the basic support of the library. Newer infrastructures are created by combining multiple standards-based tools that act as the building blocks for complex functionalities or user interfaces. Ideally, these integration services are of two types: context management services and functional services. Context management services, as their name suggests, maintain context about the user and the session. Context variables include items such as search history, selected databases, items marked to be printed or saved, and certificates to identify the user. The session context provides an environment that is passed on, or otherwise available, to all of the basic integration services. Functional integration services, the services depicted below the dashed line in the integration layer of Figure 1, are software programs that perform individual tasks (e.g., a single Z39.50 search). These basic services should provide single, reusable modules that are the building blocks for more complex services.

The lower layer of the diagram includes the information resources. The categories of information resources that are depicted in this layer represent the types of content that must be integrated within the portal environment. Each resource within this layer must be configured within the portal so that it is accessible within the common session context. Aspects of the configuration may include the service by which it can be accessed (e.g., Z39.50), information about the form and structure of the metadata and authorization rules.

Along the right and left sides of the diagram are columns of services that may be accessed by all services at all layers of the library portal architecture. The column on the left includes services that are provided by the library or the library's home institution (e.g., the University). The columns on the right include global services that should be available to all libraries.

Not all portals have all of the functionality listed. In fact, as will be described later, some of the functionality is not yet available in any portal product. An installed software component often encompasses more than one of the functionalities depicted in the architecture. For example, a typical commercial portal includes the services related to discovery and access of information. The following sections of this chapter will discuss technical issues related to some of the services provided within each section of the architecture. The dependencies among layers and services will be noted.

INTEGRATION SERVICES

The purpose of the integration services layer, depicted above the dashed line in Figure 1, is to link the underlying services together in ways that are meaningful to users. Tools such as metasearching, reference and help, result set management, and knowledge management use the lower-layer services within a common session context to seamlessly support the users' tasks. The session context stores items that are useful between components. These items may include authentication information, search history and e-mail address. There is no widely adopted standard for the contents of the session information.

Metasearching can be used as an example to conceptualize the purpose of this layer. Metasearching uses lower-layer services such as Standard Harvesters and Standard Broadcast Searching to allow users to query multiple information resources without knowing the relationships between resources or the technical standards necessary to search each resource. At this layer, it is important to manage workflow issues, such as the functional relationship between metasearching, result set management, and seeking help. The details of lower layer services and of presentation (e.g., icons, color, and pull-down vs. static menus) are also not specified at this layer. The focus of the attention is on the workflow and information needs of the metasearching function. The following section provides a more in-depth discussion of issues related to metasearching and other examples of the components that integrate several services including result set management, knowledge management, and reference and help.

Metasearching

In an environment in which library users are accustomed to search tools such as Google and Amazon.com, it is essential to redesign library search tools to streamline the discovery process. Metasearching provides a robust tool that aids library users in their efforts to discover relevant information from a variety of sources comprehensively. Users can locate information from abstracting and indexing databases, image repositories, locally digitized content, and more in a single discovery process. Metasearching is an important strategy for removing the barriers to library use that result from multiple data sources and multiple user interfaces.

Metasearching, however, changes the traditional searching paradigm in which information resource providers are able to distinguish themselves by providing exceptional searching interfaces that have been optimized for their dataset. Metasearching allows the native search interface to be bypassed and the vendor's content accessed through an interface that has been developed to work adequately with a wide variety of data sets. There is reluctance on the part of some information resources vendors to provide standard, but less optimized, access to their content. When metasearching standards are not implemented by a resource provider, a library must use time-consuming techniques (i.e., screen scraping) that employ locally developed scripts to imitate a user's commands and extract result information from the native search interface. These searches are expensive for the library to develop or configure (estimates range from 10-40 hours of personnel time per interface). These non-standard searches are also expensive for the information resource vendor because instead of using optimized computer-level interfaces, the scripts act like a user and require the information resource provider to generate all of the code associated with a user session. Some information vendors contractually forbid libraries from using these scripting methods to access information. Maintenance of such scripts, if allowed, is also staff-intensive, as screen-scraping techniques are sensitive to changes in user interface.

Another important point about metasearching is that the library cannot adopt a widely used standard protocol (e.g., common Web services) unless that protocol is supported by the information resources. This does not allow the library the flexibility they might want in adopting new technology. Sensing no market demand, information resource vendors have been slow to adopt new technologies.

Currently there are two categories of metasearching standards that are supported by information resource providers–broadcast searching that query the information resource at the time of user request and locally federated searching that query large amounts of information periodically and store and index the information locally. These categories of standards will be discussed in the following sections.

Broadcast Search

One category of standards used in metasearching is broadcast searching. With these approaches, a metasearching system accepts a user query, sends it to a target data source, then formats the returned metadata so that results from all resources will appear in a common structure. The searching of resources is done at the time of the request and no result information is cached locally. This is the most practical method of including data sources that change frequently, such as abstracting and indexing databases. As with all metasearching approaches, there are problems using an identical search string to search across multiple data resources. A search that is reliable in one domain may produce less reliable results in databases designed for other domains. This shortcoming is not entirely insurmountable, and can be ameliorated through efforts such as improved adherence to standards and the development of robust terminology services. The most widely adopted metasearching protocols are based on ANSI Z39.50 and will be discussed in the following paragraphs.

Z39.50

The most commonly implemented protocol supporting broadcast search is Z39.50. It is an ANSI-approved standard that defines a stateful (i.e., continuously connected) protocol for computers to communicate during information retrieval transactions. The protocol is widely implemented within the library community, being supported by virtually all integrated library system (ILS) vendors and many abstracting and indexing services. Protocol Z39.50 has also been incorporated into client applications such as citation managers to facilitate the import of bibliographic data (Library of Congress 2003b; Moen, Taylor 2003).

This protocol is an important tool for libraries. It provides powerful search features, supporting Boolean and proximity operators, truncation, and date searching. Protocol Z39.50 also facilitates the interchange of MARC records, providing not only a standard communication protocol, but also data in a usable format. Additionally, many Z39.50 clients are capable of sending multiple search requests simultaneously. This is a particularly useful feature when multiple searches need to be run in a single database, or when a single query needs to be run in multiple databases. It is also a feature that is the basis of many metasearch tools. To be used as such, the metasearch tool must be configured to search each Z39.50 target individually. The address, port number, and technical database name for each resource must be specified, search attributes (i.e., the types of searches to be completed) must be defined, and the format of both records and holdings information specified.

While Z39.50 has been an important standard for libraries, it is a complex standard and is difficult to implement. It has been subject to interpretation, leading to incompatible implementations. Profiles, such as the Bath Profile, are being developed to address these differences in interpretation and further standardize Z39.50 implementations. Another shortcoming of the protocol is that, despite the robust feature set defined within the protocol, not every Z39.50 service provider supports all possible features. Two areas where the lack of uniformity in implementations of the standard have immediate impact on library portals are the lack of support for server-based sorting of results and the lack of consistency in the data that is returned. Each of these will be discussed later in this chapter. Additionally, Z39.50 is based on technologies that predate those commonly used on the Web. This has repercussions for development efforts by libraries and library vendors, and has also prevented the protocol from being adopted widely outside of the library community.

ZING

In an effort to lower the barriers to Z39.50 implementation and increase its adoption by non-library developers, the Library of Congress has launched a number of initiatives to modernize the protocol. Collectively, these efforts are known as ZING (Z39.50-International: Next Generation) (Library of Congress 2003c, Needleman 2002). ZING projects recast Z39.50 using Web-based technologies that are increasingly popular, while continuing to support the mature Z39.50 implementations within the library community.

Search/Retrieve for the Web (SRW) and its partner, Search/Retrieve with URLs (SRU), are cornerstones of ZING efforts. SRW updates Z39.50 transforming the powerful search features to function over newer Web technologies rather than the older TCP/IP technologies. SRW provides a SOAP (Simple Object Access Protocol)-based method of access to distributed data sources. SRW uses a new standard query format, CQL (Common Query Language), which provides a standard method of expressing a user query. Additionally, XML is used for both encoding and syntax of returned records rather than the more complex ASN.1/BER formatting supplied by Z39.50. SRU provides similar functionality to SRW, but encodes queries in a URL string rather than a SOAP message. SRW is the more complicated and more robust of the ZING technologies but the Web Services technology on which it is based is gaining wide general acceptance outside of libraries. At this writing, neither SRW nor SRU are widely implemented by information resource providers.

Locally Federated Search

The other major category of standards for including data sources in metasearching is through the inclusion of both metadata and full-content hosted at the institution. Many libraries have engaged in digitization or electronic publishing efforts, and have a wealth of digital content in a variety of formats. Ideally, this content should be discoverable through a metasearching tool. Content that has been developed locally, and that is available in a structured format, may be indexed and exposed through metasearching, if the search tool is so capable. It is also increasingly possible, through such efforts as the Open Archives Initiative, to include access to content created at or hosted by other institutions in metasearching. Information that is not available through OAI-compliant harvesters can also be made available to metasearching tools by indexing local datasets. Each of these approaches will be discussed in the following paragraphs.

OAI-PMH

The Open Archives Initiative Protocol for Metadata Harvesting (OAI-PMH) is another important standard that supports interoperability, but one with a significantly different approach than Z39.50. As its name suggests, OAI-PMH is designed to facilitate the harvesting of metadata, specifically metadata in an XML format. So, instead of broadcasting a user's query to multiple databases, OAI-PMH allows metadata from multiple databases to be gathered into a local database for search and retrieval. OAI-PMH was designed to expose the "hidden Web" contained in databases, XML documents, and other formats not exposed to Internet search engines (Open Archives Initiative 2003).

In an OAI-PMH environment, content providers create collections on local servers. Software on the local server is able to answer OAI-PMH requests for metadata (either for part of a collection, or its entirety), and return the requested metadata to the requestor. The items described by the metadata (e.g., full text, images, etc.) are not transmitted to the remote machine. A library may configure local servers to harvest metadata from multiple archives, and may also select subsets of archives to harvest. The requesting program may then manipulate harvested metadata. Often, this means entering the metadata into a relational database which serves as the basis for other services. For example, the University of Michigan's OAIster project allows users to search over 1.7 million articles from over 200 collection providers. Potentially, such content could also be made available through a metasearch tool.

Indexing of Structured Data Formats

Some metasearching tools can also be configured to index locally maintained content for inclusion in a search. In general, any such content must be made available in a consistent, structured format. Full text may be indexed if it is encoded according to either a locally developed or broader standard. An example of indexable full-text sources is XML-encoded texts, tagged according to Text Encoding Initiative (TEI) standards. Structured metadata records, including MARC records and EAD-encoded archival finding aids can also be indexed by some searching tools and retrieved by the metasearching tool.

RESULT SET MANAGEMENT

Robust searching is not the only component of a library portal necessary to improve user access to content. To be successful the user must be able to make sense of the metadata returned from the heterogeneous databases. The user must be able to organize the returned metadata and to access the content.

Organizing the Returned Citation Metadata

Online databases and electronic resources have long provided support for results manipulation, including result set sorting, de-duplication, and a variety of export functions. Users have become accustomed to these features, which should not only be replicated, but improved in the library portal. In a metasearching environment, sorting and de-duplication of results are particularly challenging. Because of the lack of consistently applied standards in the returned metadata, functions that rely on algorithms that match metadata fields are not always successful. Identical items from multiple data sources may not have sufficient metadata in common to allow for de-duplication, yet it is important to the user experience that de-duplication be accomplished whenever possible.

Sorting is also of great importance to presenting the search results in an understandable manner. This is also an area that needs significant work in a metasearching environment. In a broadcast search, result sets are returned to the metasearching engine one database at a time. The lack of support by information resources providers for the server-side sort functionality adds to the complexity of the sort problem. Without server-side sort, the results from an information resource can be returned in any order. To avoid the delays of waiting for all results, including the slowest responding, to be returned before display, results are often displayed as they are returned. The display of a sorted list before all resources have completely returned their metadata will result in gaps in coverage where records from slower responding providers or poorly sorted sets have not been returned. Although it is possible for a user to reorder a search set by date of publication, author, or other metadata fields, it is difficult for users to be certain of the validity of the sort. Relevancy ranking, a computer-based sort done for the user, is another function that requires adequate metadata for success. Algorithms that perform relevancy ranking need, at minimum full information about the information resources that are available within the result set.

Linking to Full Content

Providing improved connections between metadata search services (e.g., abstracting and indexing databases) and full text or other content is central to improving the ease of use of the library, and is essential to the success of any portal effort. Many vendors of abstracting and indexing databases already provide links to full text, but these services have several shortcomings. First, they typically do not always support links to full text at the article level from all vendors limiting the choices from libraries selecting publisher and information resources. Second, these linking services are usually localized with a single vendor's product offerings. So, if a library subscribes to databases from multiple vendors providing such a linking solution, the library will typically need to maintain full-text links with each vendor's linking product. This is not ideal because it requires replication of labor for libraries, and also can result in data synchronization issues. In response to the need to integrate access to full text and other services within the context of user search in a generalizable manner, there has been work in developing the OpenURL framework.

OpenURL

OpenURL (NISO Committee AX 2003) is a proposed NISO standard that has its origins in the work of Herbert van de Soempel at the Los Alamos National Laboratory. It has since been developed into a proposed standard by the National Information Standards Organization (NISO) that defines a framework for providing context-sensitive services for a user, often full-text access. OpenURL links are dynamically generated by a source. These links point to a local institution's OpenURL resolver, and include metadata necessary to identify services relevant to the user's context. If selected, the link will connect a user to targets of possible interest. In the case of a user searching an abstracting and indexing database, an OpenURL link would be generated for each record in a search set and would contain an identifier (e.g., a DOI) or other bibliographic information about each record. This metadata can then be used to provide a number of services, including linking to full text. While full-text links are perhaps the most powerful application of OpenURL for libraries, other services may also be provided. One example of this is that a library could configure its OpenURL resolver to populate an Interlibrary Loan form if full text were unavailable. More sophisticated services can also be provided, such as launching citation searches on an article's authors or linking to chemical or genomic data.

A key challenge to providing OpenURL services is maintaining the wealth of metadata necessary to connect users with relevant service. Full-text journal holdings must be accurate and kept current in order to provide links to content accessible to a library's users, a task made difficult by the volume of online subscriptions held by many libraries and the ever-changing contents of some full-text aggregators. There are a number of commercial vendors that supply data on holdings from full-text aggregators, although the data supplied by these vendors may not be perfect for many libraries. There are also identifier resolution services, such as CrossRef, that can ease the burden of holdings maintenance but connecting article-level metadata to an article remains more of an art than a science. The resolver introduces several new types of configuration metadata that must be maintained at each site such as linking patterns (i.e., the structure of URLs to content), citation maps (i.e., the definition of the citation format for each searchable resource) and information about the prioritization of the appropriate copy.

Knowledge Management

Users of library resources ultimately want to use the results of their efforts, so it is important to provide portal features that enable them to make sense of their search results and retrieved content. Users often need to save and/or export the results of library searches. Users may need to save search results to a network-accessible space, such as a citation manager integrated into a library portal, e-mail the results to themselves or colleagues, or export them to client-based citation management programs for future use. Integration of search results with other client-based software including e-mail clients and news aggregators may also be desirable, using integration technologies such as Really Simple Syndication (RSS), an XML-based technology that provides a framework where changes in information resources are continuously made available to the client. High-end users may also wish to save search strategies for later use, or as part of an automated notification program. Annotation services, which allow users to create online notes and highlight passages of text, will also become increasingly important as users expect to be able to manipulate not only search results, but full content. These are all services that will be built upon successful implementation of the basic discovery and access services.

LOCAL AND INSTITUTIONAL SERVICES

The diverse systems and technologies of the presentation and integration services require access to information about valid users (e.g., group membership, preferences) and details regarding the configuration of information resources (e.g., Z39.50 settings). It is labor intensive to implement services that acquire, maintain and store this type of information within each of the integration services. To effectively and efficiently implement a library portal it will be necessary to use shared services that gather and store the information in a central location. Figure 2 highlights the relationship between the services that support the library portal and the services that support the broader information infrastructure. Commercial library portals generally provide services to acquire and store user preferences and configuration setting for information resources. As additional services are integrated into the portal framework, it will be necessary that these services be separated from the internal workings of the portal applications and be accessible to all services operating within the session context. User preference services that are available to all services within the library portal will increase efficiency of service development and operation and also protect the users'

FIGURE 2. Local, Institutional, and Global Services as Part of the Library Portal

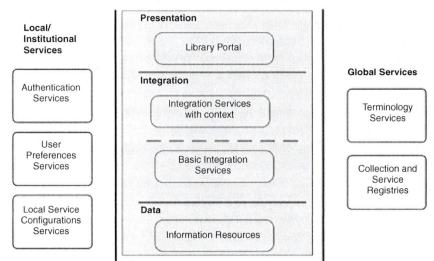

privacy. A more global approach to the configuration of information discovery and access services will be essential for the long-term success of the library portal.

Independent configuration of services by all libraries is not a sustainable model. Thousands of information resources must be configured to be accessible for both the discovery and access processes. Collaborative projects like the Scholars Portal Project (Association of Research Libraries 2003) are a step towards a more sustainable model of collaboration. Global metadata and service registries of configuration information will be required to effectively configure and manage the library portal. These registries will be discussed later in the chapter.

Authentication services provide a central mechanism to efficiently determine if a user is permitted to access information and services. Locally centralized authentication is becoming an accepted practice in libraries and will be discussed in detail in the following section.

Authentication and Authorization Services

An important aspect of seamless integration is the ability to move between resources and services without entering and re-entering passwords. To achieve the ultimate goal of single sign-on access to information, all information resources and services in the portal architecture that require authentication for use must be designed and implemented based on standard and interoperable authentication techniques.

Authentication is one part of the larger issue of access management. The two main concepts related to access management are authentication and authorization. Authentication is the process that verifies a user's identity. The authentication process usually involves the user providing username and a password, but can include any other method that demonstrates the person's identity, such as the use of a smart card. To move towards an environment of single sign-on access, it will be necessary for software systems to exchange and validate user credentials without user intervention. Authorization is the separate but often intertwined process of determining if a user is permitted to access a specific resource. The authorization process uses attributes to determine if a user should be permitted to access information or use a service. In the current library environment, authentication is performed locally by the library or institution and authorization is typically done by the resource provider.

Authentication and authorization solutions within the library environment must be designed and implemented to uphold users' right to privacy in accessing information. Lynch provides an overview of important privacy issues (Lynch 1998). The need to protect users' privacy while enforcing licensing and subscription agreements limits the possible approaches to access management. To be completely successful, an access management system must be able to grant users access to resources based on group membership and allow details regarding individual identity to be released only at user or library discretion. This type of access is commonly referred to as "role-based" access because a person is authorized to use a resource because of his or her role (e.g., law student, faculty) rather than his or her identity.

The library environment is technically complex because of the range of resources and services that require separate authorization. For example, a typical academic library will have thousands of separate information resources provided by hundreds of different vendors. In order to have a truly seamless environment, all information resources and services that require authenticated access must be designed and implemented using the same, or at least interoperable, standard access management methods. It is unlikely that a universally adopted technical approach to access management will be available in the near-term future. In the meantime, the library portal will provide a single architecture that can, at least partially, hide the complexity of access management from the user. As with all solutions that hide complexity, but do not fundamentally address the underlying technical causes of the complexity, the cost of convenience to the user will be in increased software configuration and maintenance.

Current Access Management Strategies

The library portal continues to use many of the access methods that have been developed for use in the library Web site. Information resource providers and libraries have struggled to define access management methods that are practical for both the information resources provider and the library but still guarantee privacy and ensure that access will be granted only to licensed users. As with the metasearching standards described above, both the library and the provider must agree on a common technical approach. An obvious approach is for the information resource provider to issue a user name and password to the user. Although this approach is implemented in a few cases, it is not practical for information resource providers who must maintain individual accounts and monitor changes in the status of authorized users (e.g., new hires, graduations). It is also not convenient for users who would need to keep track of distinct user names and passwords for each content provider they use. Finally, it does not allow user privacy in access because users must directly identify themselves to the information resource provider to access information.

The predominant mechanisms to manage access to licensed information combine local authentication with vendor authorization. Local authentication, once primarily performed within the Integrated Library System, is transitioning to an architecture where authentication is provided by a central institutional service. Typical authentication methods include LDAP and Kerberos. Providing a single authentication method within an organization is the first step towards a single sign-on environment. Most commercially available portal products are designed to use institutional authentication systems. Conversely, few Integrated Library Systems use centralized authentication systems (Koppel 2003). The implementation of the library portal is often the first experience the library has in working with institutional authentication systems so problems with its implementation are closely associated with the portal installation. The implementation of centralized authentication in the portal environment, however, is moving the library to a more effective service-based approach and minor problems are to be expected.

The vendor-based authorization methods have evolved in libraries to use group attributes rather than individual identity to determine if the user should be granted access to resources. The following sections will provide a brief overview of the most commonly used authorization methods: Internet Protocol (IP) address filtering with proxies, referring URL and database vendor provided scripts (Koppel 2003).

IP Address Filtering with Proxy Servers

IP address filtering, the predominant authorization method used between information resource providers and libraries, is based on the historical conception of the library as the central hub of access. Many license agreements between institutions and information resource providers allow users at all computers on the institutional network be given access to the resource. The network component of the IP address is used as a group attribute to identify the user at the computer as a member of a licensed group without the identity of the user being known. IP address filtering has low administrative overhead for both the library and the information resource provider. The library simply provides the information resource provider with a list of valid institutional addresses that typically fall into ranges that are easy to communicate and do not change frequently.

Most institutions have set up proxy servers to accommodate users demand for access outside of the physical institution. A proxy server is a computer that allows an offsite library user to appear to an information resource provider as if they are connecting from the institution's on-campus network. Remote users must authenticate with the institution in order to connect to resources through the proxy. Information about user identities is not shared with the information resource provider. Proxy servers add administrative burden for libraries that must maintain a proxy server and, at minimum, integrate with an institutional authentication system. There is no additional burden on the information resource providers, since the same range of IP addresses that was used before the proxy server was in place continues to be valid for authorization.

Referring URL

A characteristic of Web technology (i.e., HTTP) is that the URL of the page providing the link to the resource is available to the resource as an HTTP session variable when a user first connects. The information resource provider maintains a list of valid pages for each institution. Users launching the information resource from a valid referring page are granted access to the resource. The library Web site is designed so that links to resources appear on protected pages that are only accessible to valid users. Typically, validation of the user accessing the protected page is accomplished with IP address filtering. If a user is not within the licensed IP address range, the user will have to authenticate with the proxy server. Library Web sites often have numerous locations where users can link to information resources (e.g., subject guides, databases lists, etc.), so the information resource provider must maintain records for and recognize many referring URLs for each library. This method still requires that authentication take place, but as with the proxy server approach the user's identity is not closely tied with information access.

Vendor Supplied Script

Another form of authorization that also relies on links from a protected page is the vendor supplied script method. A few information resource providers provide scripts that are executed when the user activates the link to the database. The scripts create credentials for the user that are associated with the browser session. The credentials created by the vendor supplied script are specific to the browser session and often have a short expiration time (e.g., two hours for JSTOR). As with the referring URL method, the link to the information resource provider must be on a protected page that is only accessible to licensed users. However, the burden on the information resource provider is reduced because they no longer have to maintain a list of authenticated referring pages or IP addresses.

EMERGING ACCESS MANAGEMENT STRATEGIES

Each of the current authorization methods relies on assumptions about the computer location or library's Web site design to infer group membership. All authorization methods use a group identifier to determine if access, should be allowed thus protecting the privacy of the user. The proxy server, a foundational component of existing methods, can be easily mimicked by any computer in the licensed network range running an open, unauthenticated proxy server. Because of this ability to easily bypass the gatekeeping mechanism, efforts are turning to more advanced techniques. The challenge is to provide tighter control but still allow the user private access to information.

Public Key Infrastructure (PKI)/X.509 Digital Certificates

PKI and digital certificate methods are often seen as the most promising emerging authentication methods. In these methods, users must obtain a digital certificate, which is associated with their browser, that contains information that can uniquely identify them to the information resource provider. The certificate contains a public key and encrypted private key for the user. The combination of the public and private information performs the same function as the login name/password pair that is typed in by the user except that it does not require intervention by the user and can be transmitted between software systems. Although this system represents the kind of global infrastructure that will need to be in place, it has some serious shortcomings for the library portal environment.

The infrastructure is based on communities of trust. The community of trust, most likely the institution, defines how to distribute, revoke and manage keys and certificates to provide an appropriate level of security for the environment. It also defines the policies that govern the definition and standard use of the attributes associated with the certificates that it issues. Many of the policy and technical issues such as certificate expirations and the definition of sharable certificate attributes are not standard across communities (National Institutes of Standards and Technology 2002). There are development costs associated with implementing PKI within an institution. However, information resource providers will face a huge implementation burden as they understand and develop software modifications to work between multiple trust communities with differing policies and processes. Another problem for libraries with PKI is that if credentials are associated with browsers the method does not work well in a public access setting where many users will access resources with the same browser.

Shibboleth

Shibboleth is designed to provide a global standard to allow private but secure access to licensed content and resources. It defines inter-institutional trust relationships and attribute-based authorization (Internet2 2003). Shibboleth describes a group of services that each have responsibility for some aspect of the access management infrastructure. The standard provides well defined processes and is based on standard data models (e.g., SAML).

In a Shibboleth environment, users present authentication credentials to their home institution once and are issued a digital certificate that contains standard attribute definitions, which then may be used for system-to-system authentication by remote sites (e.g., electronic journal vendors, other universities, etc.) until the certificate expires. The user can take any path to the information resource, and in theory, software at the information resource (the Shibboleth Attribute Requestor or SHAR) should be able to find a way back to the home institution for authentication. The steps of the process necessary to authenticate demonstrates the number of services that must be implemented in order to create a Shibboleth infrastructure. The path may include a request from a Where Are You From Service (WAYF) and Handle service to determine the appropriate Attribute Authority (AA) to acquire the user attributes that are required for authorization. The AA is designed to use the institution's local server (e.g., LDAPs) to authenticate the user's identity. Once the user is authenticated, the AA is configured to release only the user attributes that have been approved by the user. Shibboleth specifies interfaces where individual users can control the release of their private information (Erods and Cantor 2002).

Shibboleth does not require that the information resource provider understand local issues associated with communities of trust. However, the number of services necessary to provide the separation between the user and the trust domain can make the system seem prohibitively difficult to install. Once installed, however, it will reduce the burden of resource configuration and maintenance within libraries and provide a robust and secure infrastructure for new forms of access.

It will take an investment in infrastructure like the implementation of Shibboleth to simultaneously ensure privacy and protect licensed information. Such an infrastructure is the only way to move from the current complex environment where authentication and authorization are topics of concern when an information resource is acquired or an access service is integrated within the portal (Gourley 2003).

GLOBAL SERVICES

The right side of the diagram in Figure 2 depicts examples of Global Services. The library technical infrastructure is changing rapidly. Users are demanding new forms of access and collections are no longer predominately static descriptions of physical items. To be able to provide service in the changing environment it will be necessary for libraries to collaborate to develop global services. Several groups are identifying areas where standards are required (NISO 2003) and defining the foundations for the development of standards and the accompanying services and registries (e.g., Organization for the Advancement of Structured Information Standards 2003, Dublin Core Metadata Initiative 2003, Joint Information System Committee 2002, UKOLN 2003).

Terminology Services

Libraries have long recognized the value of controlled vocabularies for information retrieval. Library catalogs, abstracting and indexing databases, and other data sources have relied on sophisticated terminologies to provide access to their contents. In a metasearch environment, terminology-based searching becomes difficult to achieve. Instead of working within the context of a single database employing a single vocabulary, users interact with an interface to multiple databases. These databases could employ numerous terminologies. Further complicating matters, designers of the search tool cannot make assumptions about which resources might be selected by a user, requiring any terminology services to be available on a dynamic basis.

In the long term, it will be necessary for metasearch tools to be developed to take advantage of centralized terminology services. This would function as both an authority server and a mapping server. Terminology services would need to contain the vocabularies in use in library resources, and would be available as a source of authority records for a range of library projects requiring structured description. These services would also provide mappings between user search terms and the terminologies used by remote data sources. Such mappings would be a powerful supplement to general or field-based keyword search.

Collection and Service Registries

In the current environment, significant staff resources are expended at each institution creating descriptions of information resources. It will be necessary for libraries to collaborate to develop registries to share information about collections. In addition, it will be necessary to develop globally available service registries that describe services, including services to access collections. Service registries might also describe other services, such as virtual reference and news feeds that are available to users.

Collection registries provide information about the resources that are available to a user, allowing the selection of appropriate information resources. The registry should include sufficient information for a user or system to find and use the information contained within the collections. This will include information such as subject coverage, and metadata forms (e.g., Dublin Core Metadata Initiative 2003, UKOLN 2003).

Service registries will contain information about services that can be used to access information. This registry describes programming-level interfaces to access collections and services. These descriptions will allow libraries developing portals to copy and include service configurations rather than independently recreating descriptions of these services. In today's environment, service registries that describe Z39.50 settings (name, port number, etc.) are available and can be used to manually configure software applications. In the future, newer services such as SRW Web Services could be described using methods that could be automatically configured by software applications (e.g., Organization for the Advancement of Structured Information Standards 2003, Joint Information System Committee 2002).

Standards-based collection and service descriptions that are discoverable by librarians or users though the portal interface and can be automatically included within the portal framework will be an essential part of the new library technical infrastructure. Without these collaborative resources, the configuration and maintenance burden to each library will not be sustainable.

CONCLUSION

The library portal is not a single technology, but is a combination of software components that unify the user experience of discovering and accessing information. Early implementations are discovering the specific areas where standards, services, and best practices are needed to transform the current environment into one that supports portals and seamless access to information (NISO 2003). While significant work remains, the current generation of portal technologies shows great promise in lowering barriers to information discovery and reducing user access issues.

Improvement and development of immature or non-existent features described in this chapter are necessary to move library portals forward. Improved results-set ranking, incorporation of controlled vocabularies and vocabulary cross-walks into the metasearching process, lower-level integration of support services (e.g., virtual reference), and development of more universal authentication will make portals even more powerful tools for users. Improved systems administration functionality, including better management of configuration information and better standards for metasearching, and the availability of global services and registries are necessary to make library staff investments in portals more manageable.

REFERENCES

Association of Research Libraries. May 2001. ARL Scholar's Portal Working Group Report. <http://www.arl.org/access/scholarsportal/may01rept.html> [2 November 2003].

Association of Research Libraries. August 2003. Access and Technology Program: Scholars Portal. August 2003. <http://www.arl.org/access/scholarsportal/> [2 November 2003].

Atkins, Daniel E., Kelvin K. Droegemeier, Stuart I. Feldman, Hector Garcia-Molina, Michael L. Klein, David G. Messerschmitt, Paul Messina, Jeremiah P. Ostriker, and

Margaret H. Wright. "Revolutionizing Science and Engineering Through Cyber-infrastructure: Report of the National Science Foundation Blue Ribbon Advisory Panel on Cyberinfrastructure." 84, 2003.

Butters, Geoff. 2003. What features in a Portal? *Ariadne* (35). <http://www.ariadne.ac.uk/issue35/butters/intro.html> [2 November 2003].

Dublin Core Metadata Initiative. 2003. DCMI Collection Description Working Group. <http://dublincore.org/groups/collections/>. [2 November 2003].

European Library Automation Group. April 2002. *ELAG 2002 Workshops.* <http://www.ifnet.it/elag2002/workshop.html> [2 November 2003].

Erdos, Marlena and Scott Cantnor. May 2002. Shibboleth Architecture v5. <http://shibboleth.internet2.edu/docs/draft-internet2-shibboleth-arch-v05.pdf> [3 November 2003].

Gourley, Don. October 2003. Library Portal Roles in a Shibboleth Federation. <http://shibboleth.internet2.edu/docs/gourley-shibboleth-library-portals-200310.html> [3 November 2003].

Internet2. Shibboleth Project. 2003. *<http://shibboleth.internet2.edu>.* [3 November 2003].

Joint Information Systems Committee. Portal Programme. April 2002. <http://www.jisc.ac.uk/index.cfm?name=programme_portals> [2 November 2003].

Koppel, Ted. May 2003. Metasearch: Issues with Authentication and Authorization. *NISO Metasearch Strategy Workshop.* <http://www.niso.org/committees/MSpapers/MSAuthAccess.pdf>.

Library of Congress. Portal Applications Issues Group Home Page. 2003a. <http://www.loc.gov/catdir/lcpaig/paig.html> [2 November 2003].

Library of Congress. Z39.50 Maintenance Agency Page. 2003b. <http://www.loc.gov/z3950/agency/> [2 November 2003].

Library of Congress. ZING–Z39.50 International: Next Generation Home Page. 2003c. <http://www.loc.gov/z3950/agency/zing/zing-home.html> [2 November 2003].

Lynch, Clifford. 1998. A White Paper on Authentication and Access Management Issues in Cross Organizational Use of Information Resources. <http://www.cni.org/projects/authentication/authentication-wp.html> [2 November 2003].

McLean, Neil and Clifford Lynch. June 2003. Interoperability Between Information and Learning Environments–Bridging the Gaps. A Joint White Paper on Behalf of the IMS Global Learning Consortium and the Coalition for Networked Information. <http://www.imsglobal.org/DLims_white_paper_publicdraft_1.pdf> (2 November 2003).

Moen, William. The ANSI/NISO Z39.50 Protocol: Information Retrieval in the Information Infrastructure. Undated. <http://www.cni.org/pub/NISO/docs/Z39.50-brochure/50.brochure.toc.html> [2 November 2003].

National Institute of Standards and Technology. February 2002. Minimum Interoperability Specification for PKI Components. <http://csrc.nist.gov/pki/mispc/welcome.html> [3 November 2003].

Needleman, Mark. ZING–Z39.50 International: Next Generation. *Serials Review* 28/3 (2002) 248-250.

NISO. Metasearch Initiative. 2003. NISO. <http://www.niso.org/committees/MetaSearch-info.html> [3 November 2003].

NISO Committee AX. 2003. Development of an OpenURL Standard. <http://library.caltech.edu/openurl/> [2 November 2003].

Open Archives Initiative. The Open Archives Initiative Protocol for Metadata Harvesting. <http://www.openarchives.org/OAI/openarchivesprotocol.html> [2 November 2003].

Organization for the Advancement of Structured Information Standards. 2003. OASIS UDDI Specifications TC. <http://www.oasis-open.org/committees/uddi-spec/tcspecs.shtml> [November 2, 2003].

Taylor, Stephanie. A quick guide to . . . Z39.50. *Interlending and Document Supply* 31(1) 2003: 25-30.

UKOLN. October 2003. Collection Development Focus. http://www.ukoln.ac.uk/cd-focus/. (2 November 2003).

Chapter 7

Issues in Planning for Portal Implementation: Perfection Not Required

Olivia M. A. Madison
Maureen Hyland-Carver

SUMMARY. Successful planning for major dynamic technical advances in library information systems now require broad-based participation and ownership across the library. Discovery tools such as portals and federated searching go far beyond the capabilities of individual traditional access tools. The external technology culture is marked with rapid change and we must also find ways to implement new sophisticated access tools that evolve quickly. Stronger integration of development and assessment as part of public releases is needed–thereby inviting our users to be strong collaborative development partners–while stressing perfection is not required. *[Article copies available for a fee from The Haworth Document Delivery Service: 1-800-HAWORTH. E-mail address: <docdelivery@haworthpress.com> Website: <http://www.HaworthPress.com> © 2005 by The Haworth Press, Inc. All rights reserved.]*

Olivia M. A. Madison (E-mail: omadison@iastate.edu) is Dean of Library Services; and Maureen Hyland-Carver (E-mail: mhylandc@iastate.edu) is Systems Analyst, both at the University Library, 302 Parks Library, Iowa State University, Ames, IA 50011-2140.

[Haworth co-indexing entry note]: "Issues in Planning for Portal Implementation: Perfection Not Required." Madison, Olivia M. A., and Maureen Hyland-Carver. Co-published simultaneously in *Journal of Library Administration* (The Haworth Information Press, an imprint of The Haworth Press, Inc.) Vol. 43, No. 1/2, 2005, pp. 113-134; and: *Portals and Libraries* (ed: Sarah C. Michalak) The Haworth Information Press, an imprint of The Haworth Press, Inc., 2005, pp. 113-134. Single or multiple copies of this article are available for a fee from The Haworth Document Delivery Service [1-800-HAWORTH, 9:00 a.m. - 5:00 p.m. (EST). E-mail address: docdelivery@haworthpress.com].

113

KEY WORDS. Portal, federated searching, broadcast searching, discovery tool, metasearch, z39.50, ZPORTAL, ARL Scholars Portal Project, Association for Research Libraries, Fretwell-Downing, Inc.

Portal technology represents a new expansive discovery tool with opportunities to change radically how we provide electronic access to library resources. This is a tool that has the potential to go far beyond identification of resources to immediate access and retrieval of information within one session. Sound institutional planning will lay the necessary framework for continual growth of the functionality, resources, and services available in a portal.

The following article seeks to describe the components of such institutional planning using the implementation of the ARL Scholars Portal Project at Iowa State University as the basis of this exploration. We begin with providing a background to this case study by defining the term *portal* for the purposes of this chapter, describing a general implementation process, and summarizing the context of the ISU Library's portal project. We then discuss the actual ISUL implementation process, detailing our portal philosophy and vision, and local project management issues. This is followed by more detailed discussions of the technical aspects of preparation and implementation, user instruction, user feedback and evaluation, and migration considerations. Throughout, the chapter underscores the general need for incorporating user feedback within the evolutionary implementation of discovery tools, rather than waiting for "perfection" before launching such pivotal new tools.

We conclude the chapter with some general observations regarding the continuing planning process and the usefulness and role of developmental user feedback in the design of new online discovery tools such as portals.

PROJECT BACKGROUND

Portal Definition

For the purposes of this chapter, we are defining a portal as a tool that provides broadcast (or federated) searching capabilities via a single metasearch across multiple information resources, with the potential of full-text retrieval (using OpenURL resolvers or direct linking) or full-text delivery through mechanisms such as fax, e-mail, etc. Information resources may represent public domain or commercially produced resources (e.g., indexing and abstracting and/or full-text resources) and a broad range of locally created resources (e.g., online catalogs, unique born digital and/or digitized full-text materials, special collections finding aids, electronic theses, reformatted audio-visual materials, and instructional learning objects). The portal may provide users the ability to vary the designated resources to be searched, according to personal interests. The portal might reside inside or outside the library holdings catalog. This definition could expand to include a seamless gateway to reference service, linkages to and integration with campus-based learning management systems, and a broad array of university-based resources and services, though these are not covered in this chapter.

General Portal Implementation Process

A portal implementation project must begin with identifying the desired specifications of the local library portal–what are the information tools, resources, and services that are envisioned to be accessed and/or created over time. Given the potentially broad nature of the specifications, discussions should include what the first phase would consist of, as well as the longer-term goals of implementing this ambitious public discovery tool.

Portals can profoundly change the concept of access, the roles of holding catalogs and indexing and abstracting tools, and our vendor access systems. This should not be underestimated. It is essential to include a wide range of librarians and staff within institutional project planning and implementation, and to create broad internal communications programs regarding all aspects of the project. The specifications for a portal must also include its placement within the internal library Web presence–where will the portal reside and how/where will one enter it, and what is its relationship to other library management systems, the holdings catalog, and, if present, the university portal and other university learning and research systems.

Following the identification of the specifications for the portal's component parts, project management must identify the roles of necessary partners and individuals for each aspect of the project (internal and external to your organization). Also, technical requirements must be determined, such as necessary hardware/software for use and/or purchase, the role of industry standards and proprietary software, etc. If an external vendor is used for supporting/providing hardware, software and/or outsourcing options, detailed specifications and an external bidding process may be required and therefore should be built into the process. Other steps include arranging a technical training program, identifying and prioritizing portal resources, determining what authentication/authorization scheme to use, identifying what usage data can and should be harvested, designing/customizing screen displays if desired, identifying the searching and personalization options, determining how the portal fits into the library's overall instruction program, understanding future migration options, and identifying the financing for both the initial project and its ongoing costs as well as any future migration costs.

Brief Overview of the Scholars Portal Project

Iowa State University Library (ISUL) is a collaborative project partner with six other Association of Research Libraries (ARL) libraries in the development of new portal technology involving federated discovery and delivery tools. The project's impetus evolved from a call by Jerry Campbell in his influential "The Case for Creating a Scholars Portal to the Web: A White Paper" (*ARL Bimonthly Report*, #211, August 2000 http://www.arl.org/newsltr/211/portal.html). A prior ARL Scholars Portal Working Group, of which ISUL was also a member, had defined a potential portal tool as an academic Google, thereby focusing its development on simple searching structures that allow students and faculty to discover and obtain vetted information resources that are critical to academic research and learning. A formal three-year project began in May 2002 following an extensive process to define the project, determine portal functionality, create the project's framework, identify participants, and select a vendor partner or partners. The current Scholars Portal Project members include Arizona State University, Dartmouth College, Iowa State University, University of Arizona, University of California–San Diego, University of Southern California, and University of Utah.

The vendor chosen by the participants in the Scholars Portal Project, Fretwell-Downing, Inc. (FD) offers portal software known as ZPORTAL. ZPORTAL is a product suite, which actually consists of several different components:

	ZPORTAL product suite
ZPORTAL	Represents the federated searching component, which enables the user to search across multiple resources transparently. It also has some limited personalization options for users, in that users can create their own search profiles and save search syntax for later re-running.
Z2WEB	Extends the federated searching capability of ZPORTAL by enabling searching of non-Z39.50 resources, generally through screen-scraping done by Perl scripts (FD has recently also begun writing Z2WEB scripts that will access the vendor's API for searching certain resources).
Z'MBOL	Also extends the federated searching by processing external database information into a static format to make the database a searchable resource through ZPORTAL.
Open Linking	Acts as the OpenURL resolver of ZPORTAL, to provide seamless linking from citations to digital content.

VISION AND PHILOSOPHY

In implementing a portal, it is essential to clearly outline the library's goals and expectations. At Iowa State, we made a series of planning assumptions based on the portal as a research and development project. The portal's implementation was to be the first step in an ongoing and changing process, in which we would create mechanisms for library staff, students and faculty to test and comment on the portal's usability and usefulness. Recognizing the need for flexibility was critical since we knew that constant change would be inevitable within the evolving Scholars Portal Project development. We did expect our initial phase to include certain established baseline requirements, sufficient to contain added value for the end-users (i.e., offering something *in addition* to the existing searching tools). Beyond that baseline, however, we did not want to wait on all the promised future features of FD's software before implementing, and instead decided to add features and enhancements as they became available.

Therefore, the concept of a "perfect," complete discovery tool with a fully integrated instructional support system on opening day was specifically ruled out. We decided to rollout the portal in our e-Library using a soft launch approach, with minimal public announcement. The intent was that subsequent feedback from a broad range of disciplines and users would help shape and improve our portal while it remained a work-in-progress.

LOCAL PROJECT MANAGEMENT

With our vision in place, we turned to the practical steps needed to make it a reality. Because we had already determined the overall expectations and selected a vendor through the work of the ARL Scholars Portal Working Group, much preliminary work was already accomplished. However, even within this environment, it was essential to define and manage this project at a local level. Local project management was provided by both the library administration and by a portal implementation team, which comprised staff from areas throughout the library.

Project management responsibilities included making key decisions (baseline requirements prior to launch, authentication/authorization scheme to use, how to integrate into the e-Library, etc.), identifying the myriad tasks to be completed and the interdependencies among tasks, assigning responsibilities for the tasks, and setting a timeline. Following the launch, the implementation team also dealt with soliciting and analyzing user feedback on the portal, and making corresponding adjustments to the project's ongoing tasks and timeline.

The nature of the portal project shaped how we handled its management. The project was (and still is) continually evolving in terms of its essential software capabilities, design of searching strategies, ongoing linking capabilities to resources, the universe of what may be searched, and integration with other services and instructional tools. As a result, our project tasks, responsibilities, and timeline for completion needed constant monitoring, and we readjusted them frequently. Also, communication among all staff was essential. Many aspects of the project were done in parallel by various cross-library task forces and administrative groups. A broad range of library constituencies were involved, including information technology, reference, collection development, instruction, cataloging, acquisitions, interlibrary loan and document delivery, service desks, and circulation.

The local project management staff concentrated on the following major responsibilities.

Decide on the phase-one baseline requirements of the portal. We organized the baseline requirements for opening day in the following three categories:

- *Content*–A sufficiently large number of resources to search, covering a number of meaningful subject areas, needed to be available, so that users would find their federated search results worthwhile.

- *Access*–An authentication/authorization scheme needed to be in place to restrict resource access to members of the ISU community, in keeping with our vendor licensing agreements.
- *Format*–The portal interface needed to be integrated with the existing e-Library design, and its initial search analogous to general Internet search engines, in order to present a unified, non-confusing tool to users that they could begin using immediately.

These baseline requirements in essence focused on the portal as a straightforward discovery tool, so they did not include services such as document delivery or interlibrary loan. Another item that was excluded from the baseline requirements was OpenLinking (the OpenURL resolver function of ZPORTAL, which would provide linkage from citations to full-text retrieval). Although OpenLinking was a much-desired feature, it had a number of unresolved issues. For example, the dataload process had yet to be developed by FD, there were schema mapping problems with various citation formats, and enhancements were still forthcoming in a later version of the ZPORTAL software. Therefore, we did not make it a phase-one requirement, and it was only minimally in place on opening day.

Select and group the resources that made up the content of the portal. The portal implementation team members initially spent a great deal of time categorizing the library's licensed resources into various subject profiles (see Appendix 1), and prioritizing those resources for which FD staff would be requested to write Z2WEB scripts. Unfortunately, it became apparent that at the time of our initial rollout, we would not have enough configured resources to make the subject profiles meaningful. Instead, we continued to revise the profiles over the next several months, as new resources continued to become available, and we made subject profiles available to users at the beginning of fall semester 2003 (see Appendix 2).

Another consideration in selecting content for ZPORTAL profiles was subscription licensing. If we had a limited number of simultaneous users for a resource, we didn't want that resource in the users' default search profile, to prevent overloading. At the time that the portal was first released to the public, we had only two profiles. The *Basic* profile, which we made the default, contained four resources that covered a broad range of subject matter, and which had unlimited user licenses: our local Library Catalog, OCLC WorldCat, Expanded Academic ASAP, ScienceDirect. The *All Find it! collections* profile contained every resource we had available through ZPORTAL at that time; this profile had a total of 58 resources (see Appendix 3).

Determine the authentication/authorization scheme to be used. We decided to use the ZPORTAL HTTP/XML method of authentication. This meant that we would need to supply ZPORTAL with XML data for users, and that data would then be entered into the ZPORTAL Oracle database. We chose to authenticate against our existing Sybase Horizon library catalog borrower file. Another option would have been to authenticate against the university's network users database, through LDAP, but we actually have more legitimate library patrons than are contained in the university's database and therefore using the university's database was not pursued. The Sybase Horizon borrower information also provided the basis for authorization. Not only do users have to be Horizon-recognized borrowers, they must also not be expired AND must be in a patron group able to access licensed electronic resources.

Name our new discovery tool, and decide where to place it within our e-Library Web site. We decided not to use "portal" as part of the name, to avoid any potential confusion with a future use of the term by the university. Ultimately, we named the application *Find it!* because we viewed it as a proactive discovery term, which would be attention-getting (particularly important due to our soft launch approach), convey the concept of federated searching, and also synchronize well with the *Get it!* term used within ZPORTAL for its OpenLinking function. We put the link to *Find it!* on the main e-Library page, next to the Library Catalog link, to implicitly show its correlation to other search tools.

Define each project task, and assign responsibility for its completion. The implementation team maintained oversight of the necessary work to be done for the project, detailed the primary/secondary relationships found between tasks, allocated the tasks to the appropriate library staff, and evaluated successful completion.

Establish the project schedule based upon the public implementation date. ISUL initially embarked upon an [overly] ambitious four-and-a-half month schedule, projecting a public launch at the beginning of spring semester 2003 (mid-January). This timeline was revised as it became apparent in December 2002 that our authentication module—one of our baseline requirements—would take more time to finalize. We then adjusted our prospective launch date to the end of February/beginning of March, and successfully met this goal. That brought us to a total six-month implementation period, from the time of our software installation in September 2002 to the public launch (see Appendix 4).

Handle internal communications, and encourage the positive buy-in of public services librarians and staff to promote the portal. We notified library staff of decisions made regarding the portal, time-frame progress, information regarding FD "fixes," new Z2WEB scripts created, new software version releases, etc. Our communication was done largely via our in-house e-mail system, through general announcements, and distribution of all meeting notes of pertinent working groups.

Assess the online help to be provided for the portal. The ZPORTAL application as distributed by FD contains a somewhat minimal set of help screens on various portal topics, which are context-sensitive. We considered whether we wished to locally augment and customize this information, but ultimately decided not to at this time, since it would have required a fair amount of manual editing which was not guaranteed to carry over to subsequent versions of ZPORTAL. To supplement the FD help screens, the portal implementation team wrote a stand-alone *About Find it!* page to introduce end-users to the portal and give brief instructions about how to use it.

Determine publicity for the launch. In the weeks immediately prior to the rollout to the public, two demo sessions were held for library staff, to show them the to-be-released portal version and its functionality. Public service desk staff were particularly encouraged to attend the demo sessions to obtain the necessary information for answering user questions. The link to *Find it!* was placed in the e-Library February 27, and a corresponding news announcement was posted in the e-Library a few days later, on March 3.

Create the framework for obtaining user questions and input, and determine how to use that input. The *About Find it!* help page that the implementation team wrote emphasized the developmental nature of our portal, and asked for user feedback. The team began the process of recording all staff and user comments and suggestions about the portal, and noting possible steps to take to respond to/resolve these issues.

Identify one-time and ongoing funding sources to fund the project. The project costs involve a variety of one-time and ongoing expenses including local hardware and software purchases, maintenance contracts and agreements, service payments, training sessions, and travel costs for a variety of different meetings due to the consortial nature of the overall project.

Participate in the ongoing collaborative work of other ARL Scholars Portal project participants, to interface our own local implementation with the overall interinstitutional project. The portal project institutions and FD have created shared listservs and Web sites for exchanging information, questions, reporting problems, etc. Iowa State staff have joined the FD-sponsored bi-weekly conference calls, and attended the interinstitutional project managers' meetings, and deans/directors' meetings. The project managers' group consists of representatives from the seven ARL Scholars Portal institutions and ARL. Its purpose is to coordinate the project direction, prioritize development and enhancement requests, and to facilitate communication between the project participants and FD. This group does most of its business via e-mail and conference calls, and holds meetings twice a year. The deans of the project participant libraries meet on an as-need basis (through conference calls and face-to-face meetings) and focus their attention on strategic issues such as governance, policies, project assessment of goals and progress, and future directions.

TECHNICAL PREPARATION AND CONSIDERATIONS

Hardware and Software

In implementing the portal, we used both existing Sun Solaris hardware plus a new Sun Solaris server. The new server was purchased specifically to run ZPORTAL's operational database, which uses Oracle software. The software for the portal implementation was installed in September 2002 by FD staff, following the local setup of the new server. We used the FD-provided runtime version of Oracle. Initially, the ZPORTAL version 2.3 pre-release build was installed; FD subsequently installed the release version of ZPORTAL 2.3 in December.

Training

Iowa State staff received training from FD during September-October 2002, shortly after the software installation. We had five days of on-site training by FD staff, for library staff from the Information Technology, Technical Services, and Public Services divisions. The sessions included ZPORTAL Introduction & Searching, ZPORTAL End-User Workshop, Introduction to the FD Windows Client, ZPORTAL Z39.50 Targets & Databases, ZPORTAL Locations, Collections & Profiles, and OpenLinking. Selected IT staff also participated in three days of more advanced training sessions at the FD offices, on Z2WEB scripting, XSL stylesheets, and Z'MBOL configuration. In addition to this start-up face-to-face training, FD subsequently provided several online informational sessions to the Scholars Portal participants on specific ZPORTAL topics.

Staff Technical Expertise

Following training, we began the process of configuring the ZPORTAL product suite to meet our local needs. We quickly discovered that the training and documentation provided by FD did not cover everything. The formal FD training sessions had concentrated on configuring ZPORTAL using the Windows Admin client, but we also found that certain parts of the configuration information were not set in this client. For some settings, it was necessary to edit configuration and properties files at the operating system level. In other cases, it was more efficient to view and edit data directly in the Oracle database tables rather than through the Admin client.

We found that the setup and configuration of ZPORTAL to match our local requirements involved a number of different skill sets. Although we could conceivably have referred all of the configuration issues encountered to FD technical staff for resolution, this would definitely have delayed the process of implementation. Having in-house expertise with the Unix operating system, Oracle, Java, XML, and XSL sped things up considerably. This meant that the issues that still needed to be referred to FD were fewer in number and (we think) more focused in nature.

Standards

The portions of ZPORTAL that build on and/or support industry standards helped facilitate the implementation. Of the two options available for providing content in ZPORTAL (Z39.50 (a standard) or FD's proprietary Z2WEB scripts), being able to connect to a resource via Z39.50 generally allowed us to immediately configure that resource. Without Z39.50 available, we were forced to wait until a Z2WEB script was written. Even then, Z2WEB scripts that are based on screen-scraping have to be continually monitored and rewritten as the vendor changes the user interface–a fairly frequent occurrence. Support for the Z39.50 standard on the part of vendors, for connecting to the resources that they offer, is very important in maximizing the amount of content that we can offer through ZPORTAL. While dated, the Z39.50 protocol remains the only usable standard for access to a number of disparate resources. Even when a vendor supports Z39.50, however, there can still be varying implementations of the standard. Some vendors used different record syntaxes, while FD requires USMARC. When the vendor-supported search attributes varied, we found it necessary to configure query adaptation in order to be able to do phrase searching against certain databases.

Other places where the ZPORTAL suite made use of industry standards were also implemented more readily than if we had started from scratch. One of the authentication methods available from FD utilizes HTTP/XML. The screen design of ZPORTAL is based on XML, XSL, and CSS, all standards. Although our implementation of authentication and screen design still required considerable time and effort to be expended, these areas would have taken even longer to finalize if we had been in completely uncharted territory.

Partnerships

Another important factor in implementing the portal was the partnership that exists between Iowa State and FD, and among all the Scholars Portal Project participants. Within the Scholars Portal Project, the institutions have shared information and expertise regarding configuring Z39.50 resources, writing preliminary Z2WEB templates, testing ZPORTAL components, etc., all of which has facilitated our local implementation. For technical issues specific to Iowa State, such as developing our authentication and authorization methodology, we have worked closely with FD staff in a one-on-one relationship, testing and re-testing on both sides.

TECHNICAL IMPLEMENTATION

Configuration of Resources

We had two types of resources to configure, those accessed through the Z39.50 protocol, and those accessed through the FD Z2WEB scripts (we have no Z'MBOL resources as of yet). We set up Z39.50 resources wherever feasible. Among our database subscriptions, we had two fairly large groups of resources from two vendors, OCLC FirstSearch and Ovid/Silverplatter, that supported Z39.50 access. Z2WEB resources could be configured only where Z2WEB scripts existed for databases or e-journal collections to which we had a subscription. At the outset, there were relatively few of these, although we did have a large group of databases from Cambridge Scientific Abstracts available through Z2WEB. (FD has added a number of Z2WEB scripts since then.)

Authentication/Authorization

We were fortunate that the ISUL authentication/authorization process could utilize FD's HTTP/XML method of authentication, with user data being retrieved from our Sybase Horizon borrower information. This allowed us to implement the portal without having to wait for more customized development from FD. The XML data was to be retrieved from Sybase using a Java servlet which would be programmed in-house. We worked in conjunction with FD staff setting the XML-tagged data fields, programming the servlet, having FD write the corresponding XSL file to read the XML data and use it to populate the ZPORTAL database, and ensuring that data was updated upon subsequent user logins.

As a result of this work, when a user logs in to ZPORTAL, our Java servlet is called via HTTP, and the user-supplied borrower ID and Pin number parameters are passed to the servlet. The Java servlet connects to Sybase Horizon, extracts the corresponding patron information from the Horizon borrower file, and generates an XML datastream (see Figure 1; the XML tags in the datastream were set in accordance with FD specifications, plus some additional tags exist that were used for debugging purposes).

The XML data is read by the FD-written XSL file, and populates the corresponding fields in the user record in the ZPORTAL Oracle database. The resulting user record can be viewed in the ZPORTAL Admin client (see Figure 2).

The Sybase Horizon data is retrieved each time a user logs into ZPORTAL, and re-populated in the ZPORTAL Oracle database. So, if a borrower ID expires in Horizon, or is moved to a different patron group, those changes will also be reflected in *Find it!* access.

Screen Design and Relationship to e-Library

The members of the implementation team found a number of places within ZPORTAL where the default terminology did not match that used by other searching tools already in use in the e-Library (e.g., ZPORTAL used "Standard Search," while our Library Catalog used "Basic Search," etc.). They identified numerous changes to be made both in wording and in elements to be added or removed from the screen

FIGURE 1. XML Datastream Tags

```
<?xml version="1.0" encoding="UTF-8" ?>
- <PatronAuthenticationData>
    <ResponseCode>0</ResponseCode>
    <PatronExpired>432</PatronExpired>
    <PatronExpireDate>Jan 9 2005</PatronExpireDate>
    <BbarcodeExpired>0</BbarcodeExpired>
    <BbarcodeExpireDate />
  - <PatronInformation>
      <Date TYPE="Expiration">Jan 09 2005</Date>
      <PatronStatus>0</PatronStatus>
      <PatronGroup>ISU_C</PatronGroup>
    </PatronInformation>
  - <Name>
      <LastName>COWLES ERIC DALE</LastName>
    </Name>
  - <ContactInformation>
    - <ElectronicAddress>
        <Address>ecowles@iastate.edu</Address>
      </ElectronicAddress>
    </ContactInformation>
  </PatronAuthenticationData>
```

FIGURE 2. User Record

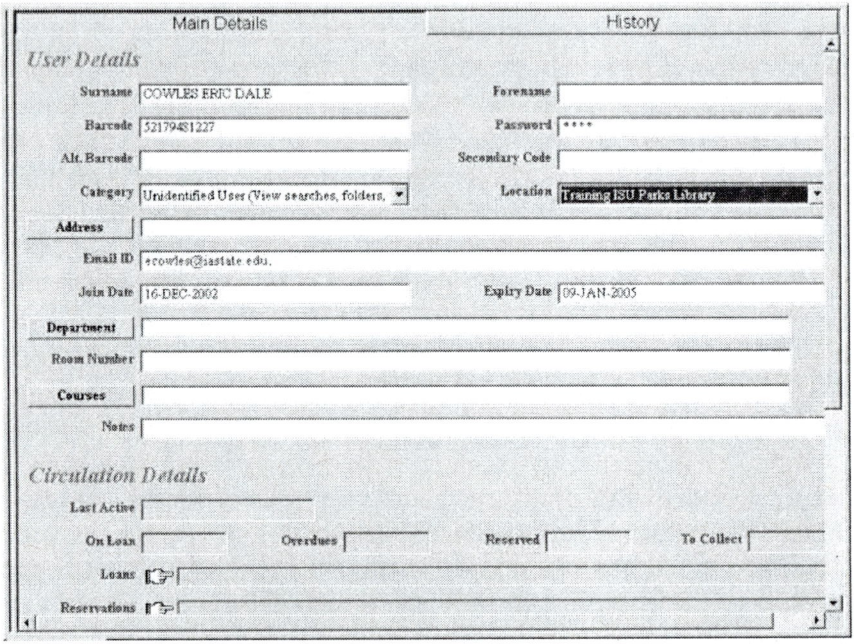

displays, and these changes were made as part of the implementation. Also, we wanted to have the portal screens match the e-Library design, which meant adding our e-Library header and footer, substituting our sidebar navigation, and using our color palette. To effect the changes required, it was necessary to edit the ZPORTAL XSL and CSS stylesheets. Figure 3 shows the "before" default ZPORTAL screen design; Figure 4 shows the "after" locally customized ZPORTAL screen.

USER INSTRUCTION

We believed that searching ZPORTAL would be sufficiently intuitive to the users to not require extensive instructions. We did provide a special *About Find it!* help page, written by the portal implementation team, as part of the portal launch (see Figure 5). A link to this page was placed in the portal sidebar navigation, as well as on the Basic search screen.

FIGURE 3. Default ZPortal Search Screen

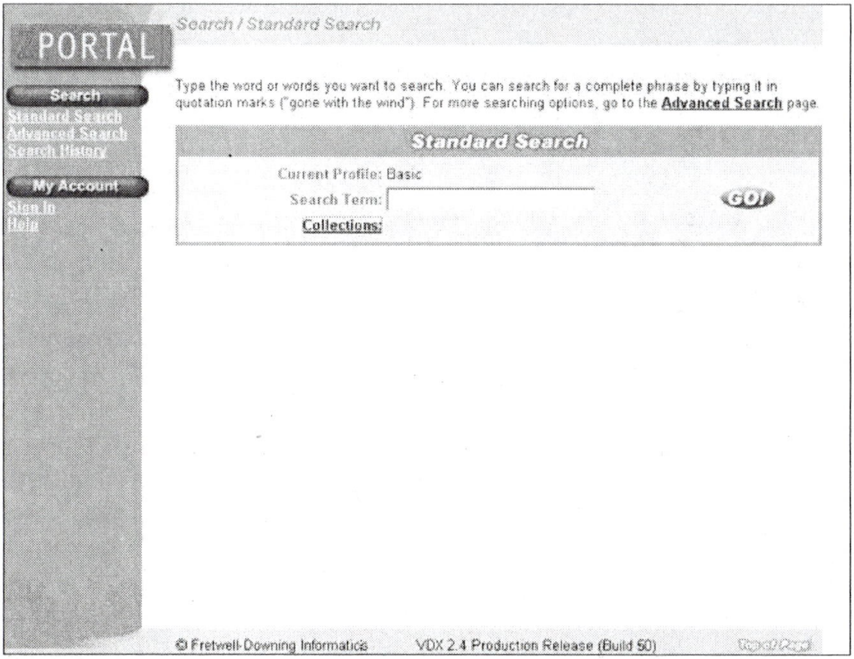

Reprinted with permission.

FIGURE 4. Customized ZPortal Search Screen

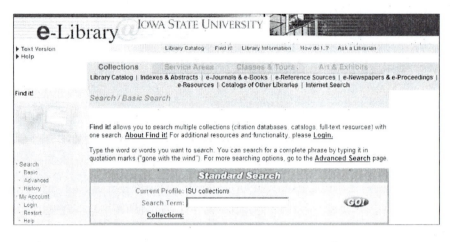

FIGURE 5. About *Find It!* Help Page

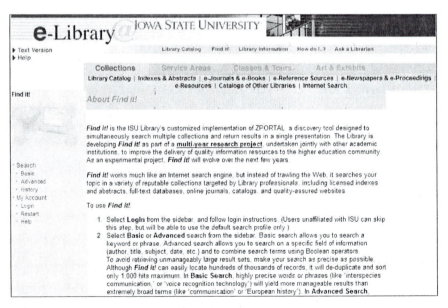

EVALUATION

Since the March 2003 public release of *Find it!*, we have received essential feedback as to its functionality and design. Of pivotal concern to us was whether or not the resources that we incorporated within *Find it!* met faculty and student needs. The feedback we examined has come from system-generated data and individual personal comments. It has been heartening to see, despite little public fanfare regarding its release, usage continuing to expand quickly–largely, no doubt, through curiosity, word of mouth, and reference and public service staff interaction.

Based upon system statistics for the first two full months of spring and fall semesters, we can see the increased number of users who have logged in to ZPORTAL for the first time and created their own user account:

2003	Number of first-time users
March	198
April	195
September	391
October	413

Another measurement from system statistics shows users who have personalized their ZPORTAL profiles. We found that only a handful of new users have created their own search profiles or have saved searches. Either these personalization features are not of great interest to users at the outset, and/or users are not fully aware that these capabilities exist (which seems most likely).

Personal comments have been extremely illuminating for shaping ongoing portal and user instruction development. Obviously scholarly content represents the core value of the portal. However, user comments have not focused on the content but rather on navigation and display. This may indeed reflect well-conceived content decisions related to faculty and student information needs. However, we believe this represents a necessary area for future formal systematic evaluation. We have received positive comments on the general portal framework of simple search mechanisms and broadcast search results.

The navigational and display issues that have been expressed fall into the following three categories:

- *What is it?* Users have expressed confusion over the difference between *Find it!* and the online catalog.
- *Where do I get it?* Users want location, call number and holdings information for serials and books that are not available electronically.
- *Where am I?* Users are often confused when they have departed from our defined *Find it!* pages and have entered a commercial resource, as to where they are and how they can return to *Find it!*

In response to the "What is it?" and "Where am I?" concerns, we have begun to incorporate information regarding *Find it!* in our reference services and our instruction program. We are addressing the "Where do I get it?" concern in our next upgrade to *Find it!* in which we will provide location, call number and holdings information from our online catalog.

MIGRATION ISSUES

We are very conscious of the fact that our portal implementation will be changing over time, and of the need for as much flexibility as possible. For example, ZPORTAL itself will continue to change and develop in future versions–we may need to implement a different authentication/authorization system in the future or we may move to a different portal product entirely. We also recognize the possibilities for other, perhaps additional, interfaces to a portal in the future. The portal may continue to be a stand-alone application, as now, or possibly contained within another application, such as our Library Catalog interface or as a channel in a future university portal. Wherever we have standards-based, non-proprietary formats and data to work with, we stand a much better chance of migrating and repurposing our current portal data.

CONCLUSION

Portal technologies offer libraries incredibly powerful integrated discovery tools that can deliver enormous efficiencies for library users in navigating a broad array of disparate resources and obtaining the information they need. The library community is in the early stages of portal development, and early adopters are presented with challenging opportunities to reexamine their basic foundational concepts for searching and retrieval strategies and to focus on integrated access to full-text resources, whether they be commercial, public domain or local.

Our own portal project planning at ISUL continues as we look to extend access within *Find it!* to local unique resources using FD's Z'MBOL software, which will provide seamless searching of our special collections finding aids, photographic collections, specialized subject guides, etc. We are continuing to refine our subject profiles and are on the verge of implementing FD's ZPORTAL version 2.4, which incorporates user-requested navigational and display features. Lastly, we are now in the planning stages for incorporating *Find it!* within our formal instructional services–particularly in so far as providing guidance on how/when to best use *Find it!* within the library's extensive discovery tool kit. Further out on the planning horizon but essential to the original vision of Jerry Campbell, as that vision was articulated within the ARL Scholars Portal Working Group, and our own local vision, will be how we integrate digital reference services and campus learning management systems within our portal environment.

Throughout these ongoing planning processes we continue to underscore the importance of incorporating user evaluative feedback in the design, functionality, content, and expansion of this amazing new discovery tool. Based on our successful design and implementation of *Find it!*, we strongly encourage libraries to step back from the common development technique of intense internal designing, testing and modeling for "perfection" of new key services and tools before public release. This model can slow down the progress of implementing and expanding new tools while we ensure the "perfect" public release–particularly as we may focus on issues that are of little concern or are a low priority to our users. Rather, the initial planning and implementation process should include a clear core definition of the basic requirements of such tools (e.g., adequate content and access control) and should value and incorporate developmental public assessment. While this approach may not be conducive to the creation and public release of all library tools, we believe it to be particularly valuable in a rapidly changing development environment. Moreover, online tools such as portals also have superficial design ties to user experiences with the Web, where expectations are less exact and more permissively forgiving. Ultimately, our users should be strong collaborative partners within an environment stressing that perfection is not required!

APPENDIX 1

Original Planned Subject Profiles

Agriculture and Life Sciences

Business and Company Information

Education Studies

Legal and Government Resources

Multicultural Perspectives

Science, Technology and Food Science

Social Sciences and Humanities

Undergraduate Student

Vet Med Student

APPENDIX 2

Subject Profiles Implemented August 2003

Agriculture and Life Sciences

Business and Company Information

Education Studies

Engineering and Computer Science

Social Sciences and Humanities

Undergraduate Student

Vet Med Student

APPENDIX 3

All Find it! collections profile, as of February 2003

AGRICOLA

AGRIS

Aerospace and High Technology Database

Alternative Press Index

Aluminum Industry Abstracts

Applied Science and Technology Abstracts

Art Abstracts

Bibliography of Native North Americans

Biography Index

Biological Abstracts

Biological Abstracts/RRM

Biological and Agricultural Index

Book Review Digest

Books in Print

CAB Abstracts

Ceramic Abstracts/World Ceramics Abstracts

Compendex

Computer and Information Systems Abstracts

Copper Data Center Database

Corrosion Abstracts

ENGnetBASE

ERIC

EconLit

Education Abstracts

Electronics and Communications Abstracts

Emerald

Engineered Materials Abstracts

Expanded Academic ASAP

Food Science and Technology Abstracts

GeoRef

IEEE Xplore

Ingenta

Ingenta Select

Internet and Personal Computing Abstracts

Iowa State University Library Catalog

Library Literature

Linguistics and Language Behavior Abstracts

MEDLINE [OCLC]; 1965+

MEDLINE [Ovid]; 1966+; includes
PREMEDLINE

METADEX

MLA Bibliography

Materials Business File

Mechanical Engineering Abstracts

Mechanical and Transportation Engineering
Abstracts

NTIS

PAIS International

Philosopher's Index

Physical Education Index

Project MUSE

PsycINFO

PubMed

ScienceDirect

Sociological Abstracts

Solid State and Superconductivity Abstracts

WELDASEARCH

Water Resources Abstracts

WorldCat

Zoological Record

APPENDIX 4. Timeline for Phase 1

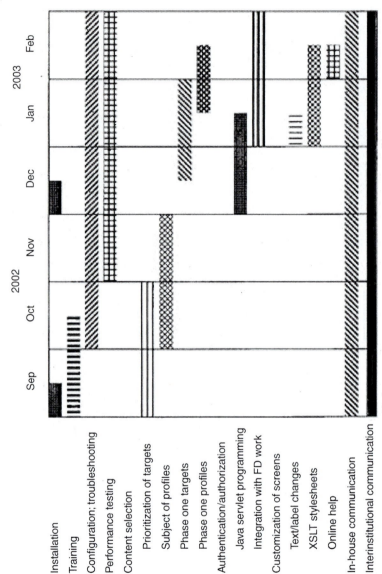

Chapter 8

Online Catalogs and Library Portals in Today's Information Environment

John D. Byrum, Jr.

SUMMARY. With the transformation of the card catalog into the online public access catalog came the expectation of its increased functionality. For the most part, today's online catalogs perform an expanded list of tasks quite effectively. Bibliographic utilities, system vendors, and individual libraries continue to improve bibliographic retrieval by providing new and better services through the catalog. In spite of these improvements, many observers believe that online catalogs have reached their maturity. Today's information environment includes a wealth of material to which online catalogs cannot provide universal and up-to-date access. Increasingly, librarians are turning to federated searching portal applications to find a means of managing the flood of digital information that threatens to engulf users. This chapter describes essential functionality of such tools, suggesting directions and strategies for improving them. The author concludes that, while the online catalog will continue to function as the principal tool for access control of the library's physical collections, the federated searching portal will ultimately serve as the library's principal Web gateway to digital resources.

John D. Byrum, Jr. is Chief, Regional and Cooperative Cataloging, Library of Congress. He also serves as Chair of the Library of Congress Portals Applications Issues Group (E-mail: jbyr@loc.gov).

[Haworth co-indexing entry note]: "Online Catalogs and Library Portals in Today's Information Environment." Byrum, John D., Jr. Co-published simultaneously in *Journal of Library Administration* (The Haworth Information Press, an imprint of The Haworth Press, Inc.) Vol. 43, No. 1/2, 2005, pp. 135-154; and: *Portals and Libraries* (ed: Sarah C. Michalak) The Haworth Information Press, an imprint of The Haworth Press, Inc., 2005, pp. 135-154.

Available online at http://www.haworthpress.com/web/JLA
Digital Object Identifier: 10.1300/J111v43n01_09

KEYWORDS. Online catalogs, integrated library systems, library portals, federated searching applications

EVOLVING FORM AND FUNCTIONS
OF LIBRARY CATALOGS

From the historical perspective, one of the 20th century's grandest information technology accomplishments was the transformation of the library card catalog into the online public access catalog, the centerpiece of today's Integrated Library Systems (ILS).[1] While many of the traditional purposes and features of the catalog have survived the transition to an online format, new and changed functionality has emerged as a result of automation.

In 1872, Charles Cutter set forth the key objectives of the catalog as: (1) enabling a person to find a book of which the author, or the title, or the subject is known; (2) showing what the library has by a given author, on a given subject, in a given kind of literature; and (3) assisting in the choice of a document as to its edition (bibliographically) and as to its character (literary or topical).[2] This vision became widely shared, especially by makers of cataloging codes, and has prevailed for more than 100 years. However, with the emergence of the online catalog, it has finally proved possible to expand this list to include additional functionality. (Other forces contributing to interest in revising these objectives included increased collection of non-book material and international standardization of bibliographic description.)

Indeed, by the time of the 1997 International Conference on the Principles and Future Development of AACR, it had become clear that

> these objectives and functions are surely inadequate for the new environment. In addition to the finding and the collocating functions, the online catalogue helps through different data fields, such as intellectual level, document type, genre, language code, geographic area code, and additional notes. Similarly, a fuller description of the item helps the online catalogue to be used as a selecting aid. . . . The locating of items is another function of the catalogue and, in this respect, online catalogues are far more capable of showing the location and status of the item(s) being sought.[3]

Interest in reformulating the functions of the catalog has continued to increase. In 2003, the first in a series of IFLA Meetings of Experts on an International Cataloguing Code was held in Frankfurt. Over a five-year period, this series is seeking to produce world-wide consensus on a "Statement of Cataloguing Principles" that might provide the basis for an International Cataloguing Code. At this initial gathering, the conferees decided to update principles comprising the "Functions of the Catalogue," both to reaffirm the traditional objectives underlying cataloging policy and practice, and also to add and change them to reflect the capacities of today's online catalogs.

The Draft Frankfurt Principles statement emerging from this Conference outlines five functional requirements for today's catalog, expanding on the traditional "finding" and "collocation" objectives and adding some entirely new tasks. Five functions are identified:

1. *The Finding function:* The catalog should enable the user to find bibliographic resources, as the result of a search using attributes or relationships of the resources.
2. *The Identifying function:* The catalog should enable the user to confirm that the entity described in a record corresponds to the entity sought or to distinguish between two or more entities with similar characteristics.
3. *The Selecting function:* The online catalog should facilitate users' selection of materials that respond to their needs with respect to content, physical format (and correspondingly, enable them to reject materials when inappropriate to their needs).
4. *The Obtaining function:* The catalog should enable access to resources described (e.g., through purchase, loan, or, in cases of electronic material through an online connection to a remote source).
5. *The Navigating function:* The online catalog should support navigation of the database through the logical arrangement of bibliographic information and the presentation of clear ways to move from one related record to another.[4]

Today, for the most part, online catalogs perform this expanded list of tasks quite effectively.

Tom Delsey–who has contributed so much to theoretical understanding of bibliographic control that he was named as the American Library Association's 2003 Margaret Mann Citation recipient for outstanding contributions in the area of cataloging and classification–has succinctly captured the adaptation of the online catalog to the evolving technological environment:

> For the past four decades the development of the library catalogue has been inextricably linked to advances in digital technology. In the sixties, libraries began experimenting with the use of digital technology to support catalogue production through the capture, formatting, and output of bibliographic data. In the seventies, software developers introduced a wide array of systems to support online access to library catalogues. In the eighties, the development and implementation of open standards added a new dimension to the networking of online catalogues. In the nineties, the development of Web technology enabled libraries for the first time to link records in their online catalogues directly to the digital resources they describe.[5]

Indeed, contemporary versions of the ILS have already developed from systems that share bibliographic records among local functions and modules to systems that can exchange information with systems outside of the library.

Even as early as 1995, Cynthia Lopata observed that "Technological developments, such as client/server architectures and standardized protocols for passing information from one system to another, are facilitating this integration of outside information sources into local systems." As an example, she pointed out that an online ordering system might allow a librarian to search a publisher's bibliographic database, select records of books to be purchased, and download those records from the publisher's database into the library catalog. She also found that some libraries were providing patron access to other bibliographic and non-bibliographic databases both inside and outside the library and to OPACs of other libraries.[6]

Into the 21st century, systems for online bibliographic retrieval have continued to improve, providing new and better services, as a few illustrations will demonstrate.

The leading bibliographic utilities are pursuing initiatives to increase the value of their online catalogs. Impressive for its efforts to further modernize the catalog is RLG's "RedLightGreen" project, proceeding with support from the Mellon Foundation, which aims "to offer rich, reliable library information that is unique in the Web environment and to deliver that information in ways that meet the expectations of Web-savvy users."[7] Directed primarily at serving undergraduate students, the goals of RedLightGreen are:

- to enable the users to search across the collections of many libraries using common words;
- to find works that are relevant and related to their interests through linkages which a more traditional online catalog does not offer;
- to select the most widely held or most authoritative works;
- to determine whether an item is on the shelf in one's own college library (or where to purchase it); and,
- to obtain a citation for the work ready to be pasted into a document in any of the several widely used formats.

RedLightGreen's service expectations are "to help undergraduates locate relevant . . . works for their research, check availability of those resources through a link to their local online catalog, and create proper citations for those resources in standard formats." Its software also aims to implement the framework of IFLA's Functional Requirements of Bibliographic Records (FRBR)[8] which distinguishes between a work, an expression, a manifestation, and an item. Programming aggregates works for which there are large numbers of editions into a manageable set of "hits" that match a user's search terms. In addition, RedLightGreen harnesses MindServer technology to find more subject correlations between works in order to increase retrieval. The RLG staff are optimistic that this service "will grow and improve in the coming months."[9]

Similarly, OCLC is mounting efforts to improve the scope and utility of its online union catalog, considered to be the world's largest bibliographic database. One current project, named the Open WorldCat Pilot, represents an effort to make library resources available from non-library Web sites. The pilot will test the effectiveness of Web search engines in guiding users to library-owned materials. The objective is to make libraries more visible to Web users and more accessible from Web sites by pointing them to local libraries that hold particular publications for which they are searching (based on holdings information recorded in WorldCat). In this initiative, OCLC's partners include Abebooks, Alibris, Antiquarian Booksellers of America, Bookcase, H. I. Bibliography, and most recently, Google.[10]

OCLC, like RLG, is also conducting research to determine the cost-benefits of an implementation of the distinctions set forth in the Functional Requirements of Bibliographic Records. Specifically, OCLC has designed four related research projects that aim to test the feasibility of implementing the FRBR structure in a large catalog database and to examine the issues associated with the conversion of a set of bibliographic records to conform to FRBR requirements. The assumption is that having resources brought together as "works" will help users sift through the myriad information resources available digitally.[11]

While the leading utilities enhance the union catalogs they maintain, the major ILS vendors are exploring improvements to the systems they market. Some improvements are similar to those pursued by RLG and OCLC, making it easier for users to navigate a library's bibliographic database through an FRBR-enabled interface. In addition, several vendors have initiated content enhancement services by which libraries are able to extend the reach of their OPACs. Such services include subscription products that provide links to tables of contents, author biographies, and reviews. Indeed, on their own, some libraries have undertaken bibliographic enrichment projects to achieve the same results. The Library of Congress, for example, is pursuing a suite of such projects aimed to link researchers, catalogs, and Web resources, to increase the content of the catalog record itself (e.g., to include tables of contents and reviews), and to link the catalog to electronic resources (e.g., Web access to individual publications within series).[12]

LIMITATIONS OF ONLINE CATALOGS IN TODAY'S INFORMATION ENVIRONMENT

Despite ongoing work to enhance the effectiveness of online catalogs, many observers believe that catalogs have reached their maturity, particularly in relation to their primary purpose of managing access to and control of the library's physical collection. Some librarians have wondered whether today's ILS's are, in fact, nearing the limits of their utility. While they efficiently provide access to the library holdings, they often do so at the level of the title for a serial publication or archival collection and generally do not extend deeper to the level of component parts. For example, the online catalog easily retrieves bibliographic information about the journal titles that a library acquires, but does not enable users to directly discover individual articles these journals contain. As the Frankfurt Draft "Statement of Cataloguing Principles" referred to earlier indicates, this reflects economic realities, as most libraries lack the staff resources necessary to create bibliographic records for works within works in all but exceptional cases. Also due to economic constraints, the online catalog will at most provide access only to a relatively small number of remotely accessible electronic resources, whether subscribed to or not, because such resources are so voluminous and so fraught with difficulties as to almost defy universal and up-to-date bibliographic control.

Marshall Breeding points out another intrinsic shortcoming regarding the ILS's ability to manage e-journals and other electronic content: "while much of the basic functionality for managing electronic content is present in a typical ILS, it lacks some of the needed features, largely due to an orientation toward print resources. Some of the complications stem from the licenses that govern the library's use of electronic content . . . where access to the content resembles a lease more than a purchase."[13] Improvements to ILS technology should and will, no doubt, be pursued, particularly to better support the navigation principle (for example, using linking fields). Another area of future focus will likely be directed at XML applications to enable accommodation of records from a variety of formats.[14]

Until recently, the online catalog functioned as the center of the bibliographic universe, surrounded by the dependent modules that it operates and feeds: Acquisitions, Serials, Circulation, and others. Although this universe also features networking capabilities, such as Z39.50 connectivity with other databases and some quite limited direct access to Web resources, today's information environment includes a wealth of material to which online catalogs cannot effectively provide access. These materials include electronic journals, citation databases, full-text aggregations, online reference tools, and other forms of remote access resources freely available to the user or available by subscriptions or licences.

Further complicating the situation, much of the material now accessible on the Web is not bibliographic in nature. As Trant observed:

> Formally published writings are now integrated with drawn or digitally photographed images, recorded sounds, reconstructed models, mathematical simulations in a fluid digital space and these new genres require different methods and structures for their description. These new genres raise new issues: much of the information required to adequately document such networked information resources is extrinsic to the resource itself. Even if a digital object could in some way technically "self-describe" through a declaration of embedded metadata, much intellectual description becomes a matter of assertion. The catalog record begins to represent opinion, rather than fact.[15]

Indeed, it is now accepted that the proliferation of all kinds of material readily available online has had an impact on the research process at all levels. "The library of the 21st century integrates a variety of technologies to provide new levels and types of services to its users," according to William Moen. He adds that "the vision for this library acknowledges that the Internet, the Web, the networked information environment and digital collections of information provide a context to offer broader and more instantaneous access to information."[16]

Users are not depending on the online catalog to reach the resources in which they are interested. Rather, the vast majority has readily turned to fast and often precise tools such as Google that were developed in response to proliferation of Web materials. Today's users want the instant gratification that such tools can produce. And, despite the limitations of these applications, particularly in relation to massive result sets, users increasingly prefer search engines to library catalogs because they are easier to use and because they return rapid responses that often yield the desired information. In fact, 30% of all Web searches are conducted through Google alone.[17] Berkeley professor Peter Lyman is quoted in the *Washington Post* as having claimed: "There's been a culture war between librarians and computer scientists." He adds that the war is over, and "Google won."[18]

CATALOG AS PORTAL?

But Professor Lyman exaggerates, and librarians have not, in fact, conceded defeat in the fulfillment of one of their most essential professional activities, the discovery and delivery of quality information. Indeed, with the advent of so many informational resources on the Web, the question has naturally arisen: Can the catalog become a portal to the Internet? At the Library of Congress Bicentennial Conference on Bibliographic Control for the New Millennium, Sarah Thomas addressed this question by stating:

> The catalog can serve as a portal to the Internet if the catalog is reinterpreted to be an information service which registers in a systematic arrangement those publications and documents of interest to a particular community, regardless of the form in which they appear. This discovery and access tool may exploit a variety of metadata schemes to locate materials, but it imparts unity, predictability, authority, and credibility to search results through the

efforts of expert knowledge managers and the application of principles, policies, and practices of their devising. In the short term, we can expand the catalog to be more inclusive and flexible. In the near future, however, we should expect a hybrid which will adopt some of the superior features of the catalog, but which will employ an increasingly sophisticated technological infrastructure to increase the yield for information seekers.[19]

In responding to these comments, Brian Schottlaender agreed with the last point, stating that "catalogs and portals are 'metadata constellations' which, when integrated–as, for the most part, they presently are not–make up, along with other such constellations, the 'universe of access.' To ask catalogs to serve as portals to the Web is asking too much of them, just as asking portals to serve as catalogs of 'the non-Web' is asking too much of them."[20]

Others have endorsed this concept of the online catalog, the library portal and other related services, as both independent and dependent partners. For example, in his introductory remarks to "The Future of Integrated Library Systems: An LJ Round Table," Brian Kenney observes:

> The potential to improve interoperability drives librarians to look more critically at ILS. Some wonder whether the information portal of the future should be based on a single ILS or instead be a collection of products from different ILS vendors. This piece-meal approach to interoperability in the library marketplace has been created by the vendors themselves, with such products as Ex Libris's SFX, a tool for reference linking, and Endeavor's ENCompass, a product for creating and managing digital content. Standalone products for linking and digital management accounted for nearly 13 percent of the ILS market last year.[21]

Other discussion participants at the LJ Round Table echoed this finding. Carl Grant, President and CEO, VTLS stated: "The functional integration of systems is absolutely where we are headed." Jack Blount, President and CEO, Dynix: "Open standards and integration [of standalone products] bring you lower costs, higher performance, and more robust solutions." Matthew Goldner, Executive Vice-President, Fretwell-Downing: "Librarians don't want all their eggs in one basket any more. They want to be able to pull things together; that's what metasearching has brought up. It's the first place where librarians can actually buy from several vendors and have the products work together extremely well."

EMERGENCE OF FEDERATED SEARCH FUNCTIONALITY AS AN INTEGRAL FEATURE OF LIBRARY PORTALS

It is to "library portals" (a term which for the purpose of the remainder of this chapter refers to federated searching portal applications and identical or similar technology often referred to as "metasearch" tools) that more and more librarians are turning to in the hope of finding a means to manage the flood of information that threatens to engulf users. While online catalogs are generally considered mature technology, federated search portals are still in their infancy. Eric Hellman, president of Openly Informatics, is quoted at the 2003 Library and Information Technology Association's National Forum as describing federated search portals as "a technology everyone thought they wanted, but it's still unproven."[22] And, indeed, as late as December 2002, only a small number of libraries–estimated to be fewer than one-half of one percent–had implemented portals.[23]

Breeding, having surveyed the environment of existing and new tools, recently concluded that so far, there is no single product that can provide comprehensive management of electronic resources. "In my mind, the many facets of electronic resource management should be delivered through a set of interconnected modules that work together, sharing common data files or at least communicating with each other through open protocols. What I see in today's set of products seems far from that ideal. I'm optimistic, however, that a more cohesive approach will emerge in the very near future."[24] Indeed, despite a slow start, federated search technology has already become a source of keen interest among librarians. Not surprisingly, a variety of products are being created to cater to this escalating interest. For example, librarians at the Houston Public Library, who were reportedly unenthusiastic about the federated search portal implemented by that library, "became more supportive when usage statistics revealed that full-text retrievals increased by 69 percent."[25] Moreover, almost all of the vendors developing and maintaining ILSs are now marketing portal applications in anticipation of increased demand for these products. Peter Noerr, CTO of MuseGlobal asserts that "Within 18 months [from late 2003], all academic and consortia RFPs will include requirements for the basic functionality for metasearch."[26] In short, both potential buyers and sellers are coming to the conclusion that federated searching applications "are the correct solution for unifying access to a variety of information resources."[27]

ESSENTIAL AND DESIRABLE FUNCTIONALITY OF FEDERATED LIBRARY PORTALS

In 2001, the Library of Congress Cataloging Directorate issued "Bibliographic Control of Web Resources: A Library of Congress Action Plan,"[28] which stemmed from the Bicentennial Conference on Bibliographic Control for the New Millennium. One of the planks in this action plan called for definition of requirements for a common interface for searching, retrieving, and sorting across a range of discovery tools, including a local catalog, other library catalogs, licensed or locally mounted full-text and A&I databases, and public domain resources. To tackle this assignment, the Library appointed the LC Portals Applications Issues Group (LCPAIG)[29] in mid-2002. In addition to pursuing efforts for development and enhancement of portal functionality for the benefit of the library community in general, the LCPAIG was tasked with examining portal products to determine whether any meet the reference and research needs of the staff and users of the Library.

The LCPAIG devoted nearly one year to performing market analysis and studying the functionality of portal products in order to identify their existing features. The group concentrated on the interface, searching, results presentation, and output capabilities of these products. Three applications in particular were examined and tested extensively by Library staff from diverse operational areas.[30]

The LCPAIG found, as have many others, that there was no single, universal understanding of the term "portal." After much deliberation, the group decided to focus its explorations and testing on portals as tools for organized knowledge discovery rather than as enterprise interfaces. For the purposes of its work, the LCPAIG settled on the following features by way of identifying the distinguishing characteristics of an effective portal service. Successful portals will assist users in identifying and selecting appropriate target resources.[31] They will also help users to determine the target resources that are most useful to their research by providing effective search interfaces and an architecture that supports groupings and rich descriptions of resources. In addition, library portals should provide federated searching and information retrieval of descriptive metadata from multiple, diverse target resources, including, but not limited to, commercial or licensed electronic resources, databases, Web pages, and library catalogs, as well as linking to full text or other related resources through OpenURL support. They should also assist users in setting up and controlling searches and ensure that search results can be reliably duplicated. Other success indicators include: the portal's ability to integrate and manage search results in an understandable, customizable format that allows users to interpret and manipulate their search result; to save and export search results including such options as printing, e-mail, and file downloads; to link search results to full text; and to reliably manage access to target resources and portal functionalities for authenticated users.[32]

The LCPAIG published its "List of Portal Applications Functionalities for the Library of Congress" in July 2003.[33] This sets out portal requirements appropriate for a general research library of a large and complex nature. The list is offered with the understanding that additions or subtractions may be appropriate according to the needs of other kinds of libraries. It differentiates between "mandatory" and "desirable" features. The category of "mandatory" not only embraces essential features but also those that existed in one or more products that were tested in developing the list, while "desirable" items are intended to identify functionality that portal service developers should seek to provide in the next few years.

The list identifies more than 200 recommended features, grouped under broad headings: General Requirements, Client Requirements, Searching and Search Results, Knowledge Database, Patron Authentication, and Portal Administration and Vendor Support.

For each of these categories, functional requirements are either mandatory or desirable.

Mandatory "General Requirements" are illustrated as follows:

1. Search queries should be processed efficiently, including queries that generate a large number of search result records.
2. The portal should guide users in identifying one or more targets most useful to their research through a combination of locally selected groupings of targets and rich descriptions for targets that can incorporate guidance from reference staff.
3. The portal should be accessible to users with various levels of skills in specifying search queries, manipulating and exporting search results and feature error messages that are readily understood.

Mandatory "Client Requirements" include:

1. The Web client must work in a browser-neutral environment on various hardware platforms and accommodate needs of persons with disabilities.
2. Screen displays must be locally customizable to support different user communities and support local branding, labeling, and search session defaults.

Mandatory "Searching/Search Result Requirements" are among the most important specifications and include:

1. The portal should enable users to perform searches in an iterative manner using the search history, saved searches, marked metadata records, and should support linking to full text or other related resources through OpenURL support.
2. The portal software should merge search results from different targets into an easy to understand display.
3. Users should be able to save and export search results from queries without additional log-in requirements and understand and select the formats in which they can receive exported data (e.g., citation, abstract, full text).

"Knowledge Database and Patron Authentication Requirements" are also significant, as illustrated by the following three mandatory functionalities:

1. The portal creator/vendor should provide and maintain basic descriptive metadata and configuration information for core databases, including target title or name, subject terms, publisher, and standard identifiers.
2. The knowledge database to which the portal provides access should be updateable online and through batch processes.
3. The portal architecture should support different methods to authenticate users and recognize various user roles or classes of users and enable security against unauthorized use as well as privacy for users.

Finally, among the mandatory "Portal Administration/Vendor Support Requirements" are expectations that:

1. The portal should provide access to Z39.50 target servers and one or more mechanisms for accessing non-Z39.50 target servers (e.g., HTML).
2. The application should interoperate with related library systems and applications, such as integrated library systems, an OpenURL resolver, interlibrary loan protocols.
3. Operation of the portal application should be well documented and supported with tools to allow local systems staff to configure and monitor the system and to transfer location configurations, customized help files, knowledge database contents, etc.

From this summary of necessary functionality, it should be clear that an effective federated portal will not only complement but also greatly extend the library's abilities to provide effective resource discovery services. Ideally, as Caroline Arms has suggested, such portal applications should accomplish a single search of a large number of high-quality bibliographic databases and full-text resources, including those within the "hidden" Web, leading users to the best material and providing comprehensive retrieval for a topic or task–with the ease of using Google.[34]

This may be the goal, but to a varying degree, products currently available fall short of realizing such an ambitious vision. As was pointed out in a recent issue of *Library Technology Reports*: "Library portal products are still new–most were introduced in 2001 and 2002. The keyword-based search tools employed in most of them usually deliver excessive quantity, poor quality, and inaccurate results."[35]

Additional shortcomings of most currently available federated search applications include issues regarding interoperability. Their inability to compensate for inconsistent metadata and differing indexing approaches among targets searched seem to be particularly challenging examples. Also, the work involved in setting up and maintaining current applications, including customization and configuration, is generally considered to be time-consuming and labor intensive (at least at the outset), and there are definitely costs related to training staff and users to make the most of the features of whichever application is installed. Moreover, as Judy Luther points out: "Metasearch also bypasses the sophisticated interface . . . such as a thesaurus that is useful in providing alternative terms for searching."[36] De-duping and relevance-ranking represent additional challenges.

Beyond addressing these serious concerns, vendors and others responsible for developing and maintaining library portals have opportunities to enhance their products to make them even more attractive in the marketplace, step-by-step. To assist them, the Library of Congress Portals Applications Issues Group devoted attention to identifying "desirable" functionality now not present in most federated search portals. Implementation of such features as those that follow should yield a higher performing portal product. For example:

- Users should be able to begin evaluating partial search results before complete search results are received.
- Unicode should be supported throughout.
- Searchers should be able to apply "search relationship identifiers" (such as Boolean operators, truncation, wildcards, and nesting) in a single advanced search query.
- Between search sessions, users should be able to save, modify, and delete both search queries and the targets associated with these queries (most likely through personalized user profiles).
- Searching options should include more than "keyword anywhere" support. Users should be able, for example, to search keywords in specified fields or browse a "left-match" display of fields in an ordered list.
- Descriptive metadata for individual electronic resources contained within aggregated targets (such as journal titles) should be available in the knowledge database.
- Institutions should be able to add local descriptive metadata and configuration information to knowledge database records; this information should be retained when records are regularly refreshed.
- For reasons of security and privacy, the application should support secure user logins and enable institutions to determine what session-specific information will be stored and purged.

Even when the limitations of today's federated search technology are taken into account, Arms found them effective for single searches of small sets (eight or less) of relatively coherent resources. In assessing the services tested at the Library and the responses of other testers, she observed that "OpenURL-enabled links to full text [are] the most uniformly popular functionality." She also felt that "ease and flexibility of administration" as well as personalization (by individual users) and customization (for groups, by librarians) should be important considerations in selecting a product.

That federated searching portal applications will evolve to increase their utility and attractiveness as tools for libraries underscores the importance of librarians closely following and exerting influence on the direction of their development. As Moen noted: "Librarians may feel that they inherit tools, technologies, and standards created by others. This has the potential of those standards not addressing problems as defined by librarians."[37] He has cited federated search portals as an example of a technology that provides the profession with an opportunity to pursue a new approach for standardization, one that defines problems to be addressed by standards within the context of a specific service. The Association of Research Libraries' Scholars Portal Project, the Library and Information Technology Association's Portals Interest Group, and the Library of Congress Portals Applications Issues Group, National Information Standards Organization among others provide opportunities by which the profession can encourage portal developers and vendors to focus resources on enhancements to their products that will meet librarians' needs and those of the users they serve. Libraries' reliance on machine-processing to support information organization, access, and use forces librarians to take an interest in encouragement of standards and agreements to ensure that applications interoperate. These groups provide mechanisms by which individual librarians can relate concerns, and they welcome recommendations for new or improved portal functionality.

ONLINE CATALOGS AND LIBRARY PORTALS: THEIR RESPECTIVE ROLES

In the twenty-first century's increasingly electronic environment, the role of the online catalog as a tool for accessing and organizing information is changing. As Tom Delsey explained:

> The technology that supports the direct linking of catalogue records to the electronic resources they describe is also being used to support links to those same resources from a wide range of network browsing services, Web directories, indexing tools, and publishers' databases. The same technology also supports direct links from references and citations embedded in an electronic document to the resources referenced. Likewise, the technology that supports the horizontal extension of the local catalogue through the virtual union catalogue or through a networked interface between the catalogue and an A&I database is being used in other sectors as well to extend local functionality for resource discovery across multiple sources of data. What all this means, of course, is that

the library catalogue functions as just one of many access paths available to the user in search of electronic resources on the network. Setting the agenda for the adaptation and development of the library catalogue to function more effectively in a networked environment is in itself a challenging task.[38]

Will ILS vendors invest the substantial resources needed to reposition the catalog to enable it to meet these challenges or will they focus their developmental efforts on increasing the effectiveness of the library portal as a separate but complementary tool to the online catalog?

In today's setting, users are not so much interested in retrieving bibliographic records, or perhaps even library materials as physical objects, as they are in accessing information within them and information from the content of the ever-expanding Web. As the networked information environment becomes increasingly complex, the operational focus is shifting to integration of management information systems in which the public access catalog and the federated search engine each will play a role. In a contemporary view of the information environment, the ILS and its apparatus operate as important parts of the bibliographic universe. The library portal in the form of a federated search application, however, serves to unite and integrate information from a variety of sources, both within and without the library. In this view, the online catalog continues to function as the principal tool for inventory and access control of the library's collections (at least to the extent that they're represented in the bibliographic database). The online catalog will also offer limited access to relatively few targeted remote electronic resources of high research value or special interest. But, in this view, it is the library portal, assuming that it ultimately achieves the full range of its functionality, that will serve as the user's principal Web gateway to digital resources and services, providing a high level of seamless integration and including a feature-rich toolkit for cross-resource searching according to the personalized needs of the users.

NOTES

1. Defined as a system comprising a number of functional modules, such as acquisitions, circulation, cataloging, serials, and an OPAC (Online Public Access Catalog). See Cynthia L. Lopata, "Integrated Library Systems," *ERIC Digests* (April 1995). Available: http://ericit.org/digests/EDO-IR-1995-02.shtml.

2. Charles A. Cutter, *Rules for a Printed Dictionary Catalog*, 4th ed. (Washington, D. C.: Government Printing Office, 1904), 12.

3. *The Principles and Future of AACR: Proceedings of the International Conference on the Principles and Future Development of AACR, Toronto, Ontario, Canada, Oct. 23-25, 1997;* Jean Weihs, editor (Ottawa: Canadian Library Association, 1998), 18.

4. IFLA Meeting of Experts on an International Cataloguing Code, 1st Frankfurt, Germany, 2003, *Statement of International Cataloguing Principles*; draft approved. Available: http://www.ddb.de/news/pdf/statement_draft.pdf.

5. Tom Delsey, "The Library Catalogue in a Networked Environment," *Proceedings of the Bicentennial Conference on Bibliographic Control for the New Millennium: Confronting the Challenges of Networked Resources and the Web* (Washington, D. C.: Cataloging Distribution Service, 2001), 43. Available: http://lcweb.loc.gov/catdir/bibcontrol/thomas_paper.html.

6. Cynthia L. Lopata, op. cit.

7. Available: http://www.rlg.org/redlightgreen.

8. *IFLA Study Group on the Functional Requirements for Bibliographic Records, Functional Requirements for Bibliographic Records: Final Report* (München: K. G. Saur, 1998). Available: http://www.ifla.org/VII/s13/frbr/frbr.htm.

9. Merrilee Proffitt, "RedLightGreen: What We've Learned Since Launch," *RLG Focus*, issue 66 (Feb. 2004). Available: http: www.rlg.org/r-focus/i66.html.

10. The initiative is more fully described at: http://www.oclc.org/worldcat/pilot/default.htm and http://www.oclc.org/worldcat/pilot/default.htm.

11. These projects are outlined at: http://www.oclc.org/research/projects/frbr/default.htm.

12. These initiatives are undertaken by LC's Bibliographic Enrichment Advisory Team (BEAT) and described at the Team's Web site at http://lcweb.loc.gov/catdir/beat/.

13. Marshall Breeding, "The many facets of managing electronic resources," *Computers in Libraries*, v. 24, no.1 (Jan. 2004). Available: http://www.infotoday.com/cilmag/jan04/breeding.shtml.

14. Roy Tennant, "Building a New Bibliographic Infrastructure," *Library Journal*, v. 129, no 1 (Jan. 2004), 38. Tenant observes: "we need to draft standards, software tools, and systems that can accept, manipulate, store, output, search and display metadata from a wide variety of bibliographic or related standards." Without this functionality, our bibliographic apparatus "maintain[s] the status quo and risk[s] becoming increasingly (and deservedly) marginalized."

15. Jennifer Trant "Comments on Tom Delsey's Paper, 'The Library Catalog in the Networked Environment'" in *Proceedings of the Bicentennial Conference on Bibliographic Control for the New Millennium: Confronting the Challenges of Networked Resources and the Web.* (Washington, D. C.: Cataloging Distribution Service, 2001), 58. Available http://lcweb.loc.gov/catdir/bibcontrol/thomas_paper.html.

16. William E. Moen, "No Longer Under Our Control: The Nature and Role of Standards in the 21st Century Library," Library of Congress Luminary Lectures @ Your Library, Dec. 3, 2003, 7. Available: http://www.unt.edu/wmoen/presentations/LuminaryLectureDecember2003.pdf.

17. Judy Luther, "Trumping Google? Metasearching's Promise," *Library Journal* (Oct. 1, 2003), 36.

18. Joel Achenbach, "Search for Tomorrow: We Wanted Answers, and Google Really Clicked, What's Next?" *Washington Post*, Feb. 15, 2004, D7.

19. Sarah E. Thomas, "The Catalog as Portal to the Internet," *Proceedings of the Bicentennial Conference on Bibliographic Control for the New Millennium: Confronting the Challenges of Networked Resources and the Web*, Washington, D. C.: Cataloging Distribution Service, 2001, 35. Available: http://lcweb.loc.gov/catdir/bibcontrol/thomas_paper.html.

20. Brian E. C. Schottlaender, "Comments," *Proceedings of the Bicentennial Conference on Bibliographic Control for the New Millennium*, op. cit. 39.

21. Brian Kenny, "The Future of Integrated Library Systems: An LJ Round Table," *Library Journal* (June 15, 2003), 37.

22. Michael Rogers, "Library Journal InfoTech," *Library Journal* (Nov. 1, 2003) 25.

23. Richard Boss, "How to Plan and Implement a Library Portal," *Library Technology Reports*, (Nov.-Dec. 2002), 5. Boss adds: "Library portals are still new–most were introduced in 2001 and 2002. The keyword-based search tools employed in most of them usually deliver excessive quantity, poor quality and inaccurate results. The solution to the problem of excessive quantity usually is relevancy ranking, filtering for relevancy, and ranking the search results according to predetermined criteria" (7).

24. Breeding, op. cit.

25. Luther, op. cit., 39.

26. Ibid.

27. Roy Tenant, "The Right Solution: Federated Search Tools," *Library Journal* (June 15, 2003), 28.

28. Available: http://lcweb.loc.gov/catdir/bibcontrol/actionplan.html.

29. For a wealth of information on the topic as well as an introductory tutorial, see the LCPAIG Web site at: http://www.loc.gov/catdir/lcpaig/paig.html.

30. The applications studied and the vendors that made them available were: ZPORTAL™, available from Fretwell-Downing, Inc.; MetaLib/SFX, available from ExLibris (USA), Inc.; and ENCompass/LinkFinder*Plus*, available from Endeavor Information Systems.

31. For the purpose of the "List," the term "Target" is used to identify the heterogeneous local and remote electronic resources accessed directly from the portal application. Examples include library OPACs, freely available Web sites, and licensed resources (e.g., ProQuest®, Academic Search™ Premier, OCLC's FirstSearch Electronic Collections Online, or RLG's Eureka®). The term "Target resources" is used to identify individual electronic resources contained in a target. Because many targets are themselves aggregators of electronic content, the term "target resources" identifies, for example, the electronic journals found in aggregator databases.

32. For an elaboration of these points, see the Cybercast of a program "Finding It Faster: Portal Applications For Information Discovery and Retrieval," given at the Library of Congress on Nov. 24, 2003, available from a link at: http://www.loc.gov/catdir/lcpaig/documents.html#programs.

33. Available: http://www.loc.gov/catdir/lcpaig/PortalFunctionalitiesList4Public Comment1st7-22-03.html.

34. See her PowerPoint presentation, "What Is a Portal? And, How Might It Help You Find Stuff Faster" (created Nov. 2003) at: http://www.loc.gov/catdir/lcpaig/arms1124.pdf.

35. Richard Boss, "How to Plan and Implement a Library," *Library Technology Reports* (Nov./Dec. 2002), 7.

36. Luther, op. cit., 38.

37. Moen, op. cit., 3.

38. Delsey, op. cit., 53.

Chapter 9

Usability Testing, Interface Design, and Portals

Jennifer L. Ward
Steve Hiller

SUMMARY. During the past decade, usability testing has become an integral component of Web design and development in libraries. Within the past five years, library portals allowing some degree of personal customization have established a presence on a number of library home pages. This chapter reviews some basic concepts of usability testing and then examines how usability testing has been employed to inform the design and use of Web sites and customized library portals at the University of Washington and at other institutions. *[Article copies available for a fee from The Haworth Document Delivery Service: 1-800-HAWORTH. E-mail address: <docdelivery@haworthpress.com> Website: <http://www.HaworthPress.com> © 2005 by The Haworth Press, Inc. All rights reserved.]*

Jennifer L. Ward is Head, Web Services (E-mail: jlward1@u.washington.edu); and Steve Hiller is Head, Science Libraries, and Library Assessment Coordinator (E-mail: hiller@u.washington.edu), both at the University of Washington Libraries, Box 352900, Seattle WA 98195.

[Haworth co-indexing entry note]: "Usability Testing, Interface Design, and Portals." Ward, Jennifer L., and Steve Hiller. Co-published simultaneously in *Journal of Library Administration* (The Haworth Information Press, an imprint of The Haworth Press, Inc.) Vol. 43, No. 1/2, 2005, pp. 155-171; and: *Portals and Libraries* (ed: Sarah C. Michalak) The Haworth Information Press, an imprint of The Haworth Press, Inc., 2005, pp. 155-171. Single or multiple copies of this article are available for a fee from The Haworth Document Delivery Service [1-800-HAWORTH, 9:00 a.m. - 5:00 p.m. (EST). E-mail address: docdelivery@haworthpress.com].

Available online at http://www.haworthpress.com/web/JLA
Digital Object Identifier: 10.1300/J111v43n01_10

KEYWORDS. Usability testing, library Web sites, library portals, interface design

INTRODUCTION

Usability testing was established in the business world to gain a better understanding of how the (potential) customer uses a specific product. By using a variety of qualitative methods, including observation and focus groups, information would be acquired that could then be used both in the design and marketing processes. We define usability testing as a structured process of getting information on the extent to which a product can be used by the intended users to achieve specified goals with effectiveness, efficiency, and satisfaction in a specified context of use.

While usability testing is most commonly associated today with human-computer interactions it can be used with almost any product or service. One of the authors took a usability workshop in the early 1990s in which the first task was to set the alarm for a clock radio and, if we were successful, to turn it off. Even though the room was well-lighted, this wasn't easy. Many of us have struggled with clock alarms in dim, unfamiliar hotel rooms and wondered why a relatively simple task could turn out to be such a complex operation. Yet relatively few libraries at that time had employed such testing with their own products and services. Some work had been done with using the library catalog (both card and online) as well as tracking how people actually found books and journals in the library. The majority of these studies showed that users experienced difficulty finding resources through the catalog and locating items on the shelf. The solution offered by many libraries was based on our assumptions on how users should act. We would provide more user education and teach them how to use libraries the "correct way," and perhaps improve signage. The idea of redesigning services based on user preferences was rarely considered or employed.

The concept of the user-centered library that began to emerge in the early 1990s shifted the library focus from how we think or assume things ought to work to understanding how and why our community used libraries, and then designing and implementing library services and programs that could best support their work. As Stoffle and her colleagues at the University of Arizona put it:

All services and activities must be viewed through the eyes of the customers, letting customers determine quality by whether their needs have been satisfied. Librarians must be sure that their work, activities and tasks add value to the customer. (Stoffle et al., 1996, p. 221)

To understand user behavior we need structured methods to observe, measure, and acquire appropriate information directly from them. Usability testing is one of these methods.

USABILITY TESTING

Usability testing generally involves creating a list of tasks that participants follow when using a product or service and then observing how they accomplish those tasks. Participants are often asked to comment on the process during the test (by thinking aloud) or afterwards and their activity may be captured through a variety of methods: observation, visual and/or audio recording, or through a computer log. The goals of usability testing are to provide data on whether participants can accomplish the task (effectiveness), do it in reasonable time and effort (efficiency), show how it is done (context), and finally their reaction to the product or service (satisfaction). The information acquired from usability testing is then shared with developers and designers and others in direct contact with the user community to better understand user behavior and as part of a user-centered design process. Rubin's influential *Handbook of Usability Testing* (1994) identifies three principles of user-centered design: (1) an early focus on users and tasks; (2) empirical measurement of product usage; and (3) iterative design whereby a product is designed, modified, and tested repeatedly.

For most libraries, usability testing is now associated with Web-based services. Many of the initial library usability studies involved questions of navigability and language on the library's Web site. Participants were often given a task or list of activities to do and their actions were observed. They are often asked to vocalize their thoughts as they go through the process and can indicate when they have difficulty navigating or finding a resource or service on the Web site as well as note any language used that is confusing or they don't understand. More recently, library Web usability studies have also included resource discovery and customizable portals.

Usability testing generally falls into the category of structured qualitative research. Substantial preparation needs to go into the design of
the usability test. Campbell notes:

> The most crucial part of doing formal usability testing is creating
> the list of tasks that participants will complete using the Web site
> or system. These tasks should be representative of actual things
> average users would do on the site. . . . When creating tasks it is
> important to pay special attention to the wording of each question
> and use words that are not leading or biased in some way. . . . It is
> also important to limit the number of tasks based upon the amount
> of time allotted for test sessions. (Campbell, 2001, p. 3)

The number of participants can be relatively small. Generally, four or
five participants should be enough to identify about 80% of the problems. When dealing with a more heterogeneous community, it is advis-
able to make sure there are some representatives from each group. Thus,
academic libraries might want to involve several undergraduates as well
a few faculty as they tend to use libraries differently. Usability testing
can be done at places ranging from a simple computer with a note taker
to a sophisticated usability lab with audio and/or video capabilities.
However, it is critical that a trained observer record not only their activities but also the comments from the participant as they "think aloud"
and other personal reactions such as body language.

Other methods for assessing usability include site statistics, focus
groups, pop-up and other Web-based surveys, card sorting and categorization, cognitive walk throughs, and heuristic evaluation by "experts."
Effective usability reviews will employ multiple methods to provide a
multidimensional evaluation from the user perspective. Conducting the
usability test is just one part of the overall process. Equally important is
communicating the results to designers, developers and those who work
directly with the customer. Usability testing is effective only if the information acquired can be used to make the design process more
user-centered. At best this is an iterative process of design, testing,
modification, employment, and retesting. More realistically it involves
a cyclical process with periodic major design or content changes followed by ongoing small tweaks that enhance use.

Library-related usability testing began to bloom in the mid-1990s
through work on digital library initiatives (Van House et al., 1996) and
in design and evaluation of library Web sites. Initial publications on
usability of library Web sites appear in 1998 based on work at the Uni-

versity of Arizona Sabio system and later at North Carolina State University. Campbell in her 2001 LITA publication, *Usability Assessment of Library-Related Web Sites: Methods and Case Studies*, provides an excellent bibliography of previously published or accessible work on library Web sites, as well as a number of case studies from different libraries. Norlin and Winters (2002) produced a short how-to manual published by the American Library Association which is designed for those interested in evaluating their library Web site. Pace's Building and Optimizing Library Web Services in *Library Technology Reports* (2002) had a strong focus on usability and contains usability instruments. Usability presentations are now a common feature at many library conferences and it's safe to say that usability testing is clearly part of a best practices suite for libraries.

Covey (2002) in her study of usage and usability assessment at Digital Library Federation member libraries listed several concerns and issues with usability testing or user protocols. These included librarian assumptions and preferences that impeded testing and use of results, lack of resources and commitment, interpreting and using the data effectively, and recruiting participants who can think aloud. She went on to note that usability testing

> requires skilled facilitators, observers, and analysts and the commitment of human and financial resources. . . . Even if the skills are available, there could be a breakdown in the processes of collecting, analyzing, and interpreting the data, planning how to use the findings, and implementing the plans, which could include conducting follow-up research to gather more information. . . . Limited resources frequently restrict implementation to only the problems that are cheap and easy to fix, which are typically those that appear on the surface of the user interface. Problems that must be addressed in the underlying architecture often are not addressed. (Covey, p. 29)

While these admonitions are important, especially for those planning to initiate usability testing, the predominant experience at libraries that have done usability testing is overwhelmingly positive. Even if a number of the issues and problems identified in usability testing cannot be resolved initially, small changes can improve site usability, and more importantly utilize a design process that recognizes the importance of ongoing user input.

LIBRARY PORTALS AND USABILITY

The basic elements of a library portal are a customizable Web interface, personalized content presentation, and powerful cross searching functionality. The definition, development, and implementation of library portals are described more fully elsewhere in this issue. While there is substantial interest in library portals, Boss (2002) estimated that only a small number of libraries, less than .5%, have implemented them. The first substantial effort to describe portal development at more than one library can be found in a special issue of *Information Technology and Libraries* (*ITAL*) (2000). Each of the libraries involved–North Carolina State University, Virginia Commonwealth University, and the University of Washington–had employed some type of usability testing in a redesign of their Web site which led to a customizable option. However, at the time those articles were written, these portals had been in operation for less than two years. Common threads among these sites are that a relatively low number of active users accounted for most of the activity and that most did not have a robust cross-search function. Ghapery (2002) provided an updated report on My Library at Virginia Commonwealth University which was first described in the *ITAL* 2000 issue. He stated that

> there have not been many follow up studies on the measured use of My Library. A possible reason for this might be the fragmented nature of library personalization. In the case of VCU Libraries, the initial concept for the My Library service was ahead of the technological infrastructure to support it. For example in the fall of 1998 the VCU legacy Integrated Library System (ILS) did not support online borrowing transactions and Interlibrary Loan was mediated through a simple web form. While the spring of 2002 finds these types of web services commonplace, a unified package of services remains to be fielded. (p. 1)

He went on to note that success would come with the "transparency of the My Library service whereby patrons have unfettered access to customized library resources and services depending on their information needs" (p. 5).

Gibbons (2003) discusses using the My Library concept to pre-identify and dynamically push Web pages to students based on the courses they take and course reserves. Librarians and students both participated in usability testing and the results "caused significant changes both to the requirements of the system as well as to its design. . . . Usability testing played a tremendous role in determining the terminology used . . . and the weight and emphasis of elements on the page." Gibbons stressed the integration of the library portal in the user's workspace and maintaining as few barriers as possible to its use. Ketchell noted in 2000 that "customization must expand to personalization to avoid a faceless virtual library; My Library functionality will be only one tier in a user's larger university and Web world" (Ketchell, 2002, p. 178). Morgan and Reade also conceded that "The NCSU Libraries may eventually need to cede the priority of our own portal . . . and develop modules that can function as channels and be plugged into a subscriber's own portal" (Morgan and Reade, 2000, p. 197).

USABILITY TESTING AND INTERFACE DESIGN AT THE UNIVERSITY OF WASHINGTON

Since 1992, the University of Washington Libraries, with strong administrative support and broad-based staff participation, has conducted extensive, ongoing assessment of user needs, focusing on needs assessment, priorities, library and information use patterns, and user satisfaction with the quality of library services and collections. The user-centered approach is in alignment with the UW Libraries' strategic goals and directions. The UW Libraries has employed a variety of methods to obtain information from faculty and students, including large-scale surveys, targeted surveys, focus groups, observation studies, usability testing, guided interviews, meetings, and both traditional and electronic suggestion boxes. Assessment results guide and inform development of services and resources with results used to improve service quality, library performance, and better support user needs.

In 1998, a group was convened to redesign the Libraries' Web site, the underlying goal of which was to move from an administratively organized site (Figure 1) to one that is more task-oriented and focused on information retrieval (Figure 2). During this process, usability testing was conducted on a prototype of the new site as part of a class project by students in the UW Technical Communications department. The tests were held in the department's Laboratory for Usability Testing and Evaluation (LUTE), a lab outfitted with the tools necessary to support a number of evaluation methods. Although familiar with broader service assessment, this was the first experience library staff had with formal usability testing and the reaction was very positive. Based on feedback

FIGURE 1. Screenshot of Libraries' Web Site (May, 1998)

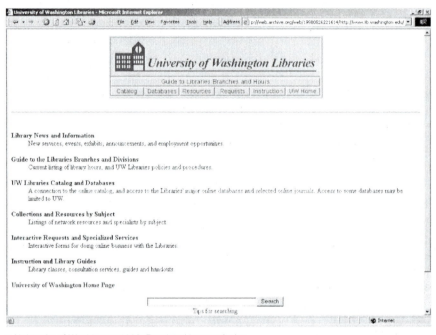

received from the testing, the group made changes to the navigation and terminology of the developing site. Staff were sold on the importance of including usability as part of the systems development life cycle.

After this experience the Libraries sought to programmatically incorporate usability testing in the development life cycle of online services and resources, a goal that was finally realized in 2001. Changes in staffing have brought a usability coordinator and a graduate student dedicated to usability efforts on board. Usability lab space is tight on campus, so equipment was purchased to conduct and monitor tests in-house.

Results from two recent broad-based surveys revealed that users were satisfied with the Libraries' Web site, the Information Gateway. The UW Libraries run large-scale user surveys every three years and the last one in 2001 showed satisfaction with the Information Gateway ranked at or near the top of a group of ten services (Table 1).

The UW Libraries also participates in the LibQUAL+™ survey which was administered at more than 300 institutions in 2003. UW re-

FIGURE 2. Screenshot of UW Libraries' Information Gateway, Showing a More User-Centered Design (December, 1998)

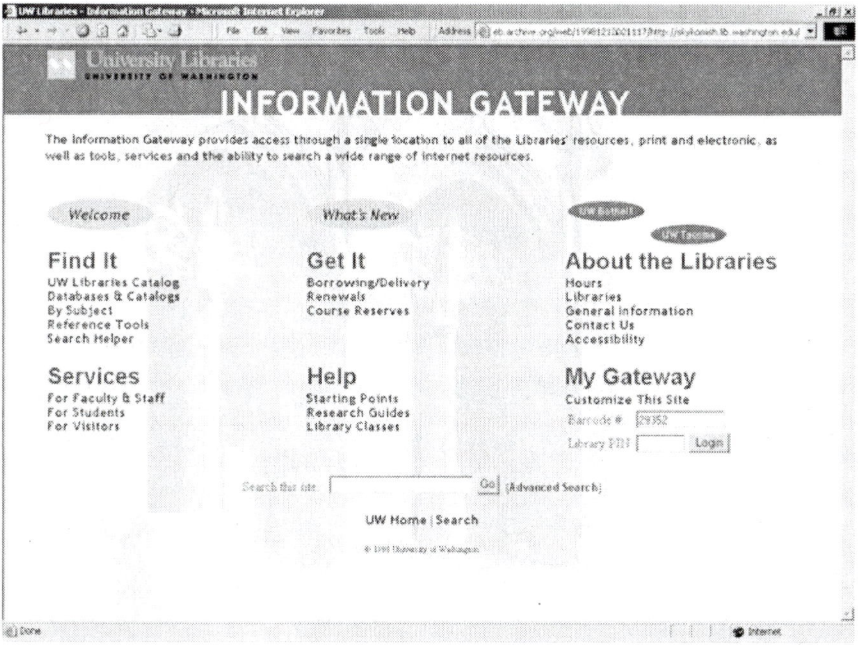

© University of Washington 1998. Reprinted by permission.

spondent satisfaction with a "library Web site enabling me to locate information on my own" was substantially higher than the mean service adequacy satisfaction for other ARL institutions. LibQUAL+™ also provides a measure for assessing importance by looking at desired levels for a specific service. Among the 25 questions asked on the LibQUAL+™ survey, the mean desired service level for a "library Web site enabling me to locate information on my own" ranked at or near the top for all 25 questions (Table 2).

While the survey results were clearly positive, more detailed information was needed about our site and how it was being used. To achieve that goal, we developed and employed a variety of assessment methods including online surveys, focus groups, interviews, field studies, prototyping, and usability testing.

In 2001, the goal for the usability group was to fix pieces of the gateway that needed improvement and since we had no real data on what ar-

TABLE 1. Satisfaction with Library Services: UW Libraries Triennial Survey 2001, Mean Scores by Group

Scale of 1 (low) to 5 (high)	Faculty (1345)	Grad Student (563)	Undergraduate (497)
Libraries Web site	**4.20**	**4.27**	**4.06**
Staff assistance in library	4.31	4.13	3.90
Article and document delivery	4.11	4.14	3.73
Access to library computers	4.09	4.12	3.90
Reshelving of library items	4.01	3.88	4.04

TABLE 2. Importance of Library Web Site: LibQUAL+™ Survey 2003, Mean Desired Service Level Scores by Group

Desired service level	Faculty		Grad Student		Undergraduate	
Scale of 1 (low) to 9 (high)	**UW**	**ARL**	**UW**	**ARL**	**UW**	**ARL**
Library Web site enabling me to locate information on my own	**8.53 (2)**	**8.49 (1)**	**8.55 (2)***	**8.47 (2)**	**7.85 (6)***	**8.20 (1)**
Information easily accessible for independent use	8.34	8.29	8.27	8.28	7.90	8.08
Electronic resources accessible from my home or office	8.68 (1)	8.49 (1)	8.58 (1)	8.50 (1)	8.02 (1)	8.20 (1)
Easy to use access tools	8.37	8.34	8.38	8.34	7.89	8.15

*Mean score was statistically indistinguishable from score above it.

eas should be targeted, user feedback was needed. Assessment practices have shown that surveys are a useful tool to help identify broad problem areas that need more in-depth investigation. A locally created tool, Catalyst's WebQ, was used to create online surveys that have been posted on the Libraries' home page in summer, 2001 and at the start of autumn quarters in 2001 (University Libraries, 2001) and 2003 (University Libraries, 2003).

The first survey was released in summer of 2001. Response rates were very low and the first valuable lesson was learned–summer is not an ideal time to get user feedback as there are few people on campus. It was, however, a great way to run a pilot test of our survey. Many of the questions went unanswered, so the survey was slightly modified and reformatted in the hopes of yielding better results when it was run again.

At the beginning of fall quarter in 2001 and 2003, surveys were linked from the Information Gateway and advertised in an electronic newsletter sent via e-mail to all students, faculty, and staff on campus. Announcing our survey in the newsletter did wonders for the response rate. In 2001, the survey was online for a week before the e-mail invitation was sent. The response rate jumped from sixteen to over sixty (of a total one hundred thirty-one) responses overnight after users received the e-mail invitation. The 2003 survey was launched about the same time the newsletter was sent, with a total response rate of two hundred and thirty-eight. Both surveys were online for almost a month, allowing users a chance to become familiar with the site before commenting. A recruiting tool was included in the survey that asked users if they were interested in participating in a future usability study. Over half the respondents from each survey provided their name; this created a built-in pool of potential participants from which we could recruit in the future.

Based on survey design, the WebQ survey tool can do some basic data analysis and that information is presented in an easy to read interface. However, it cannot analyze comments from open-ended questions. To better identify any trends that develop from the open-ended questions, library staff use "clumping" or "clustering" techniques to group comments into various subject areas. Staff read each comment, write a paraphrase of it on a sticky note and place the note on a whiteboard according to what category it falls under (e.g., catalog, navigation, new features, subject pages, etc.). This method is both low-tech and low-cost, but has proven very effective at identifying key problem areas and prioritizing next steps. Marking the respondent number at the bottom of each sticky note allows us to go back and read the comment in full if more information is needed.

The overall sentiment from the two surveys was that the Web site as a whole wasn't "broken," although there were some areas that needed improvement. Not surprisingly, the online catalog generated the most comments in both surveys; users did not discern between it and the Web site as a whole.

Experience has shown that after getting written feedback from users it is critical to follow up with observational methods such as contextual inquiry, unobtrusive studies, or usability testing (including testing on paper prototype designs). Sometimes the meaning of what is being asked is lost in translation or users think they do one thing when in fact they are observed doing something entirely different.

Using methods already cited, the redesign and usability testing of various parts of the site continued through the summer of 2003, improving many of the underlying components. Significant work was completed on the Browse Subjects, Borrowing/Delivery, and Your Library Account pages, the proxy server wizard, and the OpenURL link resolver. A group of subject librarians and technical staff was recently appointed to address ongoing usability issues with the subject guides and other resource lists, both known to be a bit difficult to use.

During the summer of 2003 it became apparent that the site needed a top-down redesign. To gather more current user feedback, we again went to an online survey, the basic design of which was similar to the successful 2001 survey. Data from this survey and follow-up focus groups will be used to inform future design decisions.

UW LIBRARIES' MY GATEWAY

During the initial Web site design in 1998, the prototyping team realized that no single organization scheme would work well for all users. The decision was made to present information in a variety of ways–resources were organized by subject, alphabetically by resource type (databases, catalogs, e-journals, etc.), and with the realization that users might want to create their own lists of useful resources, My Gateway was created.

My Gateway is the personalized component of the Libraries' Web site which allows users to create *ad hoc* lists of frequently used resources or "subscribe" to lists of resources selected by library staff. The service also allows the resource lists to be published as part of a Web page elsewhere on the site. For example, the atmospheric sciences librarian creates a list of useful databases for her subject and makes that list public. A user can subscribe to that list so it shows up on their My Gateway page. That same list can be published in a Web page elsewhere on the site via an include statement. The service will update URLs as needed, which means the resulting Web page will always remain current.

It is interesting to note the access trends to My Gateway over the last three years. In 2000, Jordan reported that "over seven thousand My Gateway accounts have been created, approximately eighteen hundred of which have been accessed at least once during the last academic quarter" (Jordan, p. 180). Yet when the statistics were pulled at almost the same time of year three years hence, the number of total accounts had doubled to over fourteen thousand, but the number that had been accessed at least once during the last academic quarter had declined by two-thirds to a little over six hundred. As in 2000, few users customize at all. Usable demographics for My Gateway users are unavailable, although anecdotal evidence suggests library staff make up a respectable portion of users entering the site.

One possible reason for the decline in use of My Gateway is the lack of a useful search function. Users prefer to search for information, not click through Web sites hunting for the right link. Nielsen (1997) states that over "half of all users are search-dominant . . . they are task-focused and want to find specific information as fast as possible." Given the popularity of search engines such as Google, that statistic could now be even higher than fifty percent. During a recent usability study of our subject guides, one of the assigned tasks was to find a resource for a Biology 101 paper on a topic of the user's choosing. One user in particular, an undergraduate, "immediately wanted to leave the subject pages. She felt uncomfortable and wanted to search on Yahoo, Looksmart, and HotBox" (University Libraries, 2002).

At a time when users' information needs are diverse and information overload is rampant, more must be done to develop richer search engines of library resources. When asked on the 2003 online survey what new feature users most wanted, over half chose multi-database searching. Focus groups and other usability testing has confirmed that users want a search engine that is capable of cross-format searching (open Web, licensed and unlicensed databases, digital libraries, OPACs, etc.) and displaying an integrated, de-duplicated set of results. Such a service would enable users to feel in control of their information seeking, highlight the breadth and depth of available resources, and get users to the information they need faster and with less frustration. Clearly this is a need that must be met.

Although staff can surmise why the portal is going largely unused, a survey was placed on the My Gateway login page to get user feedback on the service and detailed demographic data. The short survey has been up for over a month and no usable responses have been received to date.

Informal usability testing was done as part of an envisioned 1.2 release of My Gateway. Most of the proposed changes revolved around the management and display of items and categories. The prototypes also included a feature that would allow subject librarians to send short messages to their departments that would highlight a resource or new service. Due to a staffing change and the desire to move the project forward by integrating it with the campus portal, these enhancements were not implemented.

MyUW, THE UNIVERSITY OF WASHINGTON CAMPUS PORTAL

MyUW is the University of Washington's campus portal that customizes the UW Web experience for all types of users (Figure 3). It was first released to students and alumni in 1999, then to faculty and staff a year later. MyUW is the primary access point for many core campus services including registration, transcripts, course schedules, and dining card balances for students; personal benefits information for faculty and staff; and online class schedules and course information for instructors. Through the portal, users can customize content, layout, general look and feel, and add favorite links to their pages.

The delivery of dynamic Libraries' content to the MyUW portal is a goal that will soon be realized. The library currently has a presence under the "Reference" tab, which contains links to the library catalog as well as various databases and other resources. New technologies used by the Libraries will allow us to more easily publish content into MyUW via RSS (RDF Site Summary or Rich Site Summary) channels, which are required by the portal design team. A sample service would allow subject librarians to identify three key resources for a course and publish them into the MyUW student's class schedule and the faculty's class resources page. Links to the class Web site and electronic reserves are currently published within the aforementioned pages and having all course information in one place is helpful to users.

A persistent barrier to providing more library-related content to the campus portal is authentication. The Libraries currently use a 14-digit barcode (found on the back of the campus ID card) and PIN for access to functions such as patron accounts and remote resources via the proxy server. This unwieldy login is difficult for users to remember and most don't understand why they can't access licensed databases even after they have logged in to MyUW with their campus NetID. Numerous requests have been made of the MyUW team to incorporate the patron account in MyUW. Efforts are underway to use the campus authentication scheme for access to library services. Meeting these goals will allow for a more seamless integration of library content into the portal.

Before the site was released, a group in the campus Computing and Communications (IT) department conducted a usability test on MyUW. Users were asked to complete several tasks, then answer questions

FIGURE 3. Screenshot MyUW Student Page (Guest Access Available at http://myuw.washington.edu/)

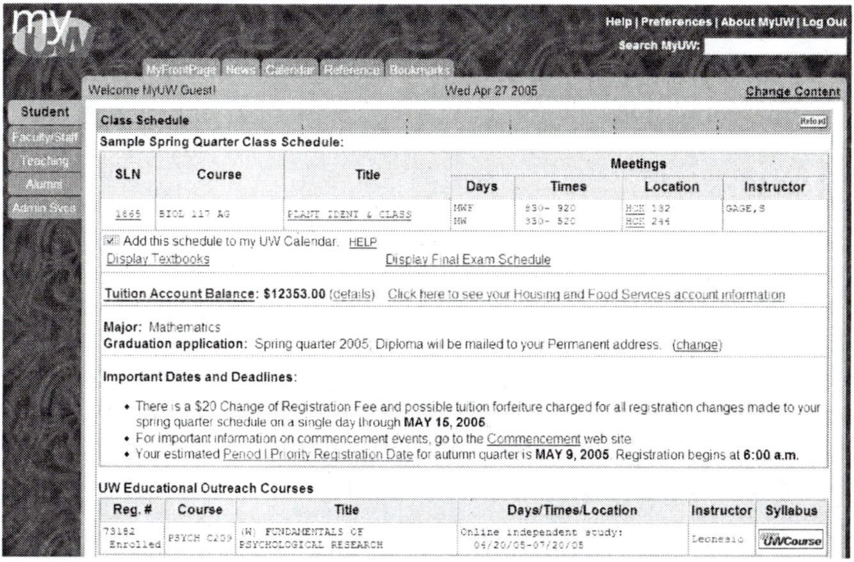

about the site and their experience. Many of the findings from this early study confirmed the top interface design heuristics as defined by Nielsen including the need for visibility of system status, match between the system and the real world, error prevention, and recognition rather than recall (Nielsen, 1994).

In addition to observing recognized usability principles, the MyUW study showed that portal interface designers should better describe the purpose of customizations and the benefits to users. By default the MyUW interface has many of the frequently used services at the top of the user's (student, faculty/staff, teaching, alumni) page. Since it was released, the MyUW team has discovered that very few users customize the content or layout of their pages. Of the "73,000 individuals who use MyUW weekly, roughly five percent personalize [content] and approximately ten percent change their preferences [look and feel]" (Jensen, 2003).

No studies have been done locally to flesh out this issue–possibly users don't see or understand the "Personalize Content" and "Preferences" links or they don't want to customize an interface that already has every-thing they need (even if it means navigating inefficient paths to informa-tion they want). Jakob Nielsen suggests that "web personalization is much over-rated and mainly used as a poor excuse for not designing a navigable website" (Nielsen, 1998). Understanding exactly why users choose to customize a portal (or not) is an area for further investigation.

CONCLUSION

Usability testing is now an accepted practice of Web site design in the contemporary academic library, and will increase in importance and use with the continued expansion of the virtual library. Usability testing is also essential in the toolkit of assessment methods and is part of that it-erative process of working directly with our users to provide the support and resources they need for their work. It can help designers and others not only to identify what doesn't work well from the user perspective but also to provide input on what would be most useful and important to potential users. Libraries will be faced with many choices on how to make available and customize library portals. Usability testing will help them make informed decisions that address customer needs.

REFERENCES

Barnum, Carol. *Usability Testing and Research*. New York: Longman, 2002. 428 pages.

Boss, Richard. "How to Plan and Implement a Library Portal," *Library Technology Reports*, 38 (6), November/December 2002, 1-61.

Campbell, Nicole (editor). *Usability Assessment of Library-Related Web Sites: Methods and Case Studies*. LITA Guide #7. Chicago: American Library Association, 2001. 125 pages.

Covey, Denise. *Usage and Usability Assessment: Library Practices and Concerns*. Washington D.C.: Digital Library Federation and Council on Library and Information Resources, January 2002. 93 pages.

Ghaphery, James. "My Library at Virginia Commonwealth University: Third Year Evaluation," *D-Lib Magazine*, 8 (7/8), July/August 2002, DOI: 10.1045/july2002-ghaphery.

Ghaperhy, Jimmy and Ream, D. "VCU's My Library: Librarians Love It. . . . Users? Well, Maybe," *Information Technology and Libraries*, 19 (4), December 2000, 186-191.

Gibbons, Susan. "Building Upon the MyLibrary Concept to Better Meet the Information Needs of College Students," *D-Lib Magazine*, 9 (3), March 2003, DOI: 10.1045/march2003-gibbons.

ISO 9241-11. *Ergonomic Requirements for Office Work with Visual Display Terminals (VDT's)–Part 11: Guidance on Usability.* London: International Standards Organization. 1998.

Jensen, Ellen. "Re: Customizations in myuw," 19 November 2003, personal e-mail (Nov. 24, 2003).

Jordan, William. "My Gateway at the University of Washington Libraries," *Information Technology and Libraries,* 19 (4) December 2000, 180-5.

Ketchell, Debra. "Too Many Channels: Making Sense out of Portals and Personalization," *Information Technology and Libraries,* 19 (4), December 2000, 175-79.

Morgan, Keith and Reade, T. "Pioneering Portals: MyLibrary@NC State," *Information Technology and Libraries,* 19 (4), December 2000, 191-198.

Nielsen, Jakob (1998). "Personalization is Over-Rated," *Alertbox* (Oct. 4, 1998). Accessed November 7, 2003, http://www.useit.com/alertbox/981004.html.

Nielsen, Jakob (1997). "Search and You *May* Find," *Alertbox* (July 15, 1997). Accessed November 16, 2003, http://www.useit.com/alertbox/9707b.html.

Nielsen, Jakob (1994). "Ten Usability Heuristics." Accessed November 14, 2003, http://www.useit.com/papers/heuristic/heuristic_list.html.

Norlin, Elaina and CM! Winters. *Usability Testing for Library Web Sites: A Hands-On Guide.* Chicago: American Library Association, 2002, 69 pages.

Pace, Andrew. "Building and Optimizing Library Web Services," *Library Technology Reports,* 38 (2), March/April 2002, 1-87.

Rubin, Jeffrey. *Handbook of Usability Testing: How to Plan, Design and Conduct Effective Tests.* New York: John Wiley & Sons, 1994, 330 pages.

Stoffle, Carla, Renaud, R. and Veldof, J. (1996). "Choosing our futures," *College and Research Libraries,* 57 (3), pages 213-225.

University Libraries, University of Washington (2001). "Autumn 2001 Survey Questions," November, 2001. Accessed November 18, 2003. http://www.lib.washington.edu/usability/aut-01/autumnsurvey.html.

University Libraries, University of Washington (2002). "By Subjects Usability Study: User Summaries," November, 2002. Accessed November 19, 2003. http://www.lib.washington.edu/usability/by-subj/bysubjectusers.html.

University Libraries, University of Washington (2003). Within the next few months this survey will be made available on the Libraries' Usability Web site. In the meantime, please contact jlward1@u.washington.edu for copies.

Van House, Nancy, Butler, M., Ogle V., and Schiff, L. "User-Centered Iterative Design for Digital Libraries," *D-Lib Magazine,* February 1996. Accessed November 17, 2003. http://www.dlib.org/dlib/february96/02vanhouse.html.

Chapter 10

Environmentalist Approaches to Portals and Course Management Systems

Alison E. Regan
Sheldon Walcher

SUMMARY. This chapter examines some of the forces, history, and language that have contributed to the current state of affairs in online learning and online library instruction. It argues that approaches to online learning should focus on making portals interactive domains where people and information can be brought together to commingle in productive ways. *[Article copies available for a fee from The Haworth Document Delivery Service: 1-800-HAWORTH. E-mail address: <docdelivery@haworthpress.com> Website: <http://www.HaworthPress.com> © 2005 by The Haworth Press, Inc. All rights reserved.]*

KEYWORDS. Electronic learning environments, course management systems, library instruction, portal, online learning

Alison E. Regan is Faculty Outreach Fellow and Interim Director of the Marriott Library Technology Assisted Curriculum Center (E-mail: alison.regan@library.utah.edu); and Sheldon Walcher is Scholars Portal Project Teaching Assistant, both at the University of Utah, 295 South 1500 East, Salt Lake City, UT 84112-0860.

[Haworth co-indexing entry note]: "Environmentalist Approaches to Portals and Course Management Systems." Regan, Alison E., and Sheldon Walcher. Co-published simultaneously in *Journal of Library Administration* (The Haworth Information Press, an imprint of The Haworth Press, Inc.) Vol. 43, No. 1/2, 2005, pp. 173-188; and: *Portals and Libraries* (ed: Sarah C. Michalak) The Haworth Information Press, an imprint of The Haworth Press, Inc., 2005, pp. 173-188. Single or multiple copies of this article are available for a fee from The Haworth Document Delivery Service [1-800-HAWORTH, 9:00 a.m. - 5:00 p.m. (EST). E-mail address: docdelivery@haworthpress.com].

Available online at http://www.haworthpress.com/web/JLA
© 2005 by The Haworth Press, Inc. All rights reserved.
Digital Object Identifier: 10.1300/J111v43n01_11

In fall 2003, the University of Utah embarked on the first phase of co-ordinated efforts to bring Scholars Portal technology to our student and faculty patrons. The J. Willard Marriot Library Technology Assisted Curriculum Center (TACC), a service center focused on helping faculty, teaching assistants, and teaching fellows to integrate technology into instruction, is working closely with a larger team from Instruction, General Reference, and Technical Services in order to plan for patron training and course integration. First, an acknowledgment: it is an occupational hazard for those involved in technology projects to underestimate the time involved in development, installation, user testing, and institutional dissemination, and we are no exception. We had hoped to be further along in our portal use and evaluation by this date, but we are still developing interfaces and testing the product with patrons and librarians. Yet while the Scholars Portal technology is both new and a work-in-progress, the general effort is not: our charge is to ensure that library resources are available in all university instruction–especially computer-mediated instruction.

It is a commonplace among library professionals that the academic library should play an integral role in all aspects of university life, but unfortunately library resources are not always a central concern for faculty, departments, and administrators as they move all or part of their courses online. TACC staff members, for example, spend a great deal of time advising instructors who ask such questions as "How do I put my course materials on the Web?" "Is it possible to add a voiceover to my PowerPoint lectures?" "Can these VHS tapes be converted into streamed media?" and "Can I post a grade spreadsheet in WebCT?" but we get few queries about library resources beyond whom to contact for online reserves or the finer points of the Technology, Education and Copyright Harmonization (TEACH) Act. Here, as elsewhere, fully online course offerings are growing steadily and blended offerings are growing by leaps and bounds–often with too little collaboration, input, or support from library professionals.

It is easy to fault instructors for this, but our own experiences as members of the teaching staff at four different ARL institutions make us sympathetic to the instructor experience. Just as libraries have been scrambling to adjust to changes in technology, information-seeking behaviors, and patron expectations, instructors have been forced to meet student expectations in new ways. Instructors must attend to usual concerns about reading lists, syllabi and students, and at the same time learn to post those lists and syllabi online and make arrangements to share lectures and communicate with students electronically. The academic library remains important, but commands attention chiefly when the difficulty of accessing its resources is perceived to have a negative impact on student learning or faculty research.

Faculty become concerned, for example, when they find that students are citing sources based on their ease of retrieval rather than relevance, but they are not especially interested in learning about IP addresses, proxy servers, or virtual private networks unless failure to do so interferes with work in the classroom. Thus, even as our own and other academic libraries have sought to creatively redefine their function and practices in the wake of dramatic changes in information technology, these efforts have sometimes gone unnoticed by the faculty. And, while academic units increasingly turn to digital learning environments and online resources to compliment and even supplant traditional methods of instruction and research, there ironically appears to be a widening gap between the ways that library professionals and students conceive of and use information resources.

Clearly we need to educate faculty and others who are involved in course design, development, and delivery about library resources so that they will help make those resources available to students and encourage students to use them. Fortunately the 60% of our students and instructors (more than 16,000 patrons) who now use WebCT or home-grown courseware each semester provide a captive audience and an opportunity for us to advertise the resources of our research libraries. Integrating portal technology is an extension of this effort–one more way to make the move from coursework to research recursive, interactive, and as seamless as possible.

Yet it would be a mistake to assume that the challenge facing those seeking to integrate library resources more fully into digital instruction is entirely a matter of outreach or communication: on the contrary, as academic departments, administrators, and library professionals have begun to engage issues of access and instruction in library resources for students working online, it has become apparent that myriad structural, bureaucratic, philosophical, and pedagogical issues must be addressed along the way. Indeed, one of the chief concerns of all of us involved in the development of new information resources and research technology is why–despite our best efforts to educate various stakeholders about the usefulness and accessibility of such materials–so many of our online students still decline to use the resources that are already available to them. That is, before addressing issues of portal design and the impact future technology may have on online instruction and research, it is necessary to re-examine some of the forces, history, and language that have contributed to this current state of affairs in online library instruction. Indeed, we contend that it is only by first understanding the unique conditions that have contributed to the positioning, status, and conceptualization of online instruction that we can begin to seriously address the underlying causes for this disconnect between outreach and use. Our hope is then to suggest several ways these issues might be reframed–theoretically and practically–in considering the advent of portal technology and the future of online library instruction and research.

REAL ESTATE:
PHYSICAL AND VIRTUAL

Although the Internet is supposed to break down geographic boundaries, one reason for the relative lack of coursework-focused attention to library resources here and elsewhere may be blamed on campus real estate: historically, at most universities, distance education–and now online or hybrid education and the administration of course management systems–has been the business of extension programs. Rarely have extension programs–the poor step-children of regular instruction–been centrally located on campuses. Relegated to the university Annex or its equivalent, these programs are often open-admissions, and they offer instruction in off-hours (evenings and weekends) and in non-traditional modes (self-study, telecourse, and online). Given that they are often faced with the mandate to be self-supporting and are almost always staffed by part-time and adjunct instructors, it is no wonder that they have failed to avail themselves of or demand the support from all campus resources, including the library.

Internet-based education has blurred longstanding distinctions between "distance" and traditional education. While many institutions are still focusing efforts on tailoring digital resources specifically in support of distance learning, the fact is that soon it may not matter where a student is when accessing library material: our "distance" student may just as well be working from a terminal or wireless connection in our buildings as from a remote site. Interestingly, just as students' location has become less relevant, we have found that physical proximity to the library is important for faculty, course-designers, and distance learning specialists. We find that face-to-face, hands-on training works best, because it provides opportunities for more extensive demonstration of available resources, and allows time for demonstration of current trends in individual disciplines. Here at the University of Utah, the management of credit-bearing, online instruction as well as the growing number of hybrid classes was moved from the Academic Outreach and Continuing Education into TACC, and TACC was located in a designated division of the main library. In addition to computer professionals and WebCT trainers, TACC is staffed by librarians and experienced university instructors. As a result, concerns of pedagogy, library instruction and public services support may more easily be addressed in tandem with administrative and technical concerns.

COURSE-WARE INVOLVEMENT

It is tempting to assign blame for lack of attention to library resources in online and hybrid education on limitations of courseware such as WebCT and Blackboard. David Cohen, Dean of Libraries at the College of Charleston and Chair of the Academic Library Advisory Committee of the Council on Library and Information Resources, for example, argues that such courseware should be fully integrated "with the educational computing applications of the institutional library."[1] We agree in principle, but until libraries and vendors agree on clear standards for library homepages, catalogs, database subscriptions, virtual reference desk software, electronic reserves, and circulation departments, it may be unreasonable to expect off-the-shelf programs to plug into individual institutions' library resources.

The fact is that programs like WebCT and Blackboard are best described as empty shells waiting to be filled: first with content, learning resources, and research tools–and then with instructors and students. At present, we may no more expect such programs to deliver library materials than we would expect a word processor to magically produce readable prose.

How then can we ensure that our own institution's resources are easily accessible? How can we leverage our institutional capital? Our libraries constitute one of most important differences between our institution and many competing education "providers"; institutions like the University of Phoenix, Capella University, and the Western Governors University deliver courses and academic programs, but they have no libraries of their own. Unless we ensure patron access, however, institutional differences that appear great to us may seem small to students as well as to the legislature that provides our funding.

Just a few years ago it seemed that every issue of the *Chronicle of Higher Education* reported on one or another company that promised, with great excitement, to deliver enough materials to students to render physical libraries and their online components obsolete.[2] The predictions, of course, proved wrong or premature: along with many dot-coms, most of those firms failed to thrive. Yet even if the threat of being outsourced was greatly overstated, the numbers make the point: the total library materials expenditures divided by total students at all ARL institutions for 2002 was $481 (our own institution spent $401). If we do not make those expenditures available for patron use we will have a difficult time justifying continuing acquisitions and subscriptions.[3] It falls, then, on the shoulders of our already beleaguered technical services librarians, IT professionals, instructional designers and any one else involved in the back-end functions of courseware and libraries to ensure that the technical and organizational infrastructure exists to support campus integration of libraries and electronic learning environments.

For the last several years we have addressed this issue by engaging in what John D. Shank and Nancy H. Dewald call "Micro-Level Library Course-Ware Involvement"–that is, developing generic links and consulting with faculty to construct customized links in order to guarantee that library resources are available in all of the fully-online or hybrid (part online, part face-to-face) classes offered at the University.[4] Figures 1 and 2 illustrate our generic library links, which are part of the WebCT course templates used by the majority of our instructors.

Yet the creation and presentation of links to library resources within online courseware does not in itself ensure that students will make use of such resources. On the contrary, while such micro-level involvement is a necessary first step in giving access to those who might otherwise be unaware of their research options, without a clear sense of purpose or additional motivation, providing such links may often simply defer the difficult issue of developing a pedagogy for library instruction online. That is, providing such links–while perhaps reassuring teachers and administrators that online students have increased access to library resources–does nothing to teach students how to use or the value of such materials. Indeed, the logic of the hyper-link is that it can be used or not, depending on the momentary curiosity of the user. Without providing a broader context and rationale for using such resources–and as we will suggest, this context and rationale must emerge from the architecture of the portal itself–such linking is at best a flanking maneuver.

FIGURE 1. Course Home Page Template

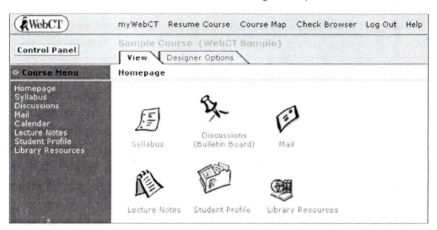

THE FUNCTION OF METAPHOR:
COURSE MANAGEMENT
vs. ELECTRONIC LEARNING ENVIRONMENTS

Thus far we have been using the generic term "courseware"–education software designed for classroom use–for programs that are now almost universally referred to as "course management systems" (CMS) but that are less often known by the competing term "electronic learning environments" (ELE). The differences between the two noun phrases are worth considering, because they shed light on the human conceptual architecture driving both the development and use of such educational software. Here we are engaging the work of University of California linguist George Lakoff, whose scholarship calls for a recognition that metaphor organizes our thoughts and shapes our judgment, and thus is not only a matter of language, but also of cognition.[5]

Lakoff's central thesis is that metaphors facilitate and organize thought by providing an experiential framework in which new concepts may be accommodated. For example, while some might see a term such as "cash flow" as a relatively neutral description of a monetary process, Lakoff contends that such phrases work and have linguistic currency because they fit into and perpetuate a cognitive framework in which "money is water." Indeed, to see how powerful such a metaphor can be

FIGURE 2. Library Resources Template

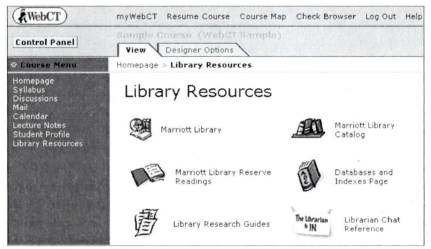

in influencing the way we come to conceive the world, consider these other common financial expressions: "liquid assets"; "the money dried up"; "He/she is just sponging off of you"; "They are solvent/insolvent"; "Don't pour your money down the drain"; "frozen assets"; "Keep your head above water"; "get in over your head"; "stay afloat"; etc.

The network of metaphors that underlie thought in this way form cognitive maps or frames that serve to focus and limit the way we come to conceptualize new experiences, as well as guide our behavior in relation to the external world. And while there is nothing inherently good or bad in any given cognitive framework–indeed, we cannot help but think in conceptual metaphors–the danger is that we are often unaware of the ways such frameworks influence our thoughts and actions. That is, we begin to forget that such conceptual metaphors are constructs, which carry and can perform a wide range of social, political, and cultural functions. They begin to seem natural to us, and in so doing, serve ideological functions that can remain unquestioned and uncontested.

Even for those who may not wholly subscribe to Lakoff's contention that conceptual metaphors serve to frame and filter our experiences of the world, the fact that two competing phrases have emerged to describe the function of this kind of "courseware" at least suggests that there remains some disagreement over the pedagogical role and value of such software. Indeed, on a purely definitional level, the components of the term "course management software" seems to limit our focus to: (1) a single course, rather than an entire educational system or plan of study; (2) the administrative aspects of teaching, with its attendant supervisory and evaluative functions; and (3) the needs and wishes of teachers or course designers, rather than the experience of students. In contrast, the phrase "electronic learning environment," which is more open ended (some might argue less clear), focuses attention both on individual students and a class as a whole.

On a deeper level, the latter phrase suggests something about an aggregate of technological, intellectual, social and scholarly conditions that contribute to the educational process. An "environment"–with its simultaneous suggestion of organic, artistic and architectural relationships–invokes notions of inclusiveness, community, development, connection and change. On a metaphoric level, then, "learning environments" are spaces that both demarcate and presumably promote an exchange between participants. They are places one enters, becomes enmeshed in, and through which one has a range of experiences that often transcend the original aims of their designers.

In contrast, "management software"–with its suggestion of instrumentality and commodification–invokes notions of functionality, aim, and limit. If an environment is a messy place you enter to have unexpected experiences, "management software" is a tool that can be wielded, an instrument that promises control, predictability, and reproducibility. Software is a mechanism to an end, and in this case, the goal is largely bureaucratic and conservative. Indeed, it is precisely when software becomes messy and unpredictable that we say it no longer performs its function.

Of course, on a conceptual level these disparate ways of imagining online learning have important implications for the development and use of library resources, particularly in regards to something that is envisioned and marketed as a *portal*. Sidestepping the problem of how exactly to define this inherently ambiguous notion (and it is important to note the degree to which most of the current literature on portals wrestles precisely with defining the term), on a metaphoric level, it is clear that a "portal" has a distinctly different cognitive relationship to the notion of "tools" than it does to that of a "space." Or perhaps it would be more accurate to say that the problems associated with defining what a portal is and does are closely related to these competing if largely under-theorized ways of imagining online education. Instrumental approaches to courseware–currently the dominant mode of approaching questions of online learning–tend to see portals largely as control panels, collections of tools selected and grouped according to function. In such articulations, library resources become a series of tools that users can select and manipulate according to need or interest. Figure 3, which provides an example of what a student might retrieve from Online Reserves from within both WebCT and the Scholars Portal, illustrates what this might look like.

"Environmental" approaches to online learning, in contrast, see portals largely in terms of their architectural metaphor, not only bridges or passageways between different spaces, but as interactive domains in themselves, places where people and information can be brought together to commingle in productive, and perhaps more importantly, unplanned ways.

Thus, we see that this disconnect between the development of new information resources and their widespread implementation and use within online learning environments is multilayered and complex. Because many programs for online instruction emerged from distance education programs–and are still housed in remote locations on many campuses–it often remains difficult for developers, information specialists and educators to meet to discuss the needs and concerns of their stakeholders. And while basic issues of access to library resources are beginning to be addressed within online and hybrid courses (largely

FIGURE 3. Online Reserves

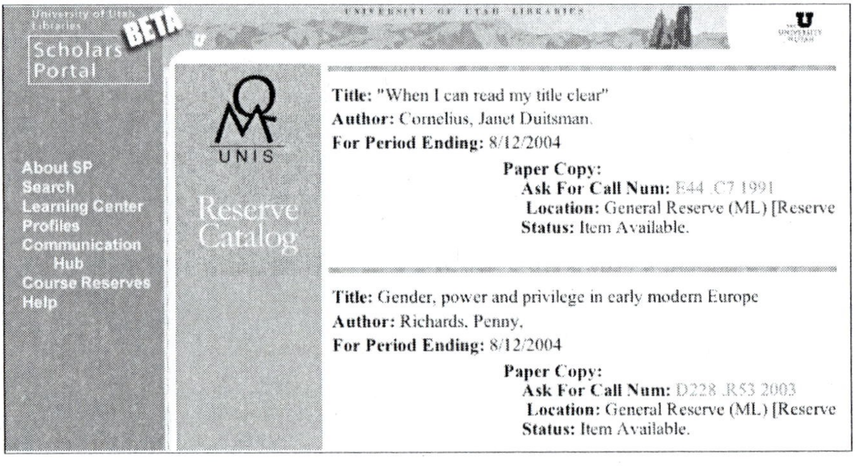

through micro-level implementation strategies), such moves remain ineffective, in part because the logic underlying much of online learning remains constrained within a metaphoric discourse of functionality and consumption, regularization and control.

ENVIRONMENTALIST APPROACHES TO LIBRARY PORTALS

All of which begs the question: what would an Environmentalist approach to Library Portals actually entail? In addition to the standard technical and systems concerns about search returns, it would almost certainly focus on providing opportunities for scholarly communication while supporting inquiry-based learning practices in ways that simply do not yet exist. Indeed, though the results of our involvement with the Scholars Portal Project will not be available for some time, the process itself has been quite suggestive, and has already yielded some provocative ideas about the future of online research and instruction.

As previously noted, in many respects the Technology Assisted Curriculum Center at the University of Utah is quite different from other units supporting–and approaches to–online education. Housed within the Marriott Library, the center is staffed by roughly equal numbers of librarians, technology specialists, and teachers. This blending of bibliographic, technical, and pedagogical expertise has meant that issues of research and online access to scholarly resources have never been understood solely in functional terms. That is, as educators, our first priority is always how new technology might better enhance the learning experiences of our students. Thus, while it is tempting to become invested in challenging back-end issues of database architecture and information delivery ambitious projects such as the Scholars Portal necessarily engender, of greater concern are questions of design, pedagogy, and use.

Though much of the financial and institutional impetus to develop new tools for online research is driven by technological innovations in information retrieval and delivery systems–guided jointly by market considerations and the priorities of system administrators and librarians–often little attention is given to the needs of end-users: the teachers and students who will ultimately work and learn with such systems. Even with the Scholars Portal Project, the focus of much of the design and development phase has been driven by technology concerns. As private sector database and networking programmers negotiate with librarians about issues of reliability, functionality and the integrity of search results, and administrators and academic units debate issues of implementation and access to the finished product, consideration of the needs and interests of students gets deferred, often to the point where if those needs and interests are registered at all, they are registered only within the context of usability testing of a nearly complete system.

Because of our somewhat unique institutional positioning, the question we asked ourselves at TACC at the outset of our involvement with the Scholars Portal Project was quite simple: how might such a portal facilitate and even enhance the research and learning experiences of our online students? Though this may strike some as a rather banal place to begin, posing such a question immediately forced our team to confront several related but distinct issues:

- The difficulty of teaching some students the advantages of using academic/scholarly/professional sources in their work, as opposed to more familiar tools and sources already available on the World Wide Web;
- The lack of quality online materials/tutorials that stress research as an inquiry-driven, dynamic process (as opposed to merely a method of obtaining facts or data);
- The impersonal and largely non-interactive design of most scholarly and professional database interfaces currently available;
- The overwhelming number of academic and scholarly resources already offered through our libraries, and the intimidation this causes less-experienced users who may not know where to begin sorting through the dizzying array of options already provided.

As we debated these issues, what emerged was a vision not merely of how to integrate the Scholars Portal interface into a pre-existing learning environment, but the creation of an entirely new space, one that was not only user-friendly, dynamic and engaging, but that might reframe the nature of the research process in the minds of our students. That is, we began to envision a true "scholarly environment"–an interface and resource center that not only would aid more experienced researchers in locating quality materials quickly and efficiently, but also would encourage students to explore and test their ideas within wider academic, scholarly, and social contexts. To this end, we have proposed three new features to the working group at the national level.

First, the creation of a "Scholarly Communication Hub" modeled in part on the outstanding work done by H-Net, a project developed initially by Matrix: The Center for Humane Arts, Letters, and Social Sciences Online at Michigan State University.[6]

Within the context of Scholars Portal, such a hub would provide an invaluable means by which students and teachers across classes and campuses could network and share information on a wide range of topics, providing both a forum and a model of scholarly communication and research (see Figure 4). Indeed, ongoing work in Rhetoric and Composition Studies has explored the usefulness of emerging digital genres–including Web logs, subject-specific discussion posts, and the design and analysis of Web pages–in the teaching of research writing and critical thinking. If one of the shared goals of information literacy instruction and writing pedagogy is cultivating in students an awareness of how knowledge production and dissemination are shaped by their contexts of use, then such a tool would certainly offer exciting possibilities for students and teachers to examine such processes in action. Password-protected course-management systems provide spaces for bounded learning communities–those that are defined by topic, course, or semester. A communication hub would support such communities and at its best it might support unbounded learning communities–those defined by interest and expertise, rather than course-requirements.

FIGURE 4. Communication Hub

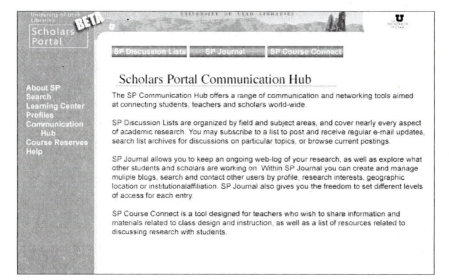

Scholars Portal Communication Hub

The SP Communication Hub offers a range of communication and networking tools aimed at connecting students, teachers and scholars world-wide.

SP Discussion Lists are organized by field and subject areas, and cover nearly every aspect of academic research. You may subscribe to a list to post and receive regular e-mail updates, search list archives for discussions on particular topics, or browse current postings.

SP Journal allows you to keep an ongoing web-log of your research, as well as explore what other students and scholars are working on. Within SP Journal you can create and manage mulipe blogs, search and contact other users by profile, research interests, geographic location or institutionalaffiliation. SP Journal also gives you the freedom to set different levels of access for each entry.

SP Course Connect is a tool designed for teachers who wish to share information and materials related to class design and instruction, as well as a list of resources related to discussing research with students.

Second, the development of an "Inquiry Driven Search Module/Tutorial," which would present a radically different sort of search interface than those currently supported in scholarly databases, one which we hope would provide a range of more intuitive and interactive options for users. Some possible features of such an interface include:

- The use of advanced Natural Language Processing. Unlike commercial sites (such as "ask Jeeves"), such an interface would use the structure of questions to organize and prioritize searching. For example, the module might distinguish between definitional questions such as "What is . . . " and analytical questions such as "Why is . . . ?" and direct patrons to different kinds of database collections.
- "Virtual Stacks" that would allow students to visually browse other titles "shelved" in the same general area as a particular hit or subject.
- A "Patrons Who Viewed This Item Also Viewed" feature similar to the ones used on commercial sites (such as amazon.com) that allows users to get a sense of how other researchers may or may not be associating certain materials.
- An "Other Possible Topics" palette that would offer suggestions of alternate search terms generated through a thesaurus function.
- A "Topic Suggestor" that would provide a boxed set of randomly selected (or parameter determined) subjects that students could choose from, as well as suggestions about how they might get started on such a topic.
- A "Most Popular Searches of the Day/Week/Month" listing that would help patrons get a sense of what other people are researching.

Third, the creation of a "Scholars Portal Dynamic Profiler" that would incorporate instruction on the options and tools available to researchers within the system, while allowing users to create, edit and manage their profiles (see Figures 5 and 6). That is, while the term "profile" is currently used generically to designate a set of selected databases in discussions of the Scholars Portal, one of the central concepts behind the Dynamic Profiler would be to broaden this definition to include a whole range of user preferences that would encompass selected databases, but might also involve such things as preferred delivery options (such as citational format, means and frequency of notification, subject/topic preferences, prioritizing media types, etc.). That is, one of

FIGURE 5. Profiler Creation Page 1

Create a name for your profile–remember, you can maintain multiple profiles in your account, so make it specific enough to distinguish from other profiles.

Profile Name:

(Insert Profile Name Here)

You can create different types of profiles in zPortal to do different sorts of things–from searching databases, participating in online discussion forums, or receiving email notices whenever new material is published on a specific topics or within a set of journals. If you aren't sure yet what sort of profile you want to set up, select "General." Remember, you can always go back and edit your profile at any time.

Profile type:

o *General Searching*
o *Research Forums*
o *Scholarly Updates*

Continue to Step 2   Save & Finish Later

FIGURE 6. Profiler Creation Page 2

ZPortal is composed of over one hundred scholarly and professional databases, with a combined holding in the tens of millions of items! Although this makes ZPortal one of the most comprehensive research tools ever created, the sheer number of choices can be overwhelming, particularly for new users. To help you get started, zPortal has created a number of "database sets" geared toward particular fields and areas of research.

From the following list, choose the fields that seem most relevant to your research interests for this profile–so if you aren't sure yet which areas you will want to search, select "General Searching" and continue to Step 3.

Remember, this is designed merely to help you get started. You will be able to add, edit, or delete specific databases in the next step.

☐ Aerospace Studies	☐ Ethnic Studies	☐ Middle East Studies
☐ Anthropology	☐ Exercise & Sport Science	☐ Military Science
☐ Architecture	☐ Family and Consumer Studies	☐ Mining Engineering
☐ Art and Art History	☐ Film Studies	☐ Modern Dance
☐ Asian Studies	☐ Foods and Nutrition	☐ Music
☐ Ballet	☐ French	☐ Naval Science
☐ Biology	☐ Gender Studies	☐ Parks, Recreation & Tourism
☐ Business	☐ Geography	☐ Philosophy
☐ Chemical & Fuels Engineering	☐ Geology & Geophysics	☐ Physical Therapy
☐ Chemistry	☐ German	☐ Physics
☐ Civil & Environmental Engineering	☐ Health Promotion and Education	☐ Political Science
☐ Classics	☐ History	☐ Psychology
☐ Communication	☐ Italian	☐ Russian & Slavic Languages
☐ Communication Science & Disorders	☐ Latin America and Caribbean	☐ Social Work
☐ Computer Science	☐ Lesbian, Gay, Bisexual, and	☐ Sociology
☐ Economics	Transgender Studies	☐ Spanish
☐ Education	☐ Linguistics	☐ Special Education
☐ Electrical & Computer Engineering	☐ Materials Science & Engineering	☐ Theatre
☐ English	☐ Mathematics	☐ Women's Studies
☐ Environmental Studies	☐ Mechanical Engineering	☐ World History
	☐ Metallurgical Engineering	

the greatest impediments in getting students to use library resources that we already own is the sheer volume of database options and choices. Thus, in addition to a more user-friendly interface, the Profiler would provide needed structure and guidance to users in customizing their searching in ways completely unavailable to students at the present time.

CONCLUSION

The advent of library portals offers librarians, teachers, and instructional designers opportunities to redefine bibliographic instruction and support and to think creatively about what portals and courseware can and should do, issues of underlying architecture and back-end information structures must be addressed, we cannot allow those concerns to overshadow larger pedagogical questions. New technologies provide us with opportunities to rethink the relationships between the library and patrons and between patrons themselves, but it is up to us to demand that they be used to create the most dynamic and robust higher education learning environments possible.

NOTES

1. David Cohen, "Course-Management Software: Where's the Library?" *Educause*, May/June 2002, 12-13.

2. See, for example, coverage of Questia Media America, Inc., the for-profit library that raised over 130 million dollars in venture capital in early 2000, but which went from 300 to a handful of employees within three years.

3. ARL Statistics at the University of Virginia Library. Accessed August 26, 2003 at http://fisher.lib.virginia.edu/arl/index.html.

4. John D. Shank and Nancy H. Dewald, "Establishing Our Presence in Courseware: Adding Library Services to the Virtual Classroom," *Information Technology and Libraries*, March 2003, 38-43.

5. Lakoff, George and Matt Johnson. "Conceptual Metaphor in Everyday Language," *Journal of Philosophy*, August 1980, 453-486.

6. H-Net: Humanities and Social Sciences Online. Accessed March 22, 2004 at http://www.h-net.org/.

Chapter 11

The Association of Research Libraries ARL Scholars Portal Working Group Final Report, May 2002

ARL Scholars Portal Working Group

SUMMARY. The ARL Scholars Portal Working Group was established in 2000 to advance the concept of a collective research library presence on the Web. On 1 May 2002, there was a public news release that a Scholars Portal Project was being launched by several ARL mem-

Original members of the Scholars Portal Working Group are Jerry Campbell, University of Southern California (Chair); Ken Frazier, University of Wisconsin-Madison; Olivia Madison, Iowa State University; Sarah Michalak, University of Utah; Sarah Pritchard, University of California, Santa Barbara; Brian Schottlaender, University of California, San Diego; Carla Stoffle, University of Arizona; and Sarah Thomas, Cornell University. Fred Heath, Texas A&M University; Richard Lucier, Dartmouth College; Sherrie Schmidt, Arizona State University; Julie Wessling, Colorado State University; Paul Willis, University of Kentucky; and Jerome Yavarkovsky, Boston College, joined the group in 2001 and 2002. Jaia Barrett served as ARL staff liaison, and Mary Jackson and Rick Johnson served as technical advisors. Throughout, the deliberations of the working group have benefited enormously from input received from various ARL colleagues, including, collectively, those on the ARL Access to Information Resources Committee.

[Haworth co-indexing entry note]: "The Association of Research Libraries ARL Scholars Portal Working Group Final Report, May 2002." ARL Scholars Portal Working Group. Co-published simultaneously in *Journal of Library Administration* (The Haworth Information Press, an imprint of The Haworth Press, Inc.) Vol. 43, No. 1/2, 2005, pp. 189-204; and: *Portals and Libraries* (ed: Sarah C. Michalak) The Haworth Information Press, an imprint of The Haworth Press, Inc., 2005, pp. 189-204. Single or multiple copies of this article are available for a fee from The Haworth Document Delivery Service [1-800-HAWORTH, 9:00 a.m. - 5:00 p.m. (EST). E-mail address: docdelivery@haworthpress.com].

Available online at http://www.haworthpress.com/web/JLA
Digital Object Identifier: 10.1300/J111v43n01_12

ber libraries (a subset of the working group) in collaboration with ARL and Fretwell-Downing, Inc. (FD). This report summarizes the work of the Scholars Portal Working Group from its inception, including the group's sense of key portal features and functionality. The report concludes with a recommendation to the ARL Board to discharge the Scholars Portal Working Group and replace it with a new ARL Working Group on Portal Applications. *[Article copies available for a fee from The Haworth Document Delivery Service: 1-800-HAWORTH. E-mail address: <docdelivery@haworthpress.com> Website: <http://www.HaworthPress.com>]*

KEYWORDS. Library.org, super discovery tool, Scholars Portal, Association of Research Libraries, Fretwell-Downing, Inc.

PREFACE

The following is not a formal chapter as are the other contributions to *Portals and Libraries*. It is the final report of an Association of Research Libraries working group and as a report it bears the characteristics of a committee-produced document.[1] There are informalities in the composition and some concepts are reiterated as the writer chronicles the events in the life of the project. The chronology begins in 1999 at the birth of the idea–"library.org"–and concludes almost three years later when the concept and project had been fully developed and implementation was about to begin. The report is valuable for two reasons. First, it communicates the time and circumstances in which a pivotal new access services concept was developed for research libraries and collects a bibliography of the early literature of the Scholars Portal. Second, it presents an interesting view of how a group of people, distributed in time and place, but nevertheless working together, evolved a sophisticated, complex and visionary idea over a three-year period and brought it successfully to the point of implementation.

BACKGROUND

The Scholars Portal Working Group was established by ARL in 2000 to advance the concept of a collective research library presence on the Web. The concept was first identified at the 1999 ARL-OCLC Strategic Issues Forum in Keystone, Colorado. Participants at the Strategic Issues

Forum agreed that libraries were in danger of losing their constituencies to commercial information services in the Web environment and that the library Web presence was not generally accepted as the entry point to the larger range of Web resources. Participants concluded that it was necessary to increase the research library presence on the Web by advancing the concept of a "library.org."

Jerry Campbell, Chief Information Officer and Dean of University Libraries, University of Southern California, advanced that idea in a white paper he prepared for discussion by the ARL membership at their May 2000 meeting. Campbell's paper asked the ARL membership to consider what role the Association should play in portal development for the scholarly community.[2] He suggested that ARL seriously pursue the feasibility of developing a "library.org" Web presence. Campbell argued for a collaborative partnership approach, and asserted that research librarians are better qualified to create a Scholars Portal than anyone else is. Campbell was the first to articulate some of the key features and functionality of such a portal. He suggested that the portal should include high-quality content, be based on standards, search across multiple and disparate databases, offer a variety of supporting tools (e.g., authoring, personalized filtering, and resource management), offer enhanced supporting services such as digital reference, and integrate electronic thesauri. Campbell asserted that this portal would be "the place to start for anyone seeking academically sound information."

The general concept of a Scholars Portal and resources to be included in it were further developed and refined in discussions at the October 2000 ARL Membership Meeting, at which then-ARL President Ken Frazier convened an open forum of approximately 45 ARL member leaders to discuss the Campbell proposal for a Scholars Portal. The discussion highlighted a range of views around the following points: the relationship of a Scholars Portal to an online integrated catalog; the role of OCLC's Cooperative Online Resource Catalog (CORC); search software; the role of a portal in supporting interactive scholarly communities; the relationship between value, quality, and traffic; audience; research on the use and effectiveness of a portal; and how to get started.

The concept of a Scholars Portal was also raised in a paper by Sarah Thomas, presented at the November 2000 Library of Congress "Bicentennial Conference on Bibliographic Control."[3] Thomas built on Campbell's thesis in her article, and was one of the first to assert that the emphasis should be on the identification of many new resources of value to the scholar and researcher, rather than on the cataloging of only a few, relatively speaking, new items. She coined a new word: "portalog."

The initiative gained real momentum with the establishment of the ARL Scholars Portal Working Group in late 2000. There were two cornerstone principles that motivated the working group in its deliberations:

- First, that access to disparate electronic resources and services can be improved through integration, both within a single institution and across multiple institutions.
- Second, that efforts to effect such integration should leverage work already being carried out in ARL libraries.

NARROWING THE FOCUS TO A "SUPER DISCOVERY TOOL" AND DEFINING REQUIREMENTS

In early spring 2001, the working group met and confirmed that the ultimate goal was the development of a suite of scholarly productivity tools and services but that it was essential to define an initial first step toward this ambitious goal. The initial step was defined as the development of what Brian Schottlaender termed a "super discovery tool." This tool needs to search, aggregate, integrate, and deliver licensed and openly available digital content across a broad range of subject fields and from multiple institutions. Members of the working group agreed early on that it was not desirable for ARL to develop the tool itself, but to identify potential partners (commercial and otherwise) with whom to collaborate in the tool's development.

At that time, finding a way to describe in any detail what the working group meant by the concept of such a "super discovery tool" was not easy. It was approached in two ways. First, Sarah Pritchard prepared a user scenario that described the concept from the point of view of an undergraduate (Appendix A). This scenario went a long way toward bringing the concept to life for the Working Group and for others. In addition, the working group developed a list of key features, functionality, and categories of content that it felt were required or highly desirable for the "super discovery tool," as well as some other general features of a portal. That list, "Portal Features and Functionality: First Phase" (included at the end of this article as Appendix B), was used in the working group's environmental scan to identify potential partners.

The critical core features of the tool can be summarized as follows:

- First, the ability to query two distinct streams of electronic resources and databases:
  - "universal stream" of unrestricted resources (Web pages and searchable databases) from Web sites targeted for quality and academic relevance, and
  - "local stream" of information, access to which is restricted to local users by license or other agreement.
- Second, the ability to map a search against different types of metadata.

The list of "Portal Features and Functionality" was enhanced and refined during the several months of the environmental scan but has not been updated since June 2001. It is included here, however, as a record of the working group efforts that led to the launch of the Scholars Portal Project.

SCANNING THE ENVIRONMENT

In an effort to identify potential partners, the working group conducted an environmental scan that identified a wide range of companies and products described as "portals." Over 30 products were identified; some were reviewed and determined to be out of scope of the goals of the Scholars Portal because they organized internal records and/or searched only Web resources. The working group was looking for an organization or company that was ready and willing to engage in a collaborative project using extant software rather than an organization wanting to develop a product from scratch. As a result, several potential collaborators were not pursued because the working group felt that they were not in a position to work in a collaborative environment with research libraries or were demonstrating signs of being overextended in their current marketplace. Several companies and products were of sufficient interest to warrant additional research and working group contact with the company.

DEVELOPING A PROJECT PLAN
AND COMMUNICATION STRATEGY

In addition to the development of the questions regarding "Portal Features and Functionality" and the completion of the environmental

scan, a third activity of the working group during this period was the development of a project plan that considered options for: phases of the
project, how to develop the discovery tool, financial strategies (developmental and operational), market deployment (integrating the tool into
the work environment of the user), and key considerations to influence
working group decisions made about the development of the project.
The working group was also in the early stages of developing a communication strategy and process for integrating feedback about their work
back into their planning process.

REPORTING AT THE MAY 2001
ARL MEMBERSHIP MEETING

The Working Group's May 2001 report to the ARL membership included the "User Scenario for the ARL Scholars Portal" developed by
Sarah Pritchard and a recommendation for the construction of a suite of
Web-based services that will connect the higher education community
as directly as possible with high-quality information resources that contribute to the teaching and learning process and that advance research.[4]
The report emphasized that the working group's initial focus was on the
"single-search" discovery tool that enables a user to search across certain limited but diverse and distributed Web sites, library catalogs, and
databases of information resources to retrieve and integrate the results
in a single presentation.

At the May 2001 ARL Business Meeting, Brian Schottlaender summarized the activities of the working group and identified 10 organizations and companies that might be potential partners on this project.[5]
Schottlaender noted that it was not clear to the working group whether it
was either necessary or desirable that the group collaborate with only
one partner to the exclusion of others. He did stress that the working
group needed to balance the impetus to move ahead expeditiously with
the need to refine further the thinking about the "Portal Features and
Functionality" for the single-search discovery tool. The working group
agreed to continue to use the term "Scholars Portal" for convenience,
even though the phrase raised questions. Schottlaender also emphasized
that the initiative's larger objective remained the development of a full
suite of scholarly productivity tools, functioning with the "single-
search" discovery tool, to create a new academic platform for members
of the research and higher education communities.

IDENTIFYING A POTENTIAL PARTNER

The working group convened by conference call on 13 July 2001 to review the results of the environmental scan, using the list of "Portal Features and Functionality" as the basis for evaluating various companies and products. Reaffirming its strong desire to implement a project in fall of 2001, the working group reviewed the strengths and weaknesses of the several products, evaluated the readiness of the various vendors to engage in a project in the fall 2001, and agreed that working with one vendor in a project was preferred over working with two or more vendors or simply calling for competition in the marketplace. The working group also briefly discussed business models and explored options for establishing an operational project. At this time, the working group considered Phase One to be the planning efforts up to the point participants implement software, and Phase Two to be the implementation of the software. From that discussion, the group submitted its recommendations to the ARL Board of Directors.

DEFINING THE PROJECT

At its July 2001 meeting, the ARL Board of Directors reviewed the working group's recommendations to take the following steps:

1. Discuss a "collaborative exploration" with the preferred vendor to lead to a project funded entirely by the participating libraries.
2. Begin discussions with the preferred vendor about the details of a project, including financial requirements, timeline, expectations, and requirements of the participating libraries, with the goal of beginning a project in fall 2001. (The working group had not excluded the other vendors, but wanted to hold them in abeyance until they saw how the contract discussions unfolded with the first vendor.)
3. Assuming ARL and the preferred vendor reached agreement on the details of the project, ARL would enter into a formal agreement with the preferred vendor on behalf of the participating libraries.
4. Supported by funds from participating libraries, ARL would provide staff assistance to work with the participating libraries and preferred vendor. (The working group recommended that Mary Jackson serve as part-time project manager.)

5. Before the agreement was signed, ARL, the working group, and the preferred vendor would reach agreement on the evaluation criteria to be used to judge the success of the project.
6. At the end of the project, the participating libraries would evaluate the success of the project and recommend any next steps.

The ARL Board supported the Scholars Portal Working Group recommendations and specified that neither the working group nor the vendor should describe the project as a commitment on the part of other ARL libraries to use the product nor that this particular product carried an "ARL imprimatur." The Board also asked ARL staff to continue to monitor other vendor developments and library applications of search engines and resource integration software tools and to develop a set of "best practices" of the functionality and service options in various portal implementations.

REPORTING AT THE OCTOBER 2001 ARL MEMBERSHIP MEETING

Jerry Campbell gave an update report at the October 2001 ARL Membership Meeting.[6] He noted that the working group had identified a vendor whose existing products offered about 80 percent of what the working group thought was needed to deploy a discovery tool that offers a critical mass, if not all, of the working group's desired features and capabilities. He also noted that the vendor was interested in collaborating with the working group to build the other 20 percent of the desired features and that they were offering to contribute some of the development time needed to do so. At that time, ARL staff had begun negotiating a contract with the vendor. Campbell extended an invitation to other ARL member libraries to join as project participants.

ARL FORUM ON "COLLECTIONS & ACCESS FOR THE 21st-CENTURY SCHOLAR," OCTOBER 2001

Brian Schottlaender gave a presentation[7] at the ARL Forum on "Collections & Access for the 21st-Century Scholar" in October 2001 on the subject of post-resource discovery portal functionality. Schottlaender reiterated to forum attendees that development of the super discovery tool was only the initial focus of the working group's attention. Their larger ambition was the development of a full suite of scholarly productivity tools and services, of which the super discovery tool will be but one feature. Schottlaender identified at least five areas of scholarly activity in which post-discovery tools would be welcome, including: capture, integration, manipulation, distribution, and consultation.

REACHING AGREEMENT WITH FRETWELL-DOWNING, INC.

Contract negotiations were more protracted than either side expected. A press release was issued on 1 May 2002 announcing the launch of the Scholars Portal Project, a collaboration between several ARL member libraries and Fretwell-Downing, Inc. (FD).[8] Taking the advice of the ARL Board, the project participants made explicit in their arrangements with FD that ARL's collaboration with the ARL member libraries on this project is not an Association endorsement of FD products. The initial libraries participating in the project are the University of Southern California; University of California, San Diego; Dartmouth College; University of Arizona; Arizona State University; Iowa State University; and the University of Utah. Plans called for expanding the number of participating libraries over the course of the three-year project. Any ARL member library interested in joining the project was invited and encouraged to contact ARL's Mary Jackson.

Initially the Scholars Portal Project would use several FD products, including ZPORTAL, as a base to deliver cross-domain searching of licensed and openly available content in a range of subject fields and from multiple institutions. The portal will aggregate and integrate the results of the search, and support delivery of the content to the user. Future phases will add other services to the portal that improve user access to, and use of, information resources. For example, planned enhancements include integration of the searching tool within the local online learning environment for a course and linkage to a 24/7 digital reference service to consult with a reference librarian.

DISCHARGING THE SCHOLARS PORTAL WORKING GROUP AND ESTABLISHING A NEW WORKING GROUP

The project with Fretwell-Downing is not the only area that the working group has been tracking. However, because "Scholars Portal" as a label is now so closely connected to the Project, members of the working group recommend discharging the Scholars Portal Working Group and subdividing the ongoing work between two new groups. First, the Scholars Portal Working Group recommends establishing a new ARL working group that would carry on with a broad charge to monitor how libraries are integrating portal technology into their new academic platforms and to identify common issues or barriers to successful implementations. In addition, as part of the Scholars Portal Project, a Project Steering Committee has been established and includes a representative from each participating library to provide project policy oversight for the duration of the project. It is hoped that some Scholars Portal Project participants will also serve on the new working group and other libraries will join this new ARL effort to monitor activity broadly in this arena.

ARL's ONGOING AGENDA REGARDING PORTALS

The Scholars Portal Working Group expects that the Scholars Portal Project will demonstrate the viability of the Scholars Portal vision with one vendor's products. The libraries participating in the project sought and received ARL's ongoing involvement because they believe that this will spur all vendors–including but not limited to Fretwell-Downing–to work even harder to create or enhance products that serve the needs of research library communities. Even as the Scholars Portal Project is launched, other ARL members are working on similar projects with other vendors. At the same time, ARL staff continue to monitor portal software applications, will host a meeting on 14 June 2002 in Atlanta where librarians and vendors may come together to hear reports by librarians on their portal implementations, and will issue a call for vendors of portal products to establish a Developers Group. Essentially, ARL's involvement in the Scholars Portal Project and related activities is aimed to encourage multiple vendors to develop and enhance portal software tools that will serve well the constituencies of academic and research communities.

NOTES

1. ARL is a not-for-profit membership organization comprising the leading research libraries in North America. Its mission is to shape and influence forces affecting the future of research libraries in the process of scholarly communication. ARL programs and services promote equitable access to and effective use of recorded knowledge in support of teaching, research, scholarship, and community service.

The Association articulates the concerns of research libraries and their institutions, forges coalitions, influences information policy development, and supports innovation and improvements in research library operations. ARL operates as a forum for the exchange of ideas and as an agent for collective action. There are currently 123 members.

2. Jerry D. Campbell, "The Case for Creating a Scholars Portal to the Web: A White Paper," ARL: A Bimonthly Report on Research Library Issues and Actions from ARL, CNI, and SPARC, no. 211 (August 2000): 1–4, <http://www.arl.org/newsltr/211/portal. html>.

3. Sarah Thomas, "Abundance, Attention, and Access: Of Portals and Catalogs," ARL: A Bimonthly Report on Research Library Issues and Actions from ARL, CNI, and SPARC, no. 212 (October 2000): 1–3, <http://www.arl.org/newsltr/212/portal. html>.

4. "ARL Scholars Portal Working Group Report," Washington, D.C.: Association of Research Libraries, May 2001, <http://www.arl.org/access/scholarsportal/ may01rept.html>.

5. "Update to the ARL Members from the ARL Scholars Portal Working Group, ARL Business Meeting," (Presented at the ARL Membership Meeting, Washington, D.C., 24 May 2001), <http://www.arl.org/access/scholarsportal/update5_24_01.html>.

6. "Report from the Scholars Portal Working Group, ARL Business Meeting," Proceedings of the 139th Association of Research Libraries Membership Meeting, Washington, D.C.: Association of Research Libraries, 18 October 2001, <http://www.arl. org/arl/proceedings/139/portal.html>.

7. Brian E.C. Schottlaender, "The New Academic Platform: Beyond Resource Discovery," (Presented at the ARL forum on "Collections & Access for the 21st-Century Scholar: A Forum to Explore the Roles of the Research Library," Washington, D.C., 20 October 2001), <http://www.arl.org/forum/schottlaender/>.

8. "ARL Announces . . . Seven ARL Libraries Launch Scholars Portal Project in Collaboration with Fretwell-Downing, Inc.," Washington, D.C.: Association of Research Libraries, 1 May 2002, <http://www.arl.org/arl/pr/scholars_portal.html>.

APPENDIX A

User Scenario for the ARL Scholars Portal "Single Search" Option

A student is at her workstation at home on a holiday, and the library is closed. She logs on through her ISP and, since library orientation included information about the Scholars Portal, she already has the bullet/logo for it added to her own start page. She clicks into the SP search page and chooses the "single search" option, and types in a few keywords for her topic. (She could also have chosen a "restricted search" option, and limited it to full-text databases, to Web resources, or other options.)

The search comes back with results of many kinds all on that topic. She sees them grouped by type of resource: books from her own library's OPAC, books from other library OPACs, individual journal article citations from databases her library licenses (some with links to full text), full-text articles and documents from publicly available sites and databases, and selected Websites on that topic.

What she sees is too broad and too voluminous, so she chooses an option from the navigation bar that allows her to further refine her keywords and to limit by other standard options (date, language, format). For each resource, if it is not already a full-text item, there is a button that gives her further delivery options: she can enter a credit card and get the full text immediately, she can transfer the citation to an ILL request, she is given the call number in the local stacks, and other such options. She chooses some sorting and printing options so she can rearrange the search results and print them out (or e-mail them to herself) in groupings useful to her.

As she goes through the results, she finds some relevant things but some of the resources are confusing and then others don't give her enough information. She goes back to the SP navigation bar and clicks to link to an online 24/7 reference/chat service to consult right away with a reference librarian who's actually located in another part of North America where the time zone and holiday schedule is such that it's still normal business hours. Although the librarian doesn't have access to every single identical resource that the student is seeing, she has many of the same things and, most of all, is able to suggest pointers to the student about refining the search terminology and limit options, and perhaps recommend additional resources that are so multi-focal that they were not identified by the automated search engine as being relevant.

Meanwhile, pages of full text are printing off from the student's printer; her university credit account is being debited where necessary; her ILL requests for monographs have gone into her library's ILL system for routing to another library based on locally defined policies; and another library (or a document delivery service) is busy getting an article to send to her digitally the next day. One of the pages that prints out is a list of just the book citations for items held in her local library, arranged in call number order so she can pick them from the stacks if she wants.

APPENDIX B

Portal Features and Functionality: First Phase

Developed by the ARL Scholars Portal Working Group, June 2001

This outline of features and functionality was developed to aid the ARL Scholars Portal Working Group in its environmental scan of potential portal products during the spring and early summer of 2001. Because the working group decided to focus initially on a "super discovery tool," this list reflects a bias toward features found in search tools. The list was not designed to be comprehensive, but represents the features and functionality that working group members articulated as their highest priority for a first step in a project. In spring 2001, the working group was not aware of any readily available list of portal features or functional requirements, so the working group developed this list as an aid in their understanding of existing products. The working group was and is aware that required and desirable features in a portal will evolve over time. This list represents the views of the ARL Scholars Portal Working Group as of June 2001 and has not been kept up to date.

1. General Information

- What is the name and version number of the product(s)?
- Does the company have additional portal-related products?

2. Fall 2001 Pilot

- Does the company have an existing product to test this fall?
- Is the prototype customizable?

APPENDIX B (continued)

3. Patron Authentication

- Does the product support 3M's SIP?
- Does the product support NCIP?
- Does the product support LDAP?
- Does the product support Kerberos?
- Does the product support PKI?
- Does the product provide a proprietary authentication system?
- Does the product support rights management tracking?
- Does the product provide a one-step login to remote databases?
- Does the product authorize users database by database?

4. User Interface

- Does the product have a clean design?
- Is the user interface customizable?
- Can the user personalize/refine/modify search and search results?
- Does the product include help screens?
- Does the product include an online tutorial?
- Can a participant integrate the "Scholars Portal" logo into the local Web pages?

5. Search Engine

- Does the product include a thesaurus? If so, which one(s)?
- Is the thesaurus static or dynamic?
- Can the product map the thesaurus vocabulary across different controlled vocabularies?
- Does the product include a crosswalk among different classification schemes?
- Can the search screen be personalized by database?
- Does the product search metadata of different types of resource formats, including multimedia?
- Can the vendor host content in a centralized database?
- Can the product search across distributed databases?
- Can the product be configured to limit a search to a specific content provider or database?
- Does the product provide access to the native search mode for advanced users?
- Does the product support keyword searching?
- Does the product support full-text indexing of digital text resources?

- Does the product support Open URL?
- Does the product support Open Archives Metadata Harvesting Protocol?
- Does the product handle foreign languages?
- Does the product handle non-Roman scripts?
- Does the product support Z39.50 searching?
- Does the product support HTTP searches of Web resources?
- What type of record structure does the product support?

  - MARC
  - EAD
  - Dublin Core
  - GILS
  - CIMI
  - RDF

- Can the product harvest all ".edu" sites?
- Can the product access OCLC's WorldCat?
- Can the product access RLG's Union Catalog?
- Does the product include push features regarding new resources?
- Does the product provide the ability to contribute and update resources or sources to be searched?

6. Search Results

- Does the product save searches for use in an alerting service?
- What is the default display of search results?
- Does the product have an ability to present search results in an unbiased manner?
- Does the product merge and de-dupe search results?
- Does the product identify the type of material (e.g., citation, full-text resource, Web page)?
- Does the search result display information on the source of the citation?
- Does the product present appropriate delivery options for each search result?
- Does the product identify if an item in a search result is owned locally?
- Can the product sort result sets by subject, target, etc.?
- Does the product present different views of resources: by task, subject, user group, data, service, locally owned/accessible, etc.?
- Does the product point to an appropriate copy?
- Does the product link to the full-text article if locally licensed?

APPENDIX B (continued)

7. Linkages with other Systems

- Does the product have a link to one or more ISO ILL Protocol-compliant messaging systems?
- Does the product have a link to one or more commercial document delivery suppliers?
- Does the product have a link to a 24/7 reference service?

8. Miscellaneous

- What types of usage statistics are provided?
- Is the product installed locally?
- Is the product vendor-hosted, or can it be?

9. Partnership

- Can the company access content from a participant's licensed resources?
- Can the company execute a library's existing license with a content provider?
- What are some examples of existing installations?
- What is the endurance of the company?
- What is the trust of the company as a partner?
- Does the company have corporate resources to deliver current and planned functionality?
- Can the company deliver on its promise?
- What is the role of ARL?
- How many libraries is the company willing to include in the initial phase of the project?
- How is the product branded?

10. Financial Issues

- Is the product purchased?
- Is the product licensed?
- What is the license fee?
- What is the annual maintenance fee?
- What is the cost to the project participants?
- What is the cost to a library using the product in an operational mode?
- Will the partner be compensated? If so, how?
- Will ARL and/or the participants own the product?
- Who owns the components and enhanced features developed in the partnership?

Chapter 12

Looking Ahead:
The Future of Portals

Mary E. Jackson

SUMMARY. This chapter identifies and describes nine key issues that will impact the future of portal development and its potential to become the preferred tool to discover quality information resources. The chapter notes the lack of consistency in how libraries currently define a portal. Key issues include metasearching, content and service description, electronic resource management, librarian/user expectations and current product functionality, single product or separate components, uniform view versus links to proprietary interfaces, open source versus proprietary software, workflow integration, and personalization and contextualization. The chapter references the Scholars Portal Project as one example of portal implementations in research libraries and how the seven libraries in the project are addressing the issues described in the article. *[Article copies available for a fee from The Haworth Document Delivery Service: 1-800-HAWORTH. E-mail address: <docdelivery@haworthpress.com> Website: <http://www.HaworthPress.com>]*

Mary E. Jackson is Director of Collections and Access Programs, Association of Research Libraries (ARL), 221 Dupont Circle, N.W., Suite 800, Washington, DC 20036 (E-mail: mary@arl.org). In that position, she serves as Project Manager for the Scholars Portal Project.

[Haworth co-indexing entry note]: "Looking Ahead: The Future of Portals." Jackson, Mary E. Co-published simultaneously in *Journal of Library Administration* (The Haworth Information Press, an imprint of The Haworth Press, Inc.) Vol. 43, No. 1/2, 2005, pp. 205-220; and: *Portals and Libraries* (ed: Sarah C. Michalak) The Haworth Information Press, an imprint of The Haworth Press, Inc., 2005, pp. 205-220. Single or multiple copies of this article are available for a fee from The Haworth Document Delivery Service [1-800-HAWORTH, 9:00 a.m. - 5:00 p.m. (EST). E-mail address: docdelivery@haworthpress.com].

Available online at http://www.haworthpress.com/web/JLA
Digital Object Identifier: 10.1300/J111v43n01_13

KEYWORDS. Portals, portal development, metasearching, Scholars Portal Project

INTRODUCTION

Portals are emerging as a preferred enabling tool to connect users with electronic information resources. As currently being designed and deployed, portals provide a single point of access to a wide variety of high-quality content and a range of appropriate supporting services. Content may vary depending on the organization implementing the portal. Services will also vary. For example, a university portal is likely to provide services that permit students to register for courses, access grades, and discover current activities on campus as well as including links to library content as well as content from other university sources. Content in a library portal includes licensed electronic resources, freely available Web resources, finding aids and other materials in rare books and special collections departments, as well as links to other university-based resources and services. Services offered by library portals include links to interlibrary loan (ILL), links to online reference services, and perhaps links to bibliographic reference tools.

Correctly predicting the future of a particular technology is challenging if impossible. Technology often evolves and is implemented in a nonlinear way, and some assert, in a non-logical manner. User acceptance, implementation, and adoption of a particular technology influences enhancements and future directions. Finally, commercial interests and needs often have a stronger influence on the direction and evolution of technology than do users of the technology, which may result in products that are commercially successful but that do not always meet user needs. Few if any predictions of the future of library services written in the early 1990s correctly identified the explosion of electronic resources and the fundamental way in which the Web has changed how users access library resources. Thus, the predictions and speculations included in this article are more likely to be wrong, perhaps even terribly off the mark. Rather than focusing completely on the specifics of how portals might operate in a decade, this article identifies issues that will influence the development and future direction of portal technology. In examining the issues, the article will predict how portals will mature and evolve, especially over the next several years, and at times, suggest preferred futures. Finally, this article focuses on the library portal, which may ultimately evolve into a channel or portlet within the university or institutional portal. Whether the library portal lives or disappears, will the functionality and services currently included in the library portal continue to be critical aspects of library information systems?

WHAT IS A PORTAL?

At times it seems that there are as many definitions and characterizations of portals as there are implementations. Some definitions are as simple as describing a portal as a search interface or a gateway to librarian-selected links to Web resources; other characterizations imply the complexity and sophistication of content and services currently offered by the most innovative libraries. The Association of Research Libraries' 2002 survey of its members' implementation of portal technology revealed a range of definitions. Several examples illustrate the diversity of definitions:

- The University of Washington defines a portal as an environment that fits specific needs, or stated another way–architecting the environment so people can do what they need to do.
- Boston College's definition is more simple–an interactive gateway to resources and services.
- Duke defines its portal as a Web gateway to digital resources and services which provides a high level of seamless integration and that includes a feature-rich kit of tools that enables use along the entire scholarly communications spectrum.
- The University of California, Irvine defines a portal as services and tools that facilitate the discovery, retrieval, and management of information from various resources in an integrated fashion that takes into account personalized needs in doing research and creating knowledge.
- The University of California, Santa Barbara defines a portal as a multi-dimensional scholarly environment; a site that allows resource discovery across disparate platforms; manipulation, customization, and enhancement of data and documents; location services (ILL, local delivery, mail-order); and tools to allow academic users to further store and organize their own subsets.

These few definitions illustrate that no consensus has yet emerged in the library community on a single definition of a portal.

The Scholars Portal Project, an effort of seven ARL member institutions, has characterized a portal as a system capable of conducting a single search across research library catalogs, licensed and unlicensed databases, indexes and abstracts, the free Web and, as it has been called, the uncontrolled Web. Retrieved resources are expected to be authoritative, scholarly, and appropriate for teaching, learning, and research in major academic institutions. Portals are expected to integrate and de-duplicate returned results, while providing full text or live-links as appropriate. The Scholars Portal features a variety of supporting services such as links to interlibrary loan and online reference systems as well as article delivery options. Customization by the library and personalization by the end user are also key features. The focus of the participants in the Scholars Portal Project has been shaped and influenced by the "User Scenario for the ARL Scholars Portal 'Single Search' Option" written by the ARL Scholars Portal Working Group.

LOOKING AHEAD

Thinking imaginatively, it is possible to envision a future in which undergraduates will have abandoned Google and other commercial search engines in favor of a faster, more powerful library portal. These portals of the future will present the most relevant resources displayed in a ranked order, and will provide immediate links to full-text resources when available, or offer options for purchasing the item or ordering a copy via interlibrary loan. In this future, the portal will be the primary place from which students conduct research as it provides seamless access to the range of supporting tools and services used by undergraduates, key among them the campus learning management system. In this future, faculty will also require students to discover, use, and cite licensed resources and other scholarly content not searchable through Google.

Librarians are beginning to have a clearer idea of what they want in portal technology. Unfortunately, current hopes for portal technology outstrip available technology. A wide variety of portal technology is marketed to the commercial sector, but most of these products have not been adapted to meet the needs of libraries. Librarians have defined functionality to be included in a portal, but few, if any, commercial or non-commercial products include all the required or desired features. The remainder of this chapter addresses a number of the issues that need to be addressed and must be solved before portal technology becomes so widespread that librarians and library patrons use the word "portal" interchangeably with the word "library."

METASEARCHING

In the idealized future, a range of issues relating to metasearching will be resolved. Current search technology requires use of multiple standards to search across different types of resources. The Z39.50 Information Retrieval standard serves as the basis for many of the current generation of commercial, library-oriented portal products in part because it is the main search standard that many information providers currently support. Z39.50 enables (more-or-less, depending on one's view) efficient searching of library catalogs and some bibliographic resources. However, the Web is not searched using Z39.50, nor will Z39.50 ever become the preferred searching standard for the Web. The Z39.50 standard is complex and originally designed for bibliographic searching. But perhaps more importantly, the Z39.50 standard is perceived as an "old and outdated" technology, although efforts are underway to bring it into a Web-friendly environment.

Not all library catalogs and online bibliographic resources are searchable using Web search protocols. As a result, portal products that search library catalogs and Web resources currently need to support Z39.50 and one or more additional searching protocols such as screen scraping, an application programming interface (API) to a remote resource, or the HTTP "get" and "post" commands. (The http specification technically defines a "GET" as form data is to be encoded (by a browser) into a URL and a "POST" as the form data is to appear within a message body.)

It is reasonable to speculate that the current exploration of and interest in moving the Z39.50 standard to an XML-based protocol, such as Search and Retrieve Web Service (SRW), may result in SRW becoming the primary standard for bibliographic searching. SRW, or SRU (Search and Retrieve via a URL) are likely to form the base for third and fourth generations of some library-oriented portal products. The Z39.50 Maintenance Agency, based at the Library of Congress, is leading the effort to move toward a searching protocol to be used on the Web.

Another possible future is that portals will become less reliant on real-time searching but will become more Google-like. In this scenario, a library portal will use the Open Archives Initiative Metadata Harvesting Protocol and harvest frequently used resources into a local repository. This discovery alternative assumes regular (perhaps daily or even hourly) harvesting of a pre-defined range of content. Searching against a "static" database (the local repository where the content is stored and indexed) enables more efficient harvesting of content, offers much faster presentation of search results, and permits results to be de-duped and ranked by relevancy.

The National Information Standards Organization (NISO) has embarked on a new initiative to explore the issues surrounding searching of disparate resources, known as cross-database, federated, or meta-searching. Intended to minimize the current challenges of using different search protocols, searching variant and incompatible metadata, and dealing with varying presentations of search results, the NISO effort expects to identify possible areas for standards development. This important effort engages three key communities: content providers, portal providers, and librarians and may well shape how the search capability in portals evolves.

Two other issues are related to searching. The first is the increased usage of a remote resource. Some commercial database providers have articulated their concerns about how portals have greatly increased searching of their content. Some also assert that some of the searching generated by portals is unnecessary and duplicative because a portal is searching multiple sources in an effort to find a few citations. Underlying their concerns is the worry that users will no longer search their Web sites directly. In this case, the corporate branding will be lost, as will enhancements or capabilities unique to that site. Some commercial publishers assume that users will prefer to go to a publisher's site, while some librarians assert that users generally do not know the publisher of a specific title or even know which publishers are well-known in certain subject areas.

The second issue relates to accessing content within a publisher's site. Assuming the publisher is willing to have a portal search its site, the next challenge is how to structure an OpenURL so that the specific journal article is found, and retrieved, if possible. NISO's OpenURL standard is the syntax to create metadata and/or identifiers about an information object that are used in the Web environment. These "packages" are at the core of context-sensitive or open link technology. Open linking using the Open URL enables a user to access the full text or digital content by clicking on a bibliographic citation and being pointed to the range of relevant resources appropriate to that user. Publisher implementation of the OpenURL will eliminate the need to construct proprietary links to each publisher's Web site and will permit users to be "directed" to resources or services they are eligible to use.

CONTENT AND SERVICE DESCRIPTION

Cross database searching using different search protocols and standards is currently available, if not well refined. To the user, the portal has undertaken a single search of different content or different resources. Accomplishing that "single" search may result in a portal invoking more than one search protocol, but that is hidden from the user.

Results are returned and displayed by differing criteria. Some portals present results as they are returned from the remote resource, while other portals wait until all remote resources return results before organizing and displaying the results to the user. Displays that present the "first-back" records satisfy the user's desire for speedy response, but more relevant records may be returned more slowly by another server, and thus, displayed lower in the search results. Portal vendors, as well as librarians, have differing views of what is most important to the user community–speed or comprehensiveness.

Fretwell-Downing's ZPORTAL software used by the Scholars Portal Project participants organizes resources into profiles; other products offer similar logical aggregations of resources. Participants in the Scholars Portal Project have suggested that users are not always choosing "the right" profile because the name of the profile may be too narrow, too general, too vague, or too specific, or the resources included in a profile may be too specific, too general, or not sufficiently comprehensive.

Missing in current portal implementations are consistent and machine-searchable descriptions of the content included in and services provided by remote resources or databases. At present, librarians need to assign the equivalent of subject headings to each and every resource added to the local portal, determine the technical requirements for searching the resource (i.e., what standard is used, what Z39.50 attributes are supported, whether any controlled vocabulary is used, etc.), identify the services offered by the resource (i.e., authentication, Open URL linking), and then configure each resource. This labor-intensive process must be repeated for each resource added to a portal.

There is no existing standard for how to describe a collection or a resource, and in fact the terms are often used inconsistently. Some use *collection* to describe an aggregated database such as Academic Search Elite and a *resource* to define an individual journal within that aggregated database. Others consider Academic Search Elite as an online *resource*. Three examples illustrate the variation in how libraries describe Academic Search Elite.

From Arizona State University Library's Web site:

(1990+) Covers a wide range of academic subjects. Features full text for selected journals, abstracts and indexing for over 3,100 scholarly journals, and coverage of *The Wall Street Journal, The New York Times* and *The Christian Science Monitor.*

From the Rochester Institute of Technology Library's Web site:

This scholarly collection provides coverage for nearly all academic areas of study including social sciences, humanities, education, computer sciences, engineering, physics, chemistry, language and linguistics, arts & literature, medical sciences, ethnic studies, and more. It features full text for over 1,800 journals, abstracts and indexing for over 3,000 scholarly journals, and coverage of *The Wall Street Journal, The New York Times* and *The Christian Science Monitor.*

From Northwestern University Library's Web site:

Multidisciplinary coverage of journal literature, including biological sciences, economics, communications, computer sciences, engineering, language and linguistics, arts and literature, medical sciences and women's studies. Provides citations and abstracts for nearly 2900 scholarly journals (1666 peer-reviewed), as well as over 1250 full-text titles. In addition to basic keyword searching options, users also may choose from a natural language search, an advanced search, and browseable and searchable indexes of subject headings and journal titles. Academic Search Elite also includes (A) a searchable Company Directory, with basic contact information, sales range and number of employees; and (B) an Image Collection that is searchable by keyword or by category. Search results may be printed, downloaded to a text file, or sent via e-mail.

These descriptions include common elements, but vary in terms of detail and comprehensiveness. This inconsistency in use of terminology or variability in description may be comparable to the early days of cataloging where each library described the same monograph in a slightly different way. Agreeing on ways to describe collections or resources will minimize current frustrations in not knowing which resource is the most appropriate. Collaborating in sharing those descriptions with other libraries will reduce the labor-intensive nature of creating and maintaining the descriptions. Collection description is one of the three areas of focus of the National Information Standards Organization's (NISO) Metasearch Initiative. The JISC Information Environment Service Registry is also addressing this issue. If these or similar efforts are successful, librarians will not need to assign a specific resource to a specific profile (or equivalent). Instead, a user will execute searches and the portal software will determine which resources are most likely to return results based on the type of user, the type of search, and the range of resources included in the portal.

The next generation of portal products will likely support some rudimentary machine-to-machine searching of collection descriptions. In the more distant future, librarians managing portals will not need to maintain details on collections and the services they offer because portals will be "aware" when new resources are added or when existing resources are enhanced.

The variations in service descriptions present similar challenges. One library may use the phrase *document delivery* to mean the delivery of locally owned material to local users, a second library may mean the ability to order from commercial document delivery suppliers, while a third library uses that phase to describe its interlibrary loan operation. Service descriptions also include the range of services provided, the clientele eligible for those services, and possible restrictions or limitations. Does a library permit an individual who is not affiliated with the university to use materials in the rare books and special collections department? Is an unaffiliated user able to submit an online reference question? What are the hours the library is open to the general public or to affiliated users? Library directories will minimize some of the variation in service description as the standard being developed by the International Organization for Standardization (ISO).

ELECTRONIC RESOURCE MANAGEMENT

In today's environment, many libraries use Serials Solution, Openly Informatics, or TDNet to manage their electronic journals and resources. Portals require accurate and current information about the library's electronic holdings to be able to link to the full text from a citation in the search result. The process of importing and maintaining detailed holdings information in a portal is very labor-intensive and not seamless. In the future, portals may not store holdings information for locally held titles. Instead, the portal will send a query to the Serials

Solution database to determine if the citation is available electronically. The integration of serials management products with portals is one example of how products developed to solve different problems will be retooled so they can exchange data without requiring manual intervention.

LIBRARIAN/USER EXPECTATIONS AND CURRENT PRODUCT FUNCTIONALITY

Several directors involved in the ARL Scholars Portal Working Group recalled a missed opportunity in the early 1990s when the next generation of integrated library systems (ILS) were being designed. These directors felt that if the library community had been more directly involved in shaping the early design of that generation of integrated library systems, library staff as well as library users of online catalogs and circulation applications would have benefited as some of the essential features and functionality would have been included in the early releases. One of the reasons the ARL Scholars Portal Working Group signed a contract with Fretwell-Downing, Inc. was to help shape ZPORTAL and other FD products to meet the specific needs of the research library community. Other ARL member libraries are working with ExLibris, Inc. so that its portal product, MetaLib, will include the functionality required by that group of research libraries. Other ARL and non-ARL libraries are in similar collaborations with other vendors of portal products. Closer collaboration between libraries and vendors is expected to improve the functionality of portal products.

Because most portal products are still first-generation, librarians and users have expectations about portals that may be more aspiration than reality. For example, not all portals integrate seamlessly and transparently into learning management systems (LMS), although some portal vendors are developing application programming interfaces (APIs) to embed portal search boxes into BlackBoard or WebCT. A growing number of undergraduates expect to be able to access the library portal from the LMS and copy citations into the bibliographies of papers they are writing or into personal bibliographic reference tools such as EndNote.

Librarians expect portals to link to local institutional repositories. At this early stage in the development of portal technology, not all portal products include all functionality deemed mandatory by the library community. Single sign-on, or the ability of the user to authenticate himself or herself one time and then search a range of licensed resources, each of which would require authorization if accessed individually, is just one example of where the library community requirements outstrip existing portal functionality.

Hopefully, portal products will catch up with the current expectations and requirements articulated by the library community. However, it is virtually certain that librarians will have developed new expectations as existing portals mature. Vendors of portals products may always be caught in a catch-up mode to meet library and user expectations.

Although many early characterizations of portals focused on features needed by users, librarians may select a product because of its administrative and back-end functionality rather than user-oriented functionality. Again, using the Scholars Portal Project as an example, discussions among the project participants about enhanced functionality illustrated the expected desire to make the software easier for library staff to manage, for example, an easier way to set up a remote resource or collect statistics, versus adding functionality to make the portal easier to use for users (e.g., integration with learning management systems). Vendors cannot be expected to incorporate all suggestions and enhancements into the next release or even next generation. Vendors will continue to receive suggestions for "backroom" enhancements aimed at library staff responsible for managing the software and user-interface enhancements geared toward users.

Librarians should not expect portal technology to be perfect or expect users to give up Google completely. At a minimum, a portal with sufficiently wide range of content and a range of commonly used services used by some portion of the campus community could be "good enough" for most users. But, many libraries are striving towards being "best in class" with the portals they are introducing to their users.

SEPARATE COMPONENTS OR COMPREHENSIVE SINGLE PRODUCT

The current design of most commercial portal products is similar to the current generation of integrated library system software–all functionality included in a single product. An alternative to a single, comprehensive product is a series of portlets, each of which includes a defined, and often narrow, set of functionality. Searching, access management/authentication, Open URL linking, and display of a news channel are examples of functionality that could be developed as stand-alone portlets and combined, again seamlessly and transparently, into a portal. In such a scenario, a library might choose the searching portlet from Vendor A, the access management portlet from Vendor B, and the Open URL functionality from Vendor C. Users of the portal would not be aware of the different software because all functionality would be accessible via a single user interface, perhaps purchased from Vendor D.

To make this level of integration work efficiently, vendors will need to agree that competing products must be able to interoperate and must support the standards used to realize that interoperability. Standards exist or appear to be emerging for searching and access management respectively. Interlibrary loan management systems, online/virtual reference systems, and learning management systems are obvious examples of other areas requiring interoperability with portals. Standards such as the ISO ILL Protocol, NISO's development of a standard for Networked Reference Services, and IMS Global Learning Consortium's Learning Resource Metadata Specification may offer some level of interoperability for these three areas. Bilateral negotiations or proprietary agreements between two vendors are neither sustainable nor scalable. For portals to succeed in the future, these, and other, interoperability issues will need to be solved. In some cases, new standards may need to be written, existing standards may need to be modified or enhanced, or vendors will be expected to implement existing standards in a standard way.

UNIFORM VIEW versus LINKS TO PROPRIETARY INTERFACE

Librarians continue to voice varying opinions about the effectiveness of searching disparate resources from a single portal interface. Some argue that a portal "dumbs down" searches so significantly that the search result will never produce appropriate results found searching via the resource's proprietary interface. Others assert that users, especially undergraduates, do not care about powerful and sophisticated searching that retrieves a comprehensive list of all possible citations, they simply want to find material and, thus, a simple search screen is required. A number of portals offer basic and advanced search screens, with the advanced screens generally offering some level of Boolean searching. The native search interface of resources or databases may provide more specialized options for searching or more detailed search results compared with a search generated from a portal. At present, some portals do not offer the ability to jump to the native search interface, but that functionality will become more commonplace in the next generation of portal products, and thus this functionality will not be as important an issue as it is currently. A countervailing view is that a small number of commercial information providers might resist, or may increasingly block, portals from searching their content by including in their licenses a requirement that their native search interfaces be used.

OPEN SOURCE *versus* PROPRIETARY SOFTWARE

The open source movement has embraced portals as a promising area of development. Open source software is source code made available without charge to others who may use it, improve it, or fix bugs. Those improvements and corrections are in turn shared with the interested community. The Scout Portal Toolkit and uPortal are two examples of open source/open standards efforts that may well influence how commercial vendors shape the next generation of portals. It is safe to say that open source and proprietary software will co-exist well into the future. Libraries without sufficient technical staff or local expertise will likely purchase commercial portal products, while other libraries will invest in implementing and enhancing open source portal software.

WORKFLOW INTEGRATION

Why are libraries and universities so interested in portals? One answer is that portals offer the promise of enabling a user to be more productive in their research and learning. Another answer is that portals will become the primary means for users to integrate separate tasks into a single workflow. The user scenario developed by the ARL Scholars Portal Working Group is one articulation of how a portal could integrate a user's work. Librarians hope that users will want to begin in libraries and integrate their workflow from that point. The university portals are being built with an assumption that users will start at the institutional portal and link to different business functions or Web services as needed.

However, in the preferred future, will users want to orchestrate their workflow from a "library portal," "my portal," or something yet to be developed? Or will the demand for support of sophisticated workflow integration models result in portals being viewed as simple integrators for a wide range of stand-alone functions, regardless of institutional affiliation? Which portal does a user with multiple affiliations use first, or should it matter? How does a graduate student working on a degree at University A and teaching at University B integrate her workflow to include a reference (or link, if permitted) to a resource licensed by University A into a paper being written at University B?

PERSONALIZATION AND CONTEXTUALIZATION

At present, some portal products permit users to select the resources they search, personalize the appearance of the interface, and perhaps select the functionality included in the portal (e.g., turning on a link to the campus learning management system, downloading citations into a personal bibliographic reference tool). Early implementations suggest that users don't often take advantage of existing personalization features. As portals become more widely deployed, the library community will gain a better understanding of the interest in and need for personalization. It is unlikely that the pre-selected sets of resources made available via current portals meet all needs of all users. It is reasonable to predict that as users gain more experience using portals, their interest in personalization will increase.

Contextualization is more challenging, and perhaps will be one of the issues that will become increasingly important. Contextualization offers users appropriate resources at appropriate times. For example, as a user is searching full-text database, the portal will "suggest" related articles. It's almost as if the software has intelligence about the user's preferences and habits.

ONE EXAMPLE OF PORTAL IMPLEMENTATION: THE SCHOLARS PORTAL PROJECT

This article identified a number of current issues that are hindering portals from realizing the vision articulated by the ARL Scholars Portal Working Group. That vision, as implemented by the Scholars Portal Project, is ambitious. The vision identifies a range of features and functionality, some of which are already available and others are yet to be implemented. The Scholars Portal Project will identify how users at the seven institutions integrate one vendor's software in support of teaching and learning. As the project passes the midpoint of the three-year effort, it is already clear that the collaboration among participants is very effective. The Scholars Portal Working Group efforts to effect integration of disparate resources should leverage work already being carried out in ARL libraries. The Scholars Portal Project Managers Group, established in early 2003, is a direct response to the Working Group's call for collaboration. The Project Managers Group has developed collaborative processes to identify priority subject areas, select specific resources for each of those subject areas, write and review templates for the resources, and reach consensus on configuration issues identified during this process. The group is also working with Fretwell-Downing on authentication issues and configuring the OL2, FD's open linking software, according to each participant's holdings.

Libraries participating in the Scholars Portal Project and other libraries implementing portal technology are trying to improve access to materials for their users. A growing number of libraries are working with vendors in new and creative ways because they want to change the way in which users access information resources and because they feel that closer collaboration and partnership with the companies developing the software will result in better products. The progress of the Scholars Portal Project and other similar efforts, even if modest at times, represents concrete steps toward the vision articulated by the ARL Scholars Portal Working Group.

AN ALTERNATIVE FUTURE

An alternative scenario might become the future of the library portal. Rather than the library portal, Google will have become the portal of choice. The convenience and ease of use will continue to be a hallmark. However, Google will have incorporated new types of content as well as the sophistication found in searching library catalogs, licensed resources, and aggregator databases. Google will also have implemented a universal authentication mechanism to permit individuals to search licensed resources available to and appropriate for that user, will have embedded links to the user's learning management system and other institution-specific services, and will provide the contextualization needed for users to select and use appropriate resources. Is this our preferred future?

CONCLUSION

Portal implementations are many and varied. Over the next decade libraries will gain valuable experience in discovering whether the technology is scalable and supportable, which services are required or optional elements of a portal, and the range of information resources most useful to most users. As a result portals will continue to evolve. Will portals become the preferred methods of delivering digital library services? Or, will portals become an invisible enabling tool?

Portals may well be more about change than about technology. Portals will change how individuals use information resources and portals will change how libraries are staffed, structured, and offer services. A library that offers its users a successful portal will need to ensure that library staff feel comfortable in helping users access appropriate intellectual content. That skill may well be different from how library staff currently assist users. Users will undertake a similar transition in their migration to a new set of tools to gather, manipulate, analyze, and repurpose information.

It is very likely that a decade from now that a commonly accepted definition and description of a portal will have emerged. On the other hand, it is also very possible that portals as we now understand and use them will have evolved to something very different, and the concept of a portal will become a footnote in the evolution of providing access to quality information resources. Whatever the future, librarians involved in defining and implementing the current generation of portal technology will have helped shape the preferred future.

SOURCES CITED

Arizona State University Library
    http://www.asu.edu/lib/resources/db/ebscohst.htm
JISC Information Environment Service Registry
    http://www.mimas.ac.uk/iesr/
NISO Metasearch Initiative
    http://www.niso.org/committees/MS_initiative.html#plan
Northwestern University Library
    http://er.library.northwestern.edu/detail.asp?id=35571
Rochester Institute of Technology
    http://wally.rit.edu/electronic/acadelite/acadelite.html
Scholars Portal Project
    http://www.arl.org/access/scholarsportal/
Search and Retrieval on the Web (SRW)
    http://lcweb.loc.gov/z3950/agency/zing/srw/

Index

Page numbers followed by "f" indicate a figure.

About Find it!, 121,127,128f
Academic librarians, challenges for, 76-77
Academic Search Elite, 211-212
Accessibility, portals and, 83-84
Access management, 102-103
  emerging strategies for, 106-108
  strategies for, 103-104
Administrative tools, for portals, 84
Advisers, online, for portals, 81
Amazon.com
  adapting library operations to, 78-79
  library services like, 77
Arms, Caroline, 148
ARPANET, 75
Assessment. *See* Usability testing
Assistance, online, for portals, 82-83
Association of Research Libraries
  (ARL), final report of, 3,190-198
Audiences
  for library portals, 15
  of Portal to the World, 40-41,52-53
  for Yahoo!, 15
Authentication services, 102-103,104, 120
  for Scholars Portal Project, 125
Authorization services, 102-103,120
  for Scholars Portal Project, 125

Berkeley Public Library's Index to the
  Internet, 12
Blackboard, 177
Blogs, 82-83

Books, research and, 60
Breeding, Marshall, 141
Broadcast searching, 65-66,93,94. *See also* Searching
  misconceptions about, 66
  Z39.50 standard for, 95
Broadnax, Lavonda, 54
Bulletin Board for Libraries (BUBL)
  Information Service, 13-14, 17-18
  audiences for, 15
  funding for, 16
Bulletin boards, 82-83
Business world, portals and, 67-68

California Digital Library, 13,17
Campbell, Jerry, 1-2,116,131,191,196
Carter, David, 8
Catalogs, 136. *See also* Online catalogs;
  Online public access catalogs
  (OPACs)
  Draft Frankfurt Principles for, 137
  evolving form and functions of, 136-140
  functional requirements of, 137
  as portals, 142-144
  reformulating functions of, 137
Chatrooms, 82-83
Citation management, 89
Clients. *See* Audiences
Cohen, David, 177
Collaboration, role of, 62-64
Collection registries, 109-110
Communication hubs, 184-185

Communities of trust, 106-107
Computer Supported Cooperative
    Work (CSCW), 62
Contextualization, portals and, 218
Corporate world, portals and, 67-68
Course management systems (CMSs),
    179-183
Course pages, publishing, on library
    portals, 25-27
Cross searching, of databases, 211
Customization, of portals, 21-25,24f
Cutter, Charles, 136

Database Finder, 28-29
Databases
    accessing, MyLibrary@NCState
        and, 28-29,30f
    cross-searching, 211
    searching multiple, portals and, 81
Data formats, indexing structured, 97
De-duplicating results, of searches, 98
Delsey, Tom, 137-138,150-151
Digital certificate methods, 106-107
Discovery services, 88
Distance education, 176
Document delivery options, for portals,
    81-82,213
Draft Frankfurt Principles, 137,140

800 numbers, for online assistance, 82
E-Journal Finder, 28
Electronic journals and resources,
    managing, 213-214
Electronic learning environments
    (ELEs), 179-183
Electronic resources
    management of, 213-214
    research and, 60
E-mail assistance, 82
Environmentalist approaches, to
        library portals, 183-188
ExLibris, Inc., 214

Extension programs, 176
Extranets, 67-68

Fabos, Bettina, 16
Faculty, online library resources and,
    174-175
Federated search, 65-66. *See also*
        Library portals
    as integral feature of library portals,
        144-145
    misconceptions about, 66
Federated search engines. *See* Library
        portals; Portals
Fenner, Joe, 67
Filo, David, 12
Find it!, 120,129-131
411 search, 80
Frank Principles. *See* Draft Frankfurt
        Principles
Frazier, Ken, 191
Fretwell-Downing, Inc. (FD),
    116-117,197,214
Functionality, integrated library systems
        and, 59
Functional Requirements of Bibliographic
        Records (FRBR), 139-140
Funding
    portals and, 15-16
    possible solutions for, 16-17

Global services, 108-110
Goldner, Matthew, 143
GoMLink, 12
Google, 16,65,142,219
Grant, Carl, 143
Graphery, Jim, 27
Group-ization, 63
Groupware, 62-64

Hane, Paula J., 66
Hellman, Eric, 144

Help screens, 82
Holland, Maurita, 9
Hubs, communication, 184-185
Hybrid education, 176

iLink, 29
Implementation processes, for portals,
    115-116
InfoMine, 14,17
    audiences for, 15
Information interrelationships, 60-62
Information management, portals and,
    89
Inquiry driven search modules, 186
Instruction
    online, course-ware for, 177-178
    online library, 175-177
Instructors, 174-175
Integrated library systems (ILSs), 136.
    See also Online catalogs
    functionality and, 59
    limitations of, 140-142
    missed opportunities in early
        development of, 214
    portals and, 57-60 .
    usability and, 59
Integration services, of library portals,
    92-97
Interface, search, portals and, 79
Interface design, at University of
    Washington Libraries,
    161-166
International Organization of
    Standardization (ISO), 213
Internet-based education, 176-177
Internet Gateway, 17
Internet Public Library (IPL), 3,6,17,54
    administration of, 9-10
    audiences for, 15
    collection content of, 10-14
    features of, 10
    funding for, 15-16
    history of, 6-8

objectives of, 8
and other portals, 12-14
as research for faculty, 8
as service provider to public, 8-9
services provided by, 9
as teaching environment, 8
Iowa State University Library, 116.
    See also Library portals;
        Scholars Portal Project
IP address filtering, 104-105
iVia, 14

Janes, Joe, 6,7
JISC Information Environment Service
    Registry, 213
Journal access, MyLibrary @NCState
    and, 28

Kenney, Brian, 143
Knowledge management, 100

Lakoff, George, 179-180
Larson, Everette, 54
Learning, online
    conceptual approaches to, 181-182
    environmental approaches to, 183-188
Leita, Carole, 12
Librarians
    academic, challenges for, 76-77
    communicating with,
        MyLibrary@NCState and,
        29-31
    evolving roles of, 89
    expectations of, for library portals,
        214-215
    online assistance and, 83
    organizing Web resources and, 2
Librarians' Index to the Internet (LII),
    12-13,54
    audiences for, 15
    funding for, 15

Libraries. *See also* Integrated library systems (ILSs)
adapting Amazon.com-like functions to operations of, 77,78-79
developing generic links to resources of, 178
proximity to, online learning and, 176-177
usability testing and, 157-159
Libraries' Web site, MyLibrary@NCState and, 28-29
Library Course Builder (LibCB), 27
Library of Congress. *See also* Portal to the World, Library of Congress
home page of, 53-54
Library of Congress Portals Application Issues Group (LCPAIG), 145-150
Library.org, 191
Library portals. *See also* Federated search; Portals; individual library portal
access management strategies for, 103-104
alternative future scenarios for, 219
authentication services for, 102
commonalities among, 14-16
conclusions about, 32-33
contextualization and, 218
emerging access management strategies for, 106-108
environmentalist approaches to, 183-188
essential and desirable functionality of, 145-150
evolving roles of librarians and, 89
federated search as integral feature of, 144-145
foundation services of, 88
generalized architecture for, 89-92,90f
implementing, 101
integration of, 215-216

IP address filtering with proxies for, 104-105
librarian/user expectations of, 214-215
online catalogs and, 150-151
open source movement and, 217
outlining library's goals and expectations for, 117
personalization and, 218
referring URLs for, 105
searches and, 216-217
services that support, 101-102
sustainable models of, 102
usability and, 160-161
vendor supplied scripts for, 105-106
workflow integration and, 217-218
Library resources, developing generic links to, 178
Library systems, integrated, portals and, 57-60
Links
developing generic, to library resources, 178
to full content, 99
Lopata, Cynthia, 138
Luther, Judy, 65
Lyman, Peter, 142

Management software, 181
MeL (library portal), 17
MetaLib, 214
Metaphors, function of, 179-183
Metasearching, 65-66,93-94,209-210. *See also* Broadcast searching; Searching
Metasearch Initiative, NISO's, 213
Michigan eLibrary, 13,17
audiences for, 15
funding for, 15
MLink, 12
Moen, William, 142,150
Mouse-overs, 82
My Gateway (University of Washington Libraries), 166-168

MyLibrary@NCState, 3,80. *See also*
        Library portals; Portals
    campus portal and, 31-32
    communicating with librarians and,
        29-31
    conclusions about, 32-33
    course pages on, 25-27
    customization of, 21-25,24f
    database access and, 28-29,30f
    future and, 33
    history of, 20
    information overload problems and,
        21
    journal access and, 28
    layouts for, 26f
    Libraries' Web site and, 28-29
    personalization of, 21,22f,23
    personal pages for course use on,
        27-28
    purposes of, 20
    usage and, 20-21
My.library software, University of
        Toronto, 25-27
My Library (Virginia Commonwealth
        University)
    usability of, 16-161
MyUW, 168-170

National Information Standards
        Organization (NISO), 210,
        213
Natural language searching, 80
Neilsen, Jakob, 77
Noerr, Peter, 144
North Carolina State University. *See*
        MyLibrary@NCState
Nyirady, Ken, 38,54

OCLC (Ohio College Library
        Catalog), 139-140
Olave, Carlos J., 54
Online advisers, for portals, 81

Online catalogs. *See also* Catalogs;
        Integrated library systems
        (ILSs)
    adapting, to evolving technologies,
        138
    library portals and, 150-151
    limitations of, 140-142
    as portals, 142-144
Online instruction, course-ware for,
        177-178
Online learning
    conceptual approaches to, 181-182
    environmental approaches to,
        183-188
Online library instruction, 175-176
    proximity to libraries and, 176-177
Online public access catalogs (OPACs),
        59,60,136
Open Archives Initiative (OAI), 96-97
Open Archives Initiative Protocol for
        Metadata Harvesting
        (OAI-PMH), 97,209-210
OpenLinking, 119
Openly Informatics, 213
Open Project Directory, 54
Open source movement, portals and,
        217
OpenURL, 99-100,210
Organizing results, of searches, 98

Passwords, 102,103
Pathfinders, 48
Patrons. *See* Audiences
Pennsylvania State University Libraries,
        27
Personalization, of portals, 21,22f,23,
        79-80,218
Personalization, role of, 62-64
Portals. *See also* Library portals;
        individual portal
    accessibility and, 83-84
    accessing local content and, 96-97
    administrative tools for, 84
    assistance on, 82-83

audiences for, 15
catalogs as, 142-144
collaboration and, 62-64
common traits of, 14
contextualization and, 218
cooperation and, 17
corporate world and, 67-68
customization of, 21-25,24f
defined, 2-3,58,67,72-73,114-115,
    207-208
designing online advisers for, 81
document delivery options for,
    81-82
411 searching and, 80
funding and, 15-16
future of, 4,208-209
historical perspective of, 75-76
ideal, 77
implementation process for, 115-116
importance of search and retrieval
    tools for, 64-67
information management and, 89
instrumental approaches to
    courseware and, 181-182
integrated library systems and,
    57-60
national virtual library, 17
natural language searching and, 80
need for, 16-18
online assistance for, 82-83
personalization of, 62-64,79-80
predicting future of, 206-207,
    208-209
relevancy ranking for, 80-81
Scholars Portal Project's definition
    of, 208
searching multiple databases and, 81
services and, 72,77
simplicity of interface and, 79
strengths of, 73
subject groupings for, 79
terminology for, 3
too much choice and, 76
users and, 73-75,77

Portal to the World, Library of Congress,
    3. *See also* Library portals;
    Portals
collaboration for, 44
development of, 41-44
future and, 55-56
general design concept of, 42-43
home page of, 53-54
major audiences of, 52-53
marketing of, 54-55
objective of, 41-42
organizational framework for, 44-48
overview of, 38
quality control and, 49-50
reasons for creating, 38-41
reception of, 52
selection criteria for, 43-44
staff development and, 51-52
technical framework for, 48
Prichard, Sarah, 192,194
Privacy issues, 103
Profilers, 186-188
Profiles, 211
Project management, 118-122
Proxy servers, 105
Public key infrastructure (PKI) method,
    106-107

Rasmussen, Gary, 1-2
Really Simple Syndication (RSS), 100
Ream, Dan, 27
RedLightGreen (RLG) project, 138-140
Reference services, 17
Regalado, Jesus Alonso, 54
Registries
    collection, 109-110
    service, 109-110
Relevancy ranking, 80-81
Research, books *vs.* electronic resources
    for, 60
Resources, library, developing generic
    links to, 178
Results, organizing and de-duplicating,
    98
Role-based access, 103

"Scholarly Communication Hub,"
184-185
"Scholars Portal Dynamic Profiler,"
186-187
Scholars Portal Project, 102,218-219.
See also Library portals;
Portals
authentication/authorization for,
125
configuration of resources for,
124-125
definition of portal by, 208
e-Library relationship for, 125-127
hardware and software for, 122
history of, 191-192
launching of, 197
librarian/user expectations of, 214-215
local project management for,
118-122
outlining goals and expectations
for, 117
overview of, 116
partnerships for, 124
screen design for, 125-127
software for, 122
staff technical expertise for, 123
standards for, 123-124
training for, 122-123
user instruction and, 127
Scholars Portal Working Group, final
report of, 190-198
Schottlaender, Brian, 143,192,194,
196-197
Schwartz, Barry, 72,76
Scout Portal Toolkit, 217
Search and Retrieve Web Service
(SRW), 209
Searching, 79-81. *See also* Broadcast
searching; Federated search;
Metasearching
bucket approach to, 66-67
411, 80
importance of potent tools for, 64-67
library portals and, 216-217
natural language, 80

relevancy ranking and, 80-81
sorting and de-duplicating results
of, 98
Serials Solution, 213
Service registries, 109-110
Services
discovery, 88
portals and, 72,77
Seuss, C. David, 62,63
Shibboleth, 107-108
Sirsi Unicorn integrated library
system, 29
Sorting, results of searches, 98
Structured data formats, indexing, 97
Subject groupings, portals and, 79

TDNet, 213
Technology Assisted Curriculum
Center (TACC), 174,177
Thomas, Sarah, 142-143,191-192
Trust, communities of, 106-107
Tutorials, 82,186

University of Rochester Library, 27
University of Toronto, my.library
software, 25-27
University of Utah, 174. *See also*
Technology Assisted
Curriculum Center (TACC)
online instruction at, 177
University of Washington Libraries
My Gateway of, 166-168
MyUW and, 168-170
usability testing and interface
design at, 161-166
uPortal, 217
Usability
integrated library systems and, 59
library portals and, 160-161
Usability testing
designing tests for, 158
libraries and, 157-159

overview of, 156-157
at University of Washington
    Libraries, 161-166
User instruction, for ZPORTAl, 127
User names, 103-104

Vertical search, 64-65
Virginia Commonwealth University
    My Library, 27
Virtual library portals. *See* Portals

Watson, James, 67
WebCT, 175,177
Web resources, organizing, librarians
    and, 2

Workflow integration, portals and,
    217-218
Writing toolkits, 83

Yahoo!, 12,15,16
Yang, Jerry, 12

Z39.50 Information Retrieval standard,
    95,123,124,209
ZING, 96
ZPORTAL software, 116-117,119-121,
    129-130,211,214. *See also*
    Scholars Portal Project
    user instruction and, 127